DISTRESSING LANGUAGE

CRIP: NEW DIRECTIONS IN DISABILITY STUDIES

General Editors: Michael Bérubé, Robert McRuer, and Ellen Samuels

Committed to generating new paradigms and attending to innovative interdisciplinary shifts, the Crip: New Directions in Disability Studies series focuses on cutting-edge developments in the field, with interest in exploratory analyses of disability and globalization, ecotheory, new materialisms, affect theory, performance studies, postcolonial studies, and trans theory.

Crip Times: Disability, Globalization, and Resistance
Robert McRuer

Accessible America: A History of Disability and Design
Bess Williamson

Literary Bioethics: Animality, Disability, and the Human
Maren Tova Linett

Disabilities of the Color Line: Redressing Antiblackness from Slavery to the Present
Dennis Tyler

Distressing Language: Disability and the Poetics of Error
Michael Davidson

Distressing Language

Disability and the Poetics of Error

Michael Davidson

NEW YORK UNIVERSITY PRESS

New York

NEW YORK UNIVERSITY PRESS
New York
www.nyupress.org

References to Internet websites (URLs) were accurate at the time of writing. Neither the author nor New York University Press is responsible for URLs that may have expired or changed since the manuscript was prepared.

Library of Congress Cataloging-in-Publication Data
Names: Davidson, Michael, 1944–   author.
Title: Distressing language : disability and the poetics of error / Michael Davidson.
Description: New York : New York University Press, [2022] | Series: Crip: new directions in disability studies | Includes bibliographical references and index.
Identifiers: LCCN 2021030643 | ISBN 9781479813827 (hardback) | ISBN 9781479813841 (paperback) | ISBN 9781479813865 (ebook) | ISBN 9781479813858 (ebook other)
Subjects: LCSH: Communication and the arts. | People with disabilities and the arts. | Miscommunication in art. | Miscommunication in literature.
Classification: LCC NX180.C65 D38 2022 | DDC 700.1—dc23
LC record available at https://lccn.loc.gov/2021030643

New York University Press books are printed on acid-free paper, and their binding materials are chosen for strength and durability. We strive to use environmentally responsible suppliers and materials to the greatest extent possible in publishing our books.

Manufactured in the United States of America

10 9 8 7 6 5 4 3 2 1

Also available as an ebook

For Peter Middleton

JUTE.—Are you jeff?

MUTT.—Somehards.

JUTE.—But you are not jeffmute?

MUTT.—Noho, Only an utterer.

JUTE.—Whoa? Whoat is the mutter with you?

MUTT.—I became a stun a stummer.

JUTE.—What a hauhahhauhaudibble thing, to be cause!

(James Joyce, *Finnegans Wake*, 16)

CONTENTS

LIST OF FIGURES

Introduction

Distressing Language

Say Again

This book is full of errors: typos, misheard lyrics, cracks in the cement, music without sound, captioning errors, sound distortion, interference, speech impediments, printing overstrikes, smudged drawings, erased words, computer glitches, interrupted conversations, broken glass. The latter refers to Marcel Duchamp's *Large Glass* (*The Bride Stripped Bare by Her Bachelors, Even*) that, while returning from its inaugural exhibition at the Brooklyn Museum in 1926, was damaged in transit, its double glass panes shattered into multiple cracks. In an interview, Duchamp remarked that fortuitously, the cracks imitated the pattern of lines in his 1914 work *Network of Stoppages* and now seemed like an integral part of the work: "It's a lot better with the breaks, a hundred times better. *It's the destiny of things*" (75). It is worth pondering the idea that things have destiny or that, in Sara Ahmed's terms, they can be "happy" and can organize relations both past and future (*The Promise of Happiness* 21–49). Duchamp's continuing legacy is testimony to this fact. For Duchamp, breaks in the glass are not flaws or mistakes but intentional events integral to the evolution of the work. The transformation of an error into new art—or a new discourse about art—is characteristic of Duchamp's oeuvre in general in which dust particles in the artist's studio or random commercial objects (urinals, bottle driers, shovels) become "works" of art. It marks a moment when the glass of retinal art is broken, its cracks exposing the material nature of transparency upon which a certain ideal of mimesis is based.

Duchamp's belief that a flaw is intentional constitutes a major event in modern art whose destiny can be read in the chance operations of John Cage, the paronomasia of *Finnegans Wake*, the mathematical procedures of Oulipo, the situationist *dérive*, musique concrète, happenings, and conceptualism. The materialization of the Word coincides with an equally important emphasis on the cultural values assigned to that materiality—the social value ascribed to sound, sight, and the integrity of the body—and as with Duchamp, with the status of the observer. The incorporation of error into the work acknowledges the fragile nature of aesthetic value and complicates any presumption of a gap between art and life.

One might say that modernism itself was born in error. The mimetic mirror is fractured when, in Cézanne's rendering, Mont St. Victoire becomes a grid of discrete facets, mountain and foreground blended into a single plane. A horizon broken by a tree suddenly reappears slightly below its presumptive continuation, violating the continuity of the retinal image but reimagining the landscape as a phenomenological experience. Speaking of the salon paintings of the 1860s, John Roberts notes that "[no] longer are errors of execution to be chastised as a failure of technique or tone; they are to be recognized as the marks of a new expressiveness, in line with the sensory demands of 'modern life'" (212). The work of art as immanent self-critique establishes an entirely new criterion for truth—an authenticity of expression rather than one of fidelity. The distortion of the body, the rupture of figure and ground, the challenge to Western tonality, the materialization of the medium are all violations of classical values of harmony, perspective, and verisimilitude. Of course, every generation's error becomes the next generation's orthodoxy as artists and writers incorporate the various permutations of novelty in new work. In a famous anecdote, Gertrude Stein reports Picasso's response to a critic who said his portrait of her did not resemble her, saying, "It will."

In a previous book, *Invalid Modernism*, I discuss a specific form that error assumes in modernism by looking at cultural depiction of the disabled, mad, and traumatized body as a challenge to classical aesthetics. The fragmentation of the body in cubism or the disarticulation of body parts in surrealism or the representation of mental illness and madness in novels and opera respond in different ways to the idealization of bodily form in neoclassicism. While certain of these distortions derived from racist and eugenicist attitudes toward the different body (embodied in Nazi "degenerate art" exhibits), they reveal an impatience with the Vitruvian version of bodily perfection. Equally in literature, the madness of Wozzeck or the mental limitations of Benjy Compson or the physical disability of Clifford Chatterley may be "narrative prostheses" for cultural decline or the effects of war, but they allow—perhaps despite the artist or author's intention—for alternate imaginings of embodiment and cognition.[1] What the eugenicists called errors of genetic purity also defined a spectrum of human variation.

Errors often reveal the truths they displace, and artists have seized upon this fact in producing new work. Errors in literature are often sites of revelation, a mistaken word illuminating the word it replaces. In Joyce's *Ulysses*, Leopold Bloom carries on an epistolary relationship with Martha Clifford, whose letters are filled with grammatical and semantic errors. At one point, she offers to punish Bloom for remarks he included in his previous letter: "I do wish I could punish you for that. I called you naughty boy because I do not like that other world. Please tell me what is the real meaning of that word?" (210). Clifford's epistolary confusion of *world* and *word* is a concise summary of *Ulysses* itself, a novel about the creation of an alternate world in words. Bloom returns to this passage often in his perambulations around Dublin as he reflects on that "other world" he fantasizes with Stephen Dedalus as his idealized son. The latter, while walking on Sandymount Strand, muses on the question, "What is that word known to all men?" (41). The missing word, as we learn, is *love*.

My interest in the quiddities of generative error is inspired not only by aesthetics but by personal experiences resulting from hearing loss. As someone who has become progressively deaf over the past fifteen years, I am increasingly aware of the mishearings, misunderstandings, and misspeakings that constitute daily social interactions. I invariably confuse what others are saying and often correct what I *should* have said in a subsequent email or text message. Although my abilities with American Sign Language (ASL) are improving, I still use captioners and dictation services in most public venues. The transcriptions they provide are essential for social interaction but are often full of mistranslations. Some of these errors are howlers, while others are confusing and frustrating. "Say again?," my inevitable response to a misheard phrase, is more than a request for clarification; it defines the recursive character of all communication as we grope toward understanding in a world of words. This post hoc understanding, what Diderot calls *l'esprit d'escalier* (the spirit of the stairs), occurs when one understands what one should have said *after* leaving the party, at the bottom of the stairs (*"ne se retrouve qu'au bas de l'escalier"* [1023–24]). Applied to my discussion of error, such moments illustrate how meaning is produced through a kind of feedback loop in which statements must be reconsidered, tested, and tried anew. As the Latin origin of the word, *errare*, suggests, error means both freedom to wander and diversion from the correct path.[2]

Something of this duplicity is contained in my title, *Distressing Language*, which is a verbal conundrum, combining a category of design with a condition of affect. Distressed clothing, pre-ripped jeans, "aged" leather, rough-textured furniture depend on the simulation of wear and tear, a stylistic marker of use that adds a patina of history to contemporary materials.[3] Douglas Kahn quotes a shirt display card in a men's clothing store that reads "Flaws and imperfections are part of this total desired look" (20). As a form of couture, distressed clothing has been attacked by critics who decry "dressing poor" as an elite fashion statement.[4] But the term also refers to affective realms of trouble and anxiety—the distress of learning of a person's death, the anxiety produced by aggressive actions or hate speech. In *Distressing Language*, I confuse both senses to describe work that makes language strange, troubling, loud, or difficult. Language that roughens the surface, effaces clarity, dissolves in puns and homonyms offers a kind of verbal static that interrupts linear communication and calls attention to the frangible nature of language itself. It also refers to the appropriation of previous uses and associations that leave their mark on the surface. Carolyn Bergvall's *Meddle English* distresses Chaucer's Middle English to draw out the hidden "midden" in language, the traces of other places, marginal spaces, and social ruptures. Harryette Mullen's use of black vernacular in *Muse and Drudge* creates a contemporary lyric poetry out of cultural materials derived from America's racial and racist history. Christine Sun Kim's recaptioning of classic movies distresses official versions by adding new captions by deaf viewers, illustrating what else can be *heard* from the visual record. The composer Alvin Lucier distresses his own voice by recording it over and over again until it becomes a single drone. A good deal of contemporary art and literature distresses conventional visual and textual material, by repurposing canonical sources, appropriating and deconstructing public rhetoric (newspapers, legal briefs, advertisements), creating homonymic equivalents for prior works, interfering with communicational conduits, or generally messing around with expectations about who hears, speaks, and communicates.

As subsequent chapters will indicate, distressing language is seen through the optic of disability, where the totality of the social symbolic order is challenged by what James Berger calls the "disarticulate" figure. Those who, because of a speech impediment, cognitive disability, deafness, neurological condition, do not speak correctly or speak at all, constitute "disarticulate" others who live outside of language and therefore define its borders:

> The strange thing is that wherever it is, the impaired figure appears to be at the center. In a text, a verbal medium, a place composed entirely of words, the figure without words or with distorted words, the one outside the symbolic loop is placed at the moral political, significatory center. (28)

Berger's paradoxical formulation—the marginal defines the center, the wrong word or usage, implicates the authority of the appropriate word—complicates a central thesis in the preface to Wittgenstein's *Tractatus*: "For in order to be able to set a limit to thought, we should have to find both sides of the limit thinkable (i.e. we should have to be able to think what cannot be thought). It will therefore only be in language that the limit can be set, and what lies on the other side of the limit will simply be nonsense" (3). Berger spies a subject on the other side of that limit—the figure whose speech is distorted, who stammers, who is mute, whose Tourette's syndrome causes uncontrolled outbursts of speech, and whose distressing language hides a functioning, conscious individual. My various examples of artists and writers who stammer (Jordan Scott, Alvin Lucier, Henry James, Lewis Carroll), who distort or misspeak words (Charles Bernstein, Larry Eigner, Norma Cole), or who speak in sign language (Christine Sun Kim, Joseph Grigely, Peter Cook) illustrate how error has impacted their work in a variety of ways. Berger's literary examples—Billy Budd, Benjy Compson, Robin Vote—display ways of not-speaking or speaking improperly that signal flaws in what socially normative speech withholds. The wordplay of Lewis Carroll's "Jabberwocky" or the verbal experiments in Zaum or Dada or in Gertrude Stein's repetitions appeared to early readers as nonsense but became defining examples of modernism. In Berger's excellent formulation, "The dys-/disarticulate is the figure of the outside of language figured in language. But he is also a representation of a human being living as an individual subject in a social world" (2). Bringing this linguistically challenged figure into the foreground is the primary focus of what follows.

Crip Failure and Deaf Gain

> Human communication is fragile. Misunderstandings abound, and their causes are so plentiful that no amount of thoughtful design could avoid them all. And so, places designed for hearing are always sites of irony. The first irony: institutions aiming to adjudicate loss may impose loss of a different kind. (Jill Stauffer, *Ethical Loneliness* 70)

Jill Stauffer's emphasis in *Ethical Loneliness*, from which my epigraph is taken, is the isolation one feels when confronted by the experience of not being heard. Immigrant detention centers, prisons, courtrooms, truth commissions, and even classrooms might be obvious sites of irony where one recognizes the disparity between one's understanding and that of those in positions of authority. When members of a persecuted or marginalized group are not listened to, they experience "ethical loneliness" in a world that refuses to hear their concerns as legitimate. I would add that deaf persons may experience ethical loneliness in a world that cannot imagine "not hearing" as anything but a tragedy. Stauffer herself creates such an ironic space in her otherwise excellent book by not mentioning deaf persons, who would be prime examples of those who historically have not been heard. Stauffer is speaking of severely marginalized populations who have been dehumanized and isolated by power structures, whereas deaf persons have a rich cultural heritage through sign language that provides vital community and solidarity. My point is that among the "places designed for hearing" that produce ethical loneliness, Stauffer might have considered the uncaptioned movie, the non-signed presidential briefing, the DMV office without a translator, verbal announcements of gate changes in airports, a classroom with a deaf student but no interpreter, and the myriad examples of opprobrious usage: "You idiot, are you deaf?," "She was deaf to his entreaties," "It was like talking to a deaf person." She might have alluded to the loneliness experienced by students in deaf residential schools during the latter nineteenth and early twentieth-centuries whose use of sign language was punished by having their hands slapped.

Current debates surrounding cultural appropriation, cyberbullying, and hate speech might be obvious sites where not being heard arises. Language that offends or disturbs or that, in Althusser's terms, "hails" and interpellates oneself as the other is distressing for the recipient while legitimating and empowering for the one who speaks. Throughout US history, the presence of migrant populations has raised concerns about the impact of "foreign" languages on English, with the concurrent need to secure a national language standard. Such concerns are embedded in racist and xenophobic attitudes toward different populations, fueled by equally unsettling language from political figures who insist on proper pronunciation and English literacy as a mark of citizenship. In the biblical shibboleth, which I discuss in chapter 3, the imperative of proper pronunciation is used to identify and isolate an alien or enemy group. The shibboleth is currently alive and well in attempts to impose English-only restrictions on voting, immigration, education, and representation. Yet the fact that certain types of language—vulgarities, racist slurs, insensitive pronominal use, sexist language—have the power to excite political challenge reinforces the performative fact of language use; it enacts what it claims, it interpellates the other, marginalizes the different, and inculcates a plural subject ("we the people") that does not yet exist. When the performative power of language is enlisted in cultural projects, it has the ability to place speech acts in quotation marks and makes speech "say again" in a different register.

This inversionary process characterizes the current usage of *crip* to describe critical disability projects. On the model of queer politics to unseat heteronormative authorizing of gender and sexuality, crip politics appropriates a term of opprobrium from the long history of prejudice against people with disabilities and rearticulates it as a critical lens on ableist assumptions. It is also an infinitive with analytical power: to crip is to critique but also to make unstable certain assumptions about looking, sounding, and being human. Crip theory aligns with queer theory in questioning ideas of futurity that imagine a world free of distressing conditions, symptoms, diseases, desires, debility. Crip theory owes a good deal to Robert McRuer's titular book that explores the compulsory character of able-bodiedness and the analogy with Adrienne Rich's formulation of compulsory heterosexuality. The twin vectors of crip and queer theory merge around a critique of embodied normalcy—a "normate" identity, in Rosemarie Garland-Thomson's terms—that organizes social identities (8). McRuer foregrounds the intersection of queer and crip identities in exposing the limits of a productivist economy that insists on the reproduction of a unitary national subject. One of the key features of McRuer's book and his other writings is his linkage of crip/queer theory to ideas of progress and improvement embodied in neoliberal social policies. To imagine a different bodymind is also to imagine a different narrative of community, kinship, and nation not dependent on capitalist accumulation and the requirement that "things must get better."[5] To imagine a body that doesn't fit, that fails to comport with heterosexual reproduction and kinship norms, is to make that disidentification a site for new languages and art. In Jack Halberstam's terms, queer (and I would add crip) failure contains the ability to "poke holes in the toxic positivity of contemporary life" (3).

Crip failure comes into conflict with cultural nationalist attempts to validate the gains of deafness and disability. Deaf activists have used the phrase *Deaf gain* to challenge the ideology of audism—the belief in hearing as communicational norm and deafness as defect or loss—and to argue for the capabilities, not liabilities, of being deaf. For Dirksen Bauman and Joseph Murray, deafness is not a "loss of hearing" but a cultural advantage based on the use of sign language and participation within the Deaf community. To say that one is "partially deaf" or experiences "hearing loss" is to align with a hearing culture for which deafness can be imagined only as a defect. "How can a deaf person simply not be deaf?" Kristen Harmon asks (125). "Do the modifying adjectives *mildly* or *partially*—as opposed to *profoundly*—ameliorate, pacify, the requirements of a hearing bias?" (125) Arguing from within deafness rather than from without, Deaf activists have uncovered the advantages and gains that deafness offers—a "different center," as Carol Padden and Tom Humphreys call it (*Deaf in America* 39–55). Deaf gain involves reordering of priorities not around sound but around sight, of signed rather than spoken or written language, of communication written *on* the body, not about it.

The "paradigm shift," as Bauman says, from hearing loss to Deaf gain has been a positive step forward in claiming deafness for diversity. But this value is weakened when it excludes large portions of the non- or partially hearing public who occupy various positions on what Christopher Krentz has called "the hearing line." Many of us cross that line on a daily basis, experiencing the alienating features of living in a hearing environment yet without fluency in ASL or with friends and family who do not sign. Hearing loss is an inevitable condition of aging, and many older persons, especially those on fixed incomes, may find the cost of hearing aids (not covered in most insurance policies) prohibitive. Aaron Williamson, who inspired the phrase *Deaf gain*, is a successful deaf performance artist whose work about being deaf is everywhere and yet who does not himself sign and who reads lips.[6] Many deaf persons who lose their hearing at a later stage of life nevertheless maintain extensive contact with hearing friends and family. Deafness—and disability more broadly—has not been included under the broad umbrella of diversity, and the claims of Deaf gain go a long way toward reversing this fact. At the same time, the claims need to include a broader constituency of persons who live closer to the hearing line and who support the political goals of Deaf World. In this book, I use *deaf communities*, plural, to indicate the multiple manifestations of deaf identity but retain capital-*D* Deafness to speak of the cultural and political meaning of communities formed through sign language. I might add that these communities are further diversified by whether one is congenitally deaf or has acquired deafness later in life.[7]

To return to the issue of queer/crip failure, I would include the importance of cross-cultural encounters as among the constitutive features d/Deaf experience. The work of significant deaf and hard-of-hearing artists and writers whom I discuss in this book—Christine Sun Kim, Alison O'Daniel, Joseph Grigely, Liza Sylvestre, David Wright, Gerald Shea, Peter Cook—is often about their varying and vexed relationships to the hearing world. Kim's installation at the 2019 Whitney Biennale, discussed in chapter 2, is called *Deaf Rage* and features large panels depicting different geometric angles whose roughly sketched captions describe the artist's anger at institutions and spaces that exclude or minoritize persons with hearing problems—lack of interpreters or captions, inadequate signage, insensitive service personnel. Her foregrounding of *Deaf Rage* in a significant art venue like the Whitney Biennale is an art of distress that celebrates Deaf identities through art—a gain—but that does not stint the complexities of living in a world that does not hear what a deaf person might see.

For my own part, I have certainly gained from deafness. My previous life as a poet and scholar was upended when I could no longer attend poetry readings or hear those readings on websites like PennSound or teach without captioners and interpreters. I had to rethink the canonical prosodic terms by which poetry is defined—rhyme, rhythm, voice, ear, ear rhymes, assonance, and so on—by considering what those terms mean when the poem is signed on the body. As someone who now relies more on visual than acoustic information, I appreciate other ways of communicating beyond the verbal or textual, and I draw information from bodily movement, facial features, spatial proximity, and lip movement. Basic categories of time and space must now be refined to include varying temporalities of meaning production and proximity. Social intercourse has become as much a spatial phenomenon as a communicational one. Most important, my slow and gradual ability to use ASL has brought a keener sense of embodied social relations, the ability to read facial expressions and body language as components of language. I also appreciate the beauty of a signed language that condenses persons and actions, pronouns and verbs, in a single motion. The kinds of economies and condensations I appreciate in poetry are embedded in the linguistic structure of ASL.[8] And this incipient understanding of a new language has acquainted me with a range of deaf artists and writers whose work challenges the generic terms of a given medium and renegotiated the usual venues and generic terms for a variety of media. But my understanding of Deaf gain is tempered by an awareness of the stresses and social tensions that subtend it.

Distributed Voice

In Ferdinand de Saussure's *Cours de linguistique générale* communication, what he calls the "speech circuit" is represented by a schematic drawing of two (somewhat degendered) male speakers in conversation. The circuit between A and B is reciprocal; A sends an utterance from his mouth to B's ear, and B responds in the same manner to A. The speech act, *parole*, consists of an active role by the speaker and a passive role for the receiver. The result, when successful, is what we call "mutual understanding." Each interlocutor draws from a common reservoir of socially approved signs, *langue*, separate from the speech act. Speaking is individual; language is collective and social, its formation the result of arbitrary relations between an individual sign and its meaning. *Parole* requires the production of sounds that are reconstituted in the brain of the interlocutor. Institutional variables (church, school, salons, the court, national academies) impact the structure of *langue* but not *parole*.

What would happen if we complicated Saussure's famous diagram by introducing a person who is hard of hearing and uses a hearing aid or a cochlear implant? Or imagine that this person reads his interlocutor's voice on a caption-phone screen? What if the interlocutor is a woman whose native language is Spanish and whose accent is difficult for the captioning system to translate? What about ambient noise in the background that interferes with the signal? What if A and B are deaf and their conversation is being conducted on Zoom or FaceTime in ASL? Is audible speech necessary to the circuit? What about distortion, temporal interruption, feedback as factors? And to what extend do gender, racial, and national power dynamics affect the otherwise unmediated circuit?

I mention these complicating circumstances to suggest that Saussure's speech circuit is, like the drawing, highly schematic and does not account for the real-time experience of most conversations, let alone those between deaf and hard-of-hearing persons and the hearing world. In 1916, when the *Cours* first appeared, Saussure could not have anticipated the multiple and varied forms of mediation that "voice" would experience through electronic and then digital platforms. The idea of voice itself, as Derrida has pointed out with respect to Saussure, is not the originary source of meaning but in fact an *effect* of linguistic difference (*différance*) embodied by writing.[9] In this book, I refer to voice as "distributed" to describe communication as mediated by electronic and digital media, prosthetics, accent, temporal delays, ambient noise, neurological and psychological distortions.[10] I am not referring to the heteroglossia of social speech, as described by Bakhtin, nor am I thinking of collaborative projects involving multiple or choral voices as in sound poetry, although these areas have contributed to my thinking about the limits of the unitary voice. Rather, my focus is on the plurality of the voice itself as it is multiplied, distorted, and diffused among various media platforms, sign systems, and vocal capabilities. In chapter 4, I discuss, for example, Vygotsky's idea of "inner speech," which refers to the eruptive and ongoing conversation that occurs in the mind, "a sludgy thing, thickened with reiterated quotation, choked with the rubble of the overheard," as Denise Riley describes it.[11]

The mediated, distributed nature of voice has occupied an important place in sound art and poetics, and many of my examples in this book provide instances. One example, which I do not cover in the book, is provided by Richard Serra and Nancy Holt's 1974 video *Boomerang*, in which Serra tape recorded the artist Nancy Holt as she talked and heard her words played back to her after a one-second delay. In the video, she struggles to continue speaking while listening and responding to her own voice, an experience that she describes as "a world of double reflections and refractions." As her voice echoes—"boomerangs," to use her term—back to her, "words become like things," disconnected from their individual meanings and from their contexts. The feedback of her voice interrupts her forward-moving thought processes and focuses on itself *as voice*. "I'm throwing things out in the world and they are boomeranging back . . . boomeranging . . . eranging . . . anginging." We hear her attempts at organizing her speech around a specific word that dissolves in dislocated syllables and false starts, and we witness her discomfiture as she tests what she hears against what she says about what she hears.[12]

Rosalind Krauss has characterized *Boomerang* as the epitome of narcissism in video art in the sense that the medium, rather than an objective surface separate from the artist like canvas or film celluloid, is the "simultaneous reception and projection of an image; and the human psyche used as a conduit" (52).[13] In the case of the Serra-Holt collaboration (Krauss tends to see it as Serra's work with Holt as a "willing . . . subject"), the subject is suspended; Holt "has great difficulty coinciding with herself as a subject." This formulation tends to privilege a subject who, could she speak without earphones, would be whole and complete. But *Boomerang* foregrounds the condition of any subject being bombarded with conflicting information, a subject engaged not just with herself but with a world that expects a certain kind of discourse. Krauss is right to see video art as often focused on the artist's psyche—Vito Acconci's or Bruce Nauman's video art would be more appropriate—but here Serra has divided the art "object" and discourse in two, with him filming Holt speaking or trying to speak to her own discourse. And since Holt is an artist herself, it is a video of two artists collaborating on several levels. I agree that Holt has difficulty "coinciding with herself as a subject," if by "subject" we mean the expectation that a subject "speaks" in a normative fashion in real time. For persons whose speech is impeded through neurological or physical disabilities, that subject cannot be assumed. And in addition, nor can the temporalities of "real time" organize the experience of mediated speech—say, the speech of a person who uses a text-to-voice system or that of deaf person with an interpreter. The "delay" that Serra imposes in Holt's hearing institutes a temporal disjunction the challenges the mirror metaphor implied by narcissism.[14]

As I have been suggesting, for deaf and hard-of-hearing persons, not "coinciding" with oneself as subject means not coinciding with a presumptive hearing world. Holt's hermeneutic task of reading herself, of distributing her voice through both visual and acoustic frames, uses that non-alignment as a mark of a different, distributed subjectivity. The art of interruption–in this case a tape delay—may not address disability, but it reveals the disorientations that attend social intercourse and make "mutual understanding" a willful fantasy.[15]

Poetics of Error

Life is what is capable of error.
—Michel Foucault, introduction to Georges Canguilhem's
The Normal and the Pathological

Now I know that I would rather embrace the flaws.
—Michael Palmer, "The Danish Notebook"

Did I say "calamine"?
I meant "chamomile."
—Paul Muldoon, "Cuthbert and the Otters"

Over
that totalizing irony of incompleat
(*sic*) sentences, slipped phrases, twisted
hesitant logic, all hiccups in the syntax . . .
—Ron Silliman, *What*

Shelley's pen slipped
referring to the Sun
Isle Continent Ocean
The date July 1st 1822
across "?fury" may be
"day" or "fiery"
by mischief superimposed on *wild*
tercet mask tercet
—Susan Howe, "Melville's Marginalia"

he sees that he has written pain for paint.   and it works
better
—Tom Raworth, "South America"

I thought I saw a crumpled blanket lying on the bed, but
then I saw it was an improviser standing on his head.
—Lyn Hejinian, *My Life in the Nineties*

It goes to show you. It was not the "Eppie Sawyer." It was the
ship "Putnam." It wasn't Christmas morning, it was Christmas night, after dark. And the violent north-easter, with
snow, which we were all raised to believe did show Bowditch
such a navigator, was a gale sprung up from W, hit them outside the Bay, and had blown itself out by the 23rd.
—Charles Olson, "Maximus, to Gloucester: Letter 15"

Danger
I thought it said dancer
—Charles Tomlinson, "Autumn Piece"

Right: the poems I write and love to read often dog the fail.
When so, writing is picking at the mess.
—Dennis Kearney, "Mess"

M. NourbeSe Philip records that when she attempted to print out a draft
of her poem "Zong!," "the laser printer for no apparent reason [printed]
the first two or three pages superimposed on each other—crumped, so

to speak—so that the page becomes a dense landscape of text" (206). The error was not repeated in subsequent printings, but when she attempted to print out later sections of the book, the same thing happened. Rather than correct the error and reprint, she decided to include the overprinted version in the final published book, seeing it as a material reminder of African bodies erased in the Middle Passage that are the subject of the text. On another level, "Zong!" is written over another, more authoritative, text, a legal case, *Gregson v. Gilbert,* involving slaves who were thrown overboard from the ship Zong in 1791 when the ship foundered in the Caribbean. Printing the overstruck version of the page becomes a metaphor for an absence that is the book's subject, a "story that simultaneously cannot be told, must be told, and will never be told" (189). That double vectored story concerns the question of slaves' legibility and whether they could be regarded as human since their fate rested in legal documents and contracts. Philip incorporates the official legal summary of *Gregson v. Gilbert* at the end of the book as the source text for much of her writing in the body of the book. Or rather, the "body" of her book is made out of distortions in the textual body of *Gregson.*

I have discussed "Zong!" elsewhere, but here I want to call attention to Philip's willingness to include a printer error in her poem, creating text that is illegible.[16] As a strategy specific to the poem's interrogation of violence in the Middle Passage, her gesture makes visible the erasure of enslaved African bodies who became commodities in a maritime insurance claim. The ghostly overstriking effaces the original text yet leaves some words partly visible, instantiating the power of language over abject bodies yet illustrating the unstable nature of words used to enslave and contain. We could see Philip's gesture as one of many instances among contemporary poets of incorporating error into poetry, either to correct the record or show a mistake as a natural feature of meaning-making. My short list of examples above is only a cursory selection of passages in which a poet corrects an error, allowing the original term to resonate differently. Michael Palmer's assertion that "I would rather embrace the flaws" summarizes the reparative value of error in poetics.

Before going further into the poetics of error, I should observe that my use of error differs in significant ways from its usage in communication and information theory. As formulated by Claude Shannon in *The Mathematical Theory of Communication,* information concerns the probability of a signal's ability to transmit; it is not about the semantic content of the message but about the ability of a signal to be decoded by a receiver without interference: "The fundamental problem of communication is that of reproducing at one point either exactly or approximately a message selected at another point. . . . The significant aspect is that the actual message is one *selected from a set of possible messages*" (31). Selection is key here; the greater redundancy in a message—more letters, more words, more qualifiers—the greater the chance that it will reach its destination. Or as Kathryn Hayles summarizes, "Information is identified with choices that reduce uncertainty" (31). Error for Shannon occurs when the process of transduction, the system's ability to decode an audible signal into text, fails due to interference, noise, electronic glitches. When one uses the search function on a smart TV to locate a film, the first letter tapped creates a vast list of possible films. The second letter narrows the field, and by the third letter, we have enough information to select from a considerably reduced list. The more information—in this case, letters—the easier it is for the right answer to be chosen. Or to take another example, the dictation application on my smartphone transcribes conversation pretty accurately in one-on-one conversations in quiet rooms, but the system fails when there are competing conversations in the surrounding area. In crowded restaurants, the system shuts down due to too much noise. As I will point out, however, "too much noise" is often the very condition for aesthetic novelty. The task for Shannon was to use statistical methods to eliminate such noise so that the message can be transmitted without interruption; the task for many writers in this book is to interrupt the message and explore its possible detours and deviations.

The discourse of poetics begins in error. Aristotle's term *hamartia*, to "miss the mark" or "err," is usually translated as the protagonist's "tragic flaw." In Greek tragedy, an individual of high estate and power is laid low by his willingness, as in the case of Oedipus, to defy the gods' injunction. For Aristotle, the function of tragedy is pedagogical: to display the protagonist's hubris and to use that recognition to instruct a public. It is this performative or dramatistic function of error that has pertinence for modern art and literature where errancy is on full display—as with Duchamp's *Large Glass* prominently installed at the Philadelphia Museum of Art—even in those instances where formal closure and organic containment are stressed. Edgar Allan Poe's restatement of Francis Bacon, "There is no exquisite beauty . . . without some strangeness in the proportion," and Keats's negative capability are foundational affirmations of error in modern poetics.

To some extent, the incorporation of error in poetry recognizes a crucial fact about poetic language. Metaphor, after all, is based on such disproportion between tenor and vehicle in an attempt to make a figure clearer by making it different. Harold Bloom makes this fact the centerpiece of his theory of misreading: "A trope is a *willing* error, a turn from literal meaning in which a word or phrase is used in an improper sense, wandering from its rightful place" (qtd. in McAlpine 52). Where I differ from Bloom is the idea that there is a "rightful place" in the first place, a stable signified to ground the errant signifier. In the language of the Russian formalists, poetry "defamiliarizes" ordinary language, reimagining the ordinary to see it better or to understand its conventional character. Thus to emphasize an error of printing, speaking, or remembering is to foreground something basic about what those acts attempt to secure. In my example above, Charles Tomlinson's couplet "Danger / I thought it said dancer" hints at an act of misreading that by bringing together two seemingly antithetical terms reveals their closer proximity in the poem as a whole:

Autumn Piece
Baffled
by the choreography of the season
the eye could not
with certainty see
whether it was wind
stripping the leaves or
the leaves were struggling to be free:

They came at you
in decaying spirals
plucked flung and regathered by the same
force that was twisting
the scarves of the vapour trails
dragging all certainties out of course:

> As the car resisted it
> you felt it in either hand
> commanding car, tree, sky,
> master of chances,
> and at a curve was a red
> board said 'Danger':
> I thought it said dancer. (91)

"Autumn Piece" figures the "choreography of the seasons" through an image of swirling leaves in the wind as seen from a car. The poem describes the author's confusion of perception about whether his eye could "with certainty see / whether it was wind / stripping the leaves or / the leaves were struggling to be free." Both possibilities exist in a kind of autumnal dance of death, one force removing leaves toward winter, the other freeing leaves toward springtime rebirth. "The same / force" that is "dragging all certainties out of course" is also the confusion that haunts the last line, a misreading that is, in fact, a new understanding. A mistaken warning sign, "Danger," becomes a continuation of the dance. Recording the error in his final lines is a kind of memento mori for the mortality he intuits as he drives into the wind, an oxymoronic conjunction of opposites.

In *Distressing Language,* I am less concerned with errors of fact, grammatical usage, or printer's errors than with their use in furthering the poem's development. The classic example of the former type would be Keats's misattribution of Balboa's first sighting of the Pacific Ocean to Cortez in his sonnet "Upon First Looking into Chapman's Homer" ("Or like stout Cortez when with eagle eyes / He star'd at the Pacific— / and all his men / Look'd at each other with a wild surmise— / Silent, upon a peak in Darien." [64]). Here, his error is one of fact and history (including a requirement for a two and not three syllable explorer's name). The same holds for Ben Jonson who pointed out that Shakespeare's description of "Bohemian shores" in *Winter's Tale* provides the landlocked Bohemia with a nearby ocean. The printers who regularized Emily Dickinson's punctuation in the few poems she published, substituting colons or periods for her idiosyncratic dashes, violated the multistable syntax that is the hallmark of the poet's style. As Erica McAlpine in *The Poet's Mistake* suggests, such errors are often explained by use of Freud's *Psychopathology of Everyday Life* or justified by the implication of mistaken intentions or printer's errors. The key issue here is intentionality—whether Keats intended to violate the historical record or whether Dickinson really intended to use a semicolon where a dash appeared. McAlpine is more interested in how mistakes "open up for exploring poetry's subjectivity and its interpretation" (27). The errors that interest me are those whose recognition within the poem or artwork becomes an *element* of that poetic "subjectivity."

Poetic error is here a variant of what rhetoricians call "catachresis" as a general term for a word's improper use. In terms developed by du Marsais and Fontanier, it is a "trope of abuse" since it lacks a referent or analogue; it "abuses" metaphor by dissolving any seamless fit between tenor and vehicle. For Derrida, drawing on Fontanier's *Supplement to the Theory of Tropes*, catachresis is a master trope for metaphor, "a sign already affected with a first idea also being affected with a new idea, which itself had no sign at all or no longer properly has any other in language" (255).[17] In Derrida's usage, quoting Fontanier, catachresis marks the linguistic "supplement," a space carved out of the imposition of a "sign upon a meaning which [does] not yet have its own proper sign in language" (255). How would one represent that space? Michel Foucault, in speaking of the works of Raymond Roussel, describes it as a semantic void produced by a collision between the multiplicity of things and the paucity of words to describe them: "It is not where the canonical figures of speech originate, but that neutral space within language where the hollowness of the word is shown as an insidious void, arid and as trap" (16).[18] Tomlinson's juxtaposition of "danger" and "dancer" hints at this unresolvable gap by foregrounding it as an error of perception. NourbeSe Phillip's inclusion of a printer's overtyped copy similarly creates a catachrestic gap by a material representation of the unspeakable nature of slavery. Her gesture performs the inadequacy of language's ability to explain or justify the transformation of a human into a commodity.

Correcting also historicizes one's error. When Charles Olson, in the above example, corrects the record in the opening to one of his *Maximus Poems*, he shows himself in the act of fusing the historian and the poet. He both "corrects himself" in the sense of setting to rights a previous mistake, and also displays the instability of the historical record and his own culpability in reproducing it. In an earlier *Maximus* poem, "Letter

2," he describes the whaling boat *Eppie Sawyer* being brought to port: "as Bowditch brought the Eppie Sawyer / spot to her wharf a Christmas morning," but upon reading another account of the event, he discovers that it was "the ship Putnam" and "It wasn't Christmas morning, it was Christmas night, after dark" (11, 71). What might seem like a minor discrepancy is an occasion for Olson to display himself as historian, "as Herodotus was, looking / for oneself for the evidence of / what is said" (104). For Olson, this is a crucial aspect of poetry's claim to historicity: to embody acts of thinking, recalibrating, revising so that the poem becomes as much a record of what happened as what might have otherwise happened. To be a historian as Herodotus was is to show oneself *in* the historical moment.

One synonym for error is deviation, the study of which will, as Zachary Sng says, "reinforce the stability of the norm through the implicit suggestion that deviation could be excluded or even rehabilitated" (3). Recording an error of perception or of historical information testifies to the equivocation in language between the godhead and the material word, a supplement to the Word, codified in metaphor: bearing a cross. Emily Dickinson often meditates on this problem (and indeed the metaphor of incarnation) in her poetry by imagining herself violating the word of God by presuming to speak through her own "loved philology." But she recognizes the danger in this act since it appropriates the master's language for herself:

> A Word made Flesh is seldom
> And tremblingly partook
> Nor then perhaps reported
> But have I not mistook
> Each one of us has tasted
> With ecstasies of stealth
> The very food debated
> To our specific strength—
>
> A Word that breathes distinctly
> Has not the power to die
> Cohesive as the Spirit
> It may expire if He—

"Made Flesh and dwelt among us"
Could condescension be
Like this consent of Language
This loved Philology. (671)

Here the declaration of error illustrates a moral conundrum regarding whether her art offers the same "cohesion" and extensiveness as that of the Word of God. Dickinson's idiosyncratic Calvinism allows her to question the difference between the incarnation—the Word made flesh—and the absence it materializes. She is talking about poetry, among other things, and her own ability to make a word "that breathes distinctly." That word would be unnecessary if "He—'Made Flesh and dwelt among us'" could appear in the flesh. She rather wittily chastises herself for partaking of that original Word that condescends to speak to her. In the imperatives of Puritan theology, one must repudiate any claim to grace, yet at the same time, "Each one of us has tasted / With ecstasies of stealth / The very food debated / To our specific strength." To the early New England Puritans, this was heresy, especially the idea that the sacramental art of writing is equivalent to the communion wafer, but to the mid-century antinomian poet, it is a claim for agency. She recognizes that her stealthy appropriation of God's word is an error: "have I not mistook." It is done ecstatically, the erotic and subversive implication of that term hinting at the excitement she feels in stealing the logos for herself. Hence a poetics of error is both ecstatic and dangerous, creating art by speaking out of turn.

Sound Studies

In my concern with mishearing and deafness, I have benefited, perhaps counterintuitively, from research in sound studies.[19] The work of Jonathan Sterne, Steven Connor, Paul Carter, Douglas Kahn, Veit Erlmann, Michel Chion, Mara Mills, Michel Friedner, Nina Sun Eidsheim, and more distantly, Martin Heidegger, Jacques Attali, and Jean-Luc Nancy have introduced the importance of sound as a cultural and conceptual field in ways that have implications for the social meaning of sound.[20] As Michele Friedner and Stefan Helmreich argue, the disciplines of sound and deaf studies tend to silo sensory modes, privileging sight for deaf persons and acoustics for sound studies instead of looking for areas of convergence. Among those areas would be shared experiences of low-frequency vibration, "deaf futurist" projections through cochlear implants usage, and "relationships between signing, non-speech-based communications and phonocentric models of speech" (74). How, then, to move beyond ear and eye, "rethinking the subjects of Sound and Deaf Studies" (75). I would add to their important formulations a few other avenues for thinking of how sound and deaf studies might inter-act around the social or cultural meaning of sound and how deaf and hard-of-hearing artists have constructed alternative narratives about the presumed opposition of sight and sound.

In chapters 2 and 6, I describe the "siting of sound" in the work of various composers and sound artists who are interested in not only the acoustic properties of sound but also the social values assigned to sound, hearing, and voice and the spaces in which sound sounds. The sonic en-vironment provides information about where we are, who is approach-ing and from which side, who is speaking, why we feel threatened, when to duck, who is in the room, and if we are sight impaired, the location of the bus stop, the intersection, the oncoming car. As someone who has only slight hearing on my right side, it governs where I sit in restaurants (in corners, to the left of my interlocutors) and even whom I avoid for conversations (those who mumble or cover their mouths). And need-less to say, poetry has been concerned with the properties of sound—as heard or, as in John Stuart Mill, "over-heard." T. S. Eliot's aesthetics is everywhere concerned with what he called "the auditory imagination," "the feeling for syllable and rhythm, penetrating far below the conscious levels of thought and feeling" (111). The preeminence of auditory imagi-nation in Dante and Shakespeare (and its weakness in Milton and Ar-nold) occupies a good deal of his poetic theory. It is less the material matter of sound that motivates Eliot's discussion than poetry's ability to harness the affective quality of sound prior to our making sense of it.

In the chapters that follow, I study the effect and affect of sound as it is heard and misheard, signed and translated into words. This interest in sound conflicts, as I have already indicated, with many of the prin-ciples of Deaf World and its important critique of audism—the ideology that presumes speech and sound as the norms for social identity. That critique addresses the cultural capital of sound by showing the various ways that deaf people are excluded by the presumption of hearing and speech. Sound studies shares with Deaf culture an awareness that sound is never neutral and never without a political subject. When Eric Garner shouted "I can't breathe," his speech was unheard by the New York police officers who put him in the chokehold that eventually killed him. But his eleven repetitions of that phrase were heard differently by the black community in which he lived and who responded in protests against police brutality. When Daniel Panteleo, the white officer who put him in the chokehold, was acquitted, riots ensued that furthered the Black Lives Matter movement, often invoking "I can't breathe" as a mantra and writing the phrase on tapes over their mouths. The ownership of language depends on the ears of the listener. Speech is not the product of the speaker but, as Nina Eidsheim says, of the one who hears it.[21]

The "cultural work" of hearing, in Paul Carter's terms, occurs when the contract between speaker and listener is broken, when the pronunciation of a word marks the speaker as foreign, where the misheard word marks the listener as obtuse or inattentive. When the ground rules for listening are broken, in Carter's words, power imbalances are revealed, permitting what he calls "echoic mimicry" within the mishearer to provide "a means by which the relatively weak resist silencing, preserving instead a degree of historical agency" (44). And as I have discussed earlier, the cultural work of hearing is the subject of many deaf artists who foreground the misuses of speech and lipreading in oralist education that oppressed many generations of deaf persons. To mishear and misspeak may lead to odd semantic trajectories far from the original intent that frustrate progress in a conversation as demonstrated by Mr. Magoo and Mrs. Malaprop.

Or by Gilda Radner's dotty newscaster, Emily Litella, on *Saturday Night Live*. In one skit, Litella expresses her ire at a recent Supreme Court decision: "What's all this fuss I hear about the Supreme Court decision on a 'deaf' penalty? It's terrible! Deaf people have enough problems as it is!" There may be more at stake in Litella's confusion over *death* and *deaf* that she realizes. Such mishearings are pretty inventive, and it would be churlish to exclude the pleasures of verbal error from our consideration of sound and communication studies. In my final chapter, I discuss the wild inventiveness of captioning errors, whether produced by closed captioning of news broadcasts or stenographers or through dictation applications on one's smartphone. I occasionally allude to actual conversational errors in my own experience and compare them to the work of avant garde poets who have exploited the sonic properties of words released from their semantic obligations. On the way to the signified, the signifier becomes seduced by a chance encounter with a familiar phoneme and brings forth a new logos—or as Jack Spicer called it, a "low-ghost."[22]

Overview

Distressing Language traces the various strands in my title as it applies to hearing, speaking, and understanding. It is a book informed by disability studies, but I hope that it offers insights into the work of art in an age of technological innovation. Woven throughout is the issue of what mistakes mean when they upset a particular protocol of behavior or comprehension and how error is constitutive of novel ways of thinking and doing. At issue is the ownership of language and what it means to use another person's words or images to mean differently. One person's critical art project is another's "excitable speech." And the question extends to matters of genre and sensation: What is music if it can't be heard? What is sculpture if it can't be seen. What is speech if it can't be understood? What is understanding if it is belated, like Minerva's owl at the falling of the dusk?

My increasing deafness has been my guide through each of these questions, pointing me toward the sensory logics that organize what passes for truth and providing alternative paths when the trail is blocked or its trajectory hard to see. It has organized the choice of chapter topics and the rather circuitous paths through various artistic and theoretical encounters. To that extent, my archive extends to include poets, visual artists, composers, filmmakers, novelists, and performance artists in an attempt to complicate fixed generic categories. I see this as an essential work of critical disability studies in organizing fields of study around embodiment rather than the distinct features of different media.

Chapter 1 offers an overview of the relationship between hearing and understanding and the manifestations by poets and artists who foreground mishearing in their work. In this and other chapters, I am making an implicit argument for expanding the genre of poetry to include a wide spectrum of cultural productions for which error is a constitutive feature. This aspect is central to my treatment of Christine Sun Kim in chapter 2 and her exploration of cultural meanings of sound for deaf and hearing audiences. It also provides me with a concrete example of an artist who distributes the senses, in terms developed by Jacques Rancière, across several media and platforms. In this chapter, I also discuss the work of Christian Marclay, whose photographic work in *Things I've Heard* displays the representation of sound in vernacular culture. Like Kim, Marclay is interested in sites where signs of sound occur in specific social environments.

In like manner, chapter 3, on misspeaking, looks at the valorization of speech in Western society and the political and social stakes for persons who stutter, interrupt, confuse syllables, and violate speech protocols. My major example is the political use of the shibboleth to isolate and minoritize individuals based on their mispronunciation of language. The chapter concludes with the work of Canadian poet Jordan Scott, in whose work misspeaking due to a lifelong stutter is rearticulated as an archaeological dig into physiological sources of sound and geological and animate forms of life. Chapter 4 continues the issue of misspeaking by focusing on vocal impairment and temporal displacement in the work of the poet Larry Eigner, who lived with cerebral palsy and whose speech was difficult to understand. His constricted speech and difficulty typing contributed to his compositional method, providing an opportunity to rethink the temporalities of disability. When Eigner in one poem writes "slow / is / the poem," he speaks metaphorically about a physiological condition that contributes to his "slow poetics."

Chapter 5 looks at the problem of difficulty in recent poetry that appropriates language from public sources and legal documents. In Jena Osman's *Corporate Relations*, the poet draws on legal language in recent court cases involving corporate subjectivity. The chapter involves a close reading of the opening poem in that volume, "Persona Ficta," and its rhetorical strategies in exposing the logic by which a corporation may be considered equivalent to an individual for the purposes of donating large sums of money to political figures. By *distressing* the language of jurisprudence, Osman *diverts* language into an alternate register for the lyric.

Chapter 6, "Missing Music," deals with the absence of music due to hearing loss and the implications of "missing" for music in general. By looking at composers whose work was not written necessarily to be heard—what Seth Kim-Cohen calls "non-cochlear music"—I engage with some fundamental issues surrounding the acoustic basis of music and the audiences who are its presumed consumers. My primary example is the work of Alison O'Daniel, who refers to herself as "border dweller" between hearing and deaf worlds and who has created a vast film archive of the soundscapes of Los Angeles as seen from the standpoint of both deaf and hearing demographics. I return to this theme in my final chapter, "A Captioned Life," based to some extent on the frustrations and delays in using voice-recognition software and captioning technologies. The chapter reflects on artists who repurpose captions toward critical ends: the artists Liza Sylvestre and Carolyn Lazard and the poet Robert Fitterman. Their work foregrounds the caption as an ideological site of meaning-making where the imperative to explain or translate becomes its own text.

My afterword, "Redressing Language," confronts the rhetoric surrounding the coronavirus pandemic that has raged during the writing of this book. The Trump administration's refusal to acknowledge the severity of COVID-19 and the president's presentation of "alternate facts" to those of epidemiologists and medical experts is a vivid example of distressing language whose propagation had the effect of proliferating the disease. If we live in a post-truth society, where objective facts for one are fictions for others, what is the value of talking about error at all? As a response, I look briefly at another model of validation in the work of Georges Canguilhem, who looks at error from the standpoint of medical philosophy. In his book *The Normal and the Pathological*, he understands disease as an anomaly, "a fact of individual variation," within the molecular structure of the individual. Truth and error, normal and abnormal, are co-constitutive in the biological reality of the human species.

"Error is a restless border dweller, and its haunting ground is the shifting boundary between irrecuperable breakdown and potentially productive deviation" (Sng 161). In his book on error in Enlightenment philosophy, Zachary Sng observes that this "double valency" of error occurs most forcefully "at the same sites where the boldest claims about knowledge, value, and meaning were advanced in the eighteenth century" (ibid.). As applied to the postwar period in poetics and visual art, this same "double valency" haunts an ideology of authenticity and immediacy. If to err is human, then to display error, whether in dance,

music or poetry, is to display the human in its most variable and vulnerable form. Since *Distressing Language* emerges from disability and deaf
studies, the display of error in art has an especially important function
in haunting the ideologies of ableism and audism. We are, as Heidegger
says in another context, "always astray in errancy" (qtd. in Roberts 6), a
fact that becomes brilliantly clear when because of a physical or sensory
impairment we fail to "fit" in an environment that does not accommodate particular bodies. But this book also emerges from a longstanding
belief in the politics of form when the failure of language to confirm
what is expected or reasonable—as in poetry—leads us astray in errancy.

1

Poetics of Mishearing

Perhaps in this sense, all hearing is mishearing
—Steven Connor

Instead of ant wort I saw brat guts
—Bob Perelman

"Bad for Glass"

My grandson and I are driving in the car. He says from the back seat,
"Caesar salad." I ask, "What?" He repeats, "Caesar thirsty." I try again:
"Are you thirsty?" In frustration, he says, "Seize Darcy!" I say, "You mean
your cousin, Darcy?" He says, "NO, SHE'S DIRTY!" I pull over and turn
around so I can read his lips. He points at the dashboard clock; it's 6:30.
This sort of thing goes on all the time: a string of phonemes circulates
through substitutions and false starts, supplemented by body language,
inflection, and facial expression. Sometimes the exercise is productive:
6:30. Time for dinner. We'll have Caesar salad.

In a world that presumes unmediated communication, not hearing
or hearing partially can be alternately frustrating and, as my example
suggests, generative. Mishearing produces a kind of social vertigo in
which individuals, as Rachel Kolb says, "encounter their own hearing
status as a partly subjective construction" (1). When the auditory social
contract is broken, one recognizes the degree to which subjecthood is
produced through a politics of recognition confirmed both visually and
auditorily. Far from being a passive experience, mishearing is a constant
reminder of the interpretive aspects of hearing—what is usually called
"listening"—that tests the meaning of a word or phrase against its contextual possibilities. One may spend (or waste) a good deal of time feeling embarrassed at having to ask people to repeat phrases over and over

("Say again?"), but then it is possible to learn from one's mediated access to sound something important about conversational ethics. Communication, as my example indicates, is less a conduit than a feedback loop.

Paul Carter has described communicational feedback as a component of listening. He distinguishes between *hearing*—the detached, sensory reception of auditory phenomena—and *listening*, or what we make of it. Listening is "intentional hearing" where we monitor our response in relation to a shifting discursive environment and the rhetorical and pragmatic rules that govern it (44). Carter uses the example of hunters who "must anticipate a target's moves, correcting their aim by taking account of the arrow's flight and the animal's movement" (44). The feedback metaphor applies to audition as well. "To be communicative depends upon anticipating the other's moves. The aim is not to end the communication but to keep it going" (44). Thus far, Carter presumes mutual intelligibility, where the process of listening is relatively unconscious and where participants know the rules and abide by the communicational contract. Listening becomes cultural when "the ground rules [for communication] are not established" and in which "listening surfaces as a device for creating new symbols and word senses" (44–45). Carter observes that mishearing can also be creative in situations of cross-cultural encounter where power is distributed unevenly—as, for example in migrant communities or among subalterns under colonialism—where "echoic mimicry" can be a form of resistance. One of his examples of cultural engagement concerns the meeting between Columbus and the Taino people upon Columbus's arrival in the West Indies in October 1492.[1] As Carter summarizes, this encounter revolved "discursively around an ambiguously signifying word-sound, '*ca*'" out of which Columbus imagined that the native inhabitants were speaking of China, the land of the Great Khan (or *Cane Grane*), where gold was presumed to be plentiful. For Carter, echoic mimicry is a form of communication "in the absence of anything to say" (46).

It would have been interesting if Carter had tested his ideas about cross-cultural encounters against persons who are deaf or disabled. The cultural work of listening would be complicated when the "ground rules" of communication involve different sensoria. In such cases, mishearings or misunderstandings often have dire consequences. Case in point: a Norwegian student staying in Copenhagen was rushed to the emergency room after being smashed over the head with a glass during a bar fight. The student tried to explain to the medical staff that he suffered from hemophilia, a condition that retards blood clotting and requires infusions of blood factor. The attending physician felt that there was nothing wrong, since the student was saying he was a homosexual. The Danish word for hemophilia is *haemofili*, similar to the word for homosexual, *homofil*. The student was sent home, and Copenhagen police later found him dead from a brain hemorrhage at his apartment in Sydhavn less than twenty-four hours after being discharged from the hospital.[2]

A second example concerns the killing of Magdiel Sanchez in Oklahoma City in 2017. Police were investigating a hit-and-run report, and when they arrived at the address, Sanchez was sitting on his father's porch. Sanchez was developmentally disabled and deaf, and when officers approached him, he left his porch, holding a metal pipe. Witnesses reported that officers gave Sanchez commands, but when he didn't respond and continued to advance, police opened fire, killing him on the spot. Witnesses had been shouting to the police that Sanchez was deaf, but they did not hear them or else were so focused on the presumed threat that they refused to hear their pleas. "He don't speak, he don't hear, mainly it is hand movements. That's how he communicates," a neighbor told the *Guardian*.[3]

These examples display the close relationship between mishearing and misunderstanding, the latter implying some bedrock of truth that has been diverted and must be set to rights. But when misunderstanding is a constant feature of interaction, when it is injected with prejudice and stereotype, then it takes on an independent life. The ideal of mutual understanding upon which much linguistic and rhetorical theory is based does not consider the provisional nature of most communicational acts nor the metadiscursive elements ("as I was saying," "what I meant was . . .") that occur in everyday conversation, what Talbot Taylor calls "practical metadiscourse" (10–17). Nor does "mutual understanding" as a concept account for the differential relationship between an utterance and any person's ability to hear it. Is this lacuna between utterance and confirmed response a loss of understanding or a new kind of understanding in which communication's indeterminate character is exposed? How much of any conversation is totally understood, the bulk reconstituted out of contextual clues, raised eyebrows, and rhetorical convention? Is all hearing mishearing, as Steven Connor in my epigraph says? What is a poetics of mishearing and what forms does it take?

Consider, in this context, Roman Polanski's 1974 movie *Chinatown*. The film is centered around the close historical relationship between water and power in Los Angeles during the 1930s, articulated in crucial ways through the confluence of mishearing and misunderstanding.[4] Jake Gittes (Jack Nicholson) has been hired as a private detective to spy on Hollis Mulwray, chief engineer of the Los Angeles Department of Water and Power. He is hired by a woman posing as Mulwray's wife, Evelyn, who suspects her husband of having an affair with a younger woman. It turns out that this is a setup, designed to discredit Mulwray, who has opposed the building of a dam that would bring water into Los Angeles. According to his geological research, the dam would not be safe and could lead to a catastrophic flood. Jake's partner overhears an argument between Mulwray and his wife's father, Noah Cross (John Huston). When the partner returns, he says the conversation was drowned out by other noise. The only words he could hear were "apple core." "That's it?" asks Gittes. It turns out that "apple core" is a misheard version of "Albacore," the name of Cross's exclusive fishing club where Cross conducts his shady business as a landowner and, with Mulwray, as partner in Water and Power. His nefarious activities, unbeknown to his partner, include diverting water from the Owens Valley and buying up the arid property in order to develop it. The mishearing of "apple core" for "albacore" is one of several scenes in the movie in which a misheard word effaces a critical truth. "Albacore" annexes the film's emphasis on water and creatures that live—and die—in it, while "apple core" invokes that first temptation and the fruit that leads to downfall.

A more important misheard phrase occurs when Jake visits Evelyn Mulrway's (Faye Dunaway) home, having discovered that he has been hired under false pretenses to spy on her husband. While waiting for her to appear, Jake notices a Chinese gardener pulling weeds and grass from a pool next to the patio. Reaching into the pool, the gardener pulls out a clump of wet grass and mutters, "bad for glass." Gittes paraphrases what he hears as "bad for the grass" through the optic of orientalist stereotypes of Chinese "bad" pronunciation. It turns out that Gittes's mishearing misunderstands the larger implication of what the gardener is saying: that the pool is filled with seawater and is therefore bad for the grass. It is also bad for Hollis Mulwray who, we learn, was drowned in the pool by Noah Cross. But the misheard "glass" indirectly alludes to something else the gardener may have seen in the water, a pair of bifocal glasses submerged in the pool, belonging not to Mulwray but to Hollis, his murderer. Gittes, who is revealed as both obtuse and racist at the outset, must gradually come to understand the fatal connections between misheard words, just as he learns—too late—of the incest between Noah Cross and his daughter.

We can use this scene as an example of how mishearing often illustrates a form of cultural hearing beyond the acoustic. Gittes "hears" through the ears of popular representations of Asians, especially those depicted in films made during the 1930s and 1940s to which the film refers. He can never understand "what goes on in Chinatown," since Chinese persons are only projections of Hollywood movies. We could see the misheard word as central to the detective genre where a misinterpreted clue or insignificant object is revealed to be the key that unlocks the crime. A phrase by an Asian gardener misheard by a racist detective leads to a string of metonymic substitutions—grass to glass to glasses to eyes—that culminate in Evelyn's death by a gunshot through her eye.

Polanski exploits the possibilities of mishearing as a thematic trope that serves to reveal both his protagonist's limitations and a city's political corruption. As I will develop the theme, the arts of generative misunderstanding are abundant in culture—from surrealist "exquisite corpse" exercises to Fluxus and Oulipo procedural forms, from children's word games like Mad Libs, Telephone, and Chinese Whispers to the "Bad Lip Reading" YouTube videos that I discuss later in this chapter. In these examples, an ideal of understanding is purposely thwarted by associative diversions and substitutions or, in the case of Oulipo, mathematical formulas—unlocking subterranean linguistic resources in everyday communication.

My epigraph from Bob Perelman's 7 Works is one such example, derived from a collaborative enterprise, "Essay on Style," that he composed with two other poets, Kit Robinson and Steve Benson. In this work, each poet would type as fast as possible what one or other of the two would read from random books at hand. "Instead of ant wort I saw brat guts," the opening of Perelman's book, was actually Kit Robinson's misheard or mistyped version of something one of the other poets was reading aloud. As Perelman elsewhere says, "It's in '*his* voice,'" even though it becomes his (Perelman's) line (*Marginalization* 33). The collaborative nature of the line's production reinforces my contention that mishearing is not a private but a social experience of meaning (un)making. The title of the work in which the phrase appears, "Essay on Style," mocks various attempts—from Walter Pater to Strunk and White—to define or categorize a particular literary style. By creating his idiosyncratic "style" out of the words of others, mangled, reheard, and misheard, Perelman hears otherwise. As he confirms, "This was not automatic writing: automatic listening would be more like it" (32).

Gladly, the Cross-Eyed Bear

For those who live at the far end of the hearing spectrum, Sylvia Wright's 1954 essay "The Death of Lady Mondegreen" is a kind of urtext. In it, she recounts her childhood pleasure at her mother's reading of a poem from Thomas Percy's *Reliques of Ancient English Poetry* (1765):

> Ye Highlands and ye Lowlands,
> Oh, where hae ye been?
> They hae slain the Earl Amurray,
> And Lady Mondegreen. (48)

Wright's fond memories of hearing this poem as a child coincide with her subsequent realization of her own hearing loss that transformed the original couplet, "They hae slain the Earl Amurray / And laid him on the green" into a memorial for *both* Earl and Lady. Thanks to Wright's essay, such misheard words and phrases have come to be called mondegreens, and there has been a good deal of commentary on the creative pleasures that such mishearing produces. Of course, one need not be hard of hearing to encounter mondegreens; they are the very stuff of most conversations as one negotiates verbal chatter at a loud restaurant or airport. And as I will suggest, they are foundational for poetry in its ability to hear language differently.

Mishearing is not *not* hearing but rather mis-listening, imposing on acoustic material an alternate set of terms to those intended. Popular culture is full of mondegreens, the most familiar for my generation being the Jimi Hendrix line "Excuse me while I kiss the sky," which was heard as "Excuse me while I kiss this guy." Creedence Clearwater's line "There's a bad moon on the rise" became "There's a bathroom on the right." For a more recent generation, Taylor Swift's song "Blank Space" became big news after listeners heard her line "Got a long list of ex-lovers" as "All the lonely Starbucks lovers." Children trying to decode adult language live in a world of mondegreens, hearing the Lord's prayer as "Our Father who art in heaven, Harold Be Thy Name," or in Malachy McCourt's childhood version of the rosary prayer, "Hail Mary. A Monk Swimming." Perhaps one reason that mondegreens are so prevalent in song lyrics is the fact that they are embedded in other sounds—loud band instruments, the vocalist's idiosyncratic (or incomprehensible) vocalization, electronic distortion. And speakers or headphones remove visual access to the singer's lips and body movement that often provide crucial elements in communicational pragmatics.

In his work "Head Citations," Kenneth Goldsmith builds on mondegreens in popular music by creating an epic length work derived from eight hundred song lyrics. It is difficult to know whether all his examples are Goldsmith's mishearings or those of other listeners or, in fact, those invented by the author. The latter possibility raises the question of what constitutes an "authentic" mondegreen, if any utterance can be subjected to its homonymic equivalent.

Here are the opening lines:

1. This is the dawning of the age of malaria.
2. Another one fights the dust
3. Eyeing little girls with padded pants
4. Teenage spacemen we're all spacemen.
5. A gay pair of guys put up a parking lot
5.1 It tastes very nice, food of the parking lot
6. One thing I can tell you is you got to eat cheese.
7. She was a gay stripper. (1)

Lyrics by the Fifth Dimension, the Beatles, Joni Mitchell, and others undergo variations that lend a certain wackiness to lyrics that are, in some cases, pretty wacky to begin with ("Michelle, ma belle, some say monkeys play piano well, piano well" as a mishearing of "*Sont les mots qui vont très bien ensemble*" [1]). The numbered list imposes a seriality on what is obviously a random assortment. The title, "Head Citations," suggests that the results are products of. a more cerebral process, although the title is itself a mishearing of the Beach Boys lyric "She's giving me good vibrations" (1). Words are substituted in many cases to undercut more ponderous material ("One thing I can tell you is you got to be free" becomes "you got to eat cheese": "Breaking up is hard to do" becomes "Waking up is hard to do."; "Hey you, get off of my cloud" becomes "Hey you, get off of my cow"). Whether there is a source text for each line hardly matters; what seems most important is the line's diversion of a recognizable utterance into a slapstick variation that dethrones the sublime ("Somewhere over the rainbow, weigh a pie") and reinforces the absurd ("Ah, ah, ah, ah, stay in the lab, stay in the lab").

Such substitutions have been described, if a bit more ponderously, in terms of the cohort model developed by William Marslen-Wilson in the 1970s, which proposes that misheard words are a normal fact of comprehension. As summarized by Maria Konnikova, the cohort model assumes that "when we hear sounds, a number of related words are activated all at once in our heads, words that either sound the same or have component parts that are the same" ("Excuse me?"). A hearing person receives sound waves that are then transformed into semantic units, based on one's knowledge of a particular language, its syntax and morphology. I emphasize "hearing person" to indicate that the model does not imagine a cohort that is deaf or hard of hearing, nor does it consider silent lipreading, which supplements most acts of hearing. What are minor glitches in conversation among hearing persons may be the daily condition of those living a bicultural life on a deaf spectrum. What is important about the cohort model is its emphasis on understanding as a collective exchange. Kenneth Goldsmith's playful variations on song lyrics may seem monological wordplay, but they would not exist without an audience or reader who completes the translation of good vibrations into head citations.

Returning to Sylvia Wright's essay, we might understand her misheard version of the Scottish ballad as a component of a much larger category of error in poetry—hoaxes, typos, printers' errors, false attributions, puns, homonymic substitutions, and malapropisms. Error is not an anomaly in poetry but a basic condition for poetic composition. As Seth Lerer observes, "error" "embraces both the erring and errant (the Latin word *errare* means, of course, 'to wander'). Being wrong is also about being displaced, about wandering, dissenting, emigrating, and alienating" (2). Once we think of poetry as a kind of displacement of the familiar, the constitutive fact of mishearing, of hearing differently, assumes greater importance.

The opening to Robert Duncan's "Crosses of Harmony and Disharmony" contains a familiar mondegreen:

> "Gladly, the cross-eyed bear"—the cross
> rising from the eye a strain of visible song
>   that Ursa Major dances,
>   star notes, configurations
>   from right to wrong
> the all night long body strechd bare
>   sleep's guy in the game of musical shares (39)

Duncan's pleasure at the inversion of a Protestant hymn, "Gladly the cross I'd bear," into the name of a cross-eyed bear has an autobiographical dimension deriving from a visual impairment in which one of his eyes was nearsighted and the other farsighted. This ocular condition, as I can attest, made it difficult to know which eye was watching you and which was looking over your shoulder. Although technically we might say his eye "wandered," Duncan preferred to describe his condition as being "cross-eyed," thus exploiting the association as a mark of his status as a queer outsider, provocateur, and eccentric. His reference to bears also carries an autobiographical element. He claimed his totem animal as a weir bear in reference to his own hirsute body and his interest in shamanistic bear cults among the California Indians. In the longer poem, "Crosses of Harmony and Disharmony," the crossing of Christian and Pagan sources permits the cross-eyed poet to connect his visual impairment to his homosexuality. His "strain" of vision identifies the Great Bear, Ursa Major as "sleep's guy in the game of musical shares." This passage is characteristic of Duncan's use of puns and wordplay that merge the Christian incarnation of word into flesh with new configurations of flesh into words:

> Mizar, Benatnasch at the tail—
> sky of hairy distances, male
>   to the fields of earth beneath night's paw,
>   female to other orders. (39)

For Duncan, constellations among stars map the movement of desire across "hairy distances," both near and far. The lover's "all night long body stretchd bare" is reflected in the constellation Ursa Major as tutelary spirit. The allusion to "hairy distances" and male/female transvestism refers, obliquely, to his close relationship to Native American ethnologist Jaime de Angulo, whom Duncan knew in his early twenties and who did pioneering work on shamanism. Introduced to Duncan by Ezra Pound, de Angulo claimed that the poet's thick hair on his back and neck would have marked him as a weir bear in Native American moieties. Nor was transvestism an academic interest in shamanism for de Angulo, who occasionally cross-dressed in female clothing and passed as female in sexual encounters.[5]

Although he often had trouble listening, Duncan's hearing was not impaired. At the same time, he courted the metaphoric potential of hearing and seeing at cross purposes as a mark of his sexual and cultural difference. "Crosses of Harmony and Disharmony" elaborately explores metaphor as "bearing a cross" between similarity and difference, between a phrase's literal meaning and meanings submerged in the philological midden out of which language emerges. As with many of his poems, Duncan begins with a misheard phrase and uses its errant possibilities to shift bearing a cross to baring himself.[6] Speaking of his investment in "the truth and life of myth," Duncan calls attention to the aesthetic and ethical responsibility he feels toward error: "Often I must force myself to remain responsible to the error that sticks in pride's craw; not to erase it, but to bring it forward, to work with it even if this flaw mar a hoped-for success" (184).

Duncan was hardly alone in seeing the poetic potential of misheard words. The lawyer Gerald Shea, in his memoir, *Song without Words,* calls misheard phrases "lyricals" and identifies them with his lifelong misunderstandings as a severely hard-of-hearing person. From the age of six until he was thirty-three, Shea lived under the assumption either that people didn't speak clearly or that everyone had the same comprehension problems as he. By the time he had an audiogram and discovered his hearing deficit, he had accomplished an impressive academic career (Andover, Yale undergraduate, Columbia Law) and professional life, ending up as a chief counsel at Mobil Oil. His extraordinary ability to turn misunderstood words into lyricals, supplemented by lipreading, reinforced his idea that errors of hearing were interesting in themselves. Mishearing was extremely disconcerting and perilous in the fast-paced, competitive environment of corporate boardrooms and offices. Shea would write down what he thought he heard and would later translate it into English. But the frustration of parsing seeming nonsense into bureaucratic prose was exhausting, requiring periods of down time and silence following a meeting. Asked by a superior for assistance on a matter concerning indentures, Shea hears the following: "We *deep* your help." *What mixed up with, oh yes, a wreck the wreck records for a northern copy—for another company—we deep knee need we need your help* "Can you provide it?" Without knowing exactly what he might provide, Shea agrees. Later he lineates his various attempts at possible meanings:

> debt sure
>   indenture
>   were to lease
>   shoes
>   no no
>   to lee shoes
>   duly issued
>   bonds
>   tell us
>   the bonds
>   under the indenture
>   were duly issued (106)

Here we see the cohort model in action as Shea sorts through possible substitutions for "indenture" and "issued." Shea finds himself agreeing to a difficult task simply to gain time to unpack the actual request post hoc. Peter Middleton describes Shea's lyricals as a "stepwise series of rapid inner translations reaching towards a plausible guess as to the actual words that had been spoken."[7] As Middleton points out, Shea's stepwise graphic representation of potential words and phrases looks a good deal like much contemporary poetry.

Shea is unequivocal on the poetic nature of his lyricals. "Whether or not you can hear well, you will find that learning about lyricals, imagining them letting them take you along with them, can be like reading or writing poetry. If you are partially deaf, they are a defining element of your life, as they are of mine" (29). When I queried Shea about why, as a lawyer with access to stenographers, he never availed himself of captioning, he replied that in the world of corporate finance, too much was going on at any one time, too many voices vying for attention: "The pace is simply too fast for visual devices."[8] He spoke of business lunches "with more than a dozen people around the table, here someone at the left, someone at the right, sometimes talking together, dishes rattling, glass klinking (or klunking) . . . subjects changing."[9] In his memoir, Shea credits his skill at decoding lyricals to his ability to read lips, identifying the slight variations in consonants (v and f look pretty much the same) and isolating the more readable vowels. But lipreading presumes facial proximity. If the person's back is turned or if one turns away, the ability to read lips is lost. Thus, important elements in communicational feedback are space and visual access; bodies must be in proximity so that the face and lips are visible.

In his memoir, *Deafness*, the poet David Wright devotes considerable attention to this spatial aspect of communication for deaf persons. He notes that he often feels somewhat awkward, maneuvering for a seat with his back to the light so that he can see people's faces. He also speaks about his fatigue as lipreader: "Sometimes [one] has to 'play back' a phrase or sentence more than once, revisualizing the lip movements with his inner eye. . . . All the while, the lipreader's eye is engaged in taking the next sentence or two, and at the same time he is working out a reply or rejoinder to keep his end of the conversation going" (74). Wright concludes by saying that this exercise "can be fatiguing. People differ, but as I grow older I find an hour or two's solitude every day (or just being somewhere where no one is going to talk to me) a necessity" (74). We may think of hearing as a passive activity, but as Wright and Shea attest, for deaf and hard-of-hearing persons, it is a much more physical process grounded in the body and reliant on variable temporalities of alertness and exhaustion.[10]

Distressing Language: Harryette Mullen

In an interview with Barbara Henning, Harryette Mullen notes of one of her poems, "It's like a mishearing. Often when I write something literal and straightforward, I will alter it so that it is a little blurred, as if you somehow misread or misheard the line" (45–46). This remark could describe any number of poems in her book *Muse and Drudge* (1995), which celebrates African American culture in general and black women in specific:

> what you do to me
> got to tell it
> sing it shout out
> all about it
>
> ketchup with reality
> built for meat wheels
> the diva road kills
> comfort shaking on the bones
>
> trouble in mind
> naps in the back
> if you can't stand
> sit in your soul kitsch
>
> pot said kettle's mama
> must've burnt them turnip greens
> kettle deadpanned not missing a beat
> least mine ain't no skillet blond (105)

A mashup of song lyrics ("what you do to me," "Trouble in mind," "I'm blue"), puns ("ketchup with reality"), gospel singing ("shout out"), gambling ("shaking on the bones"), food ("ketchup," "built for meat wheels"), homilies mixed with comic film ("pot said kettle's mama"), hair styles ("naps in the back," "skillet blonde") creates a new narrative for racialized language. The four-quatrain poems in *Muse and Drudge* are a lexical anatomy of black women's lives, often based, as she has said, on stories she heard her mother and women friends exchange when Mullen was young.[11] We hear the mixture of cultural voices overlapping each other, appropriated from white (the Doors song "Soul Kitchen," the Perry Como song "What You Do to Me") as well as black culture (Dinah Washington's "Trouble in Mind"). We might say that she distresses language by roughing-up its edges, blending dissimilar materials—seeing the Doors song *Soul Kitchen* as "soul kitsch"—to suggest white appropriation of Afro-centric sources. The language is also distressing in its references to racial difference, racism, and the legacy of slavery. The relationship between the two meanings of *distress* reinforces the cultural fact of much black music as a language *of* distress that signifies *on* historical pain.

The double entendre in *distressing* to describe Mullen's recycling of vernacular sources illuminates her various debts to the work of Gertrude Stein. In *Trimmings* and *S*PeRM**K*T,* Mullen repurposes Stein's wordplay around domestic objects and spaces and infuses it with language derived from another social and cultural realm:

> Her red and white, white and blue banner manner. Her red and white all over black and blue. Hannah's bandanna flagging her down in the kitchen with Dinah, with Jemima. Someone in the kitchen I know. (*Trimmings*, in *Recyclopedia* 7)

The possessive pronoun evokes Stein's patriotic works like *The Mother of Us All* or her *Essays in America* but introduces into the red, white, and blue "manner" (or "banner") the black and blue of racial violence and the domestic kitchen where Aunt Jemima, not Alice B. Toklas, works. Dinah and Aunt Jemima may be "someone in the kitchen" she knows. If Stein distresses the language of women's domestic world, Mullen reminds us of who works in that kitchen.

Distressed language is elaborately displayed in "Denigration," a poem from *Sleeping with the Dictionary,* which builds on the multiple associations of the N-word:

> Did we surprise our teachers who had niggling doubts about the picayune brains of small black children who reminded them of clean pickaninnies on a box of laundry soap? How muddy is the Mississippi

compared to the third-longest river of the darkest continent? In the land of the Ibo, the Hajusa, and the Yoruba, what is the price per barrel of nigrescence? Though slaves, who were wealth, survived on niggardly provisions, should inheritors of wealth fault the poor enigma for lacking a dictionary? Does the mayor demand a recount of every bullet or does city hall simply neglect the black alderman's district? If I disagree with your beliefs, do you chalk it up to my negligible powers of discrimination, supposing I'm just trifling and not worth considering? Does my niggling concern with trivial matters negate my ability to negotiate in good faith. Though Maroons, who were unruly Africans, not loose horses or lazy sailors, were called renegades in Spanish, will I turn any blacker if I renege on this deal? (*Sleeping* 19)[12]

The title contains a good deal of the poem's subject: the denigration of blackness hidden in words of negation, erasure, and dismissal. Most of the words have no etymological relation to *Negro*, but each one has some oblique association with the unspoken N-word. One might say that these are the "heard" versions of the unspoken word, potential substitutes for an identity that must not be named. The poem appears in *Sleeping with the Dictionary*, whose title provides an apt description of her love of language and, perhaps, an erotic investment in language's errancy. The poem is a kind of philological nightmare of negation or, alternately, intercourse across false friends.

The passage is structured as a series of rhetorical questions without answers, suggesting that the response is subsumed in the very structure of the question: If I disagree with your beliefs, do you chalk it up to my negligible powers of discrimination? The negation of the speaker's identity—"trifling, trivial, nor worth considering"—is the response that racism presumes and incorporates in its catechism. Her final query, "will I turn any blacker if I renege on this deal?," assumes that the question precludes an answer, as if to say, "Would I become more clearly identified as black if I refused to negotiate on your terms?" There may be a negotiation going on, but it is clear that the black speaker does not determine the terms by which it would conclude.

In her Henning interview, Mullen speaks of a poem as a "commentary on the power of language, even when it's misheard or misapprehended" (60). We might expand this remark and say that the power of language to oppress is best *heard* when it is misheard and recycled. Mullen's work, as the titles to her books suggest—*Sleeping with the Dictionary, Recyclopedia*—is all about language, the pleasures of its unstable meanings but also the dangers of its authority in describing and containing. In her preface to *Recyclopedia*, Mullen says, "If the encyclopedia collects general knowledge, the recyclopedia salvages and finds imaginative uses for knowledge. That's what poetry does when it remakes and renews words, images, and ideas, transforming surplus cultural information into something unexpected" (vii).

Mis-lipreading

Read my lips

George H. W. Bush's well-known remark at the 1988 Republican convention, "Read my lips: no new taxes," is understood as a mark of his integrity and resolve as he accepted the nomination for president.[13] Apparently, his speechwriter, Peggy Noonan, had never met a deaf or hard-of-hearing person who might tell her that lipreading is not so straightforward as she implies. In fact, there is an entire cultural fascination with mis-lipreading that testifies to the perilous nature of lipreading as a metaphor for truth. The current YouTube channel that exploits this fact, "Bad Lip Reading" (BLR), now has over 7.3 million subscribers.[14] Apparently, there is a vast audience for badly lipread speeches by public officials, football players, movies (the *Star Wars* trilogy is a favorite), and popular music, often featuring well-known Hollywood actors (Jack Black, Maya Rudolph, Carrie Fisher, Mark Hamill) doing the lip-syncing. BLR videos overdub words and phrases that conform, more or less, to the lips and facial expressions of speakers, regardless of what is being said. The results are often hilarious—and sometimes prophetic. President Trump enters the Senate Chamber to deliver his 2019 State of the Union Speech, greeting well-wishers as he walk to the podium:

> I like your fingers, and I like your face.
> So there's shark fins all over the room tonight.
> Hey, I like your hairspray, friend,
> It's like lacquer; it's got that artful shine.

Meanwhile, Mike Pence and Nancy Pelosi stoically await Trump's arrival at the podium. Nancy asides to the vice president:

PELOSI: Don't lay a finger on my gavel.
   You know, Mike, ever since you asked what the opposite of wheat is,
   I've been avoiding you.
PENCE: Hey, I once had a cockroach named Verne, but he got lost in a
   disaster.
PELOSI: Oh, that's nice
PENCE: Well not really, 'cause he poisoned people

Mis-lipread comments from football players interviewed during the NFL 2018–19 season could be mistaken for surrealist poetry: "Night screams . . . the new fun of the kids"; "My grief has a scent like suffering"; "I'm crying on the inside; I intensely stole carpet"; The image of large, muscular men in football colors speaking such lines is, in a perverse way, comforting, as though they command linguistic resources beyond their physical prowess.

BLR is the product of an anonymous music and video producer in Los Angeles who began creating videos of lipread rock songs in 2010.[15] When the videos were premiered on the Ellen DeGeneres show, they gained a large public exposure. And no wonder. Who wouldn't like to think that Rick Perry, the former secretary of energy, could say,

"I'm bored by famine. I cannot wait for a medieval cookie, a Cinnabon,
   hot yellow Kool Aid, and save a pretzel for the gas jets!"[16]

In an interview in *Rolling Stone*, the anonymous producer told Tim Dickinson that with Perry's speech, he knew he'd struck gold:

"I didn't *write* that. My brain just . . . pulled it out," he says. "There's this
   moment where I'm responding to these lines for the first time, too; if one
   of those bizarre phrases makes me laugh, I figure there's a good chance it
   will make other people laugh too."[17]

"My brain just . . . pulled it out." Some of the fascination with the mis-lipreading phenomenon may derive from witnessing Rick Perry's darker side, a surreal alternative to his otherwise anodyne political rhetoric. The will to incoherence satisfies in direct proportion to a will to understand. For those who rely on lipreading as a major part of our lives, the pleasures of mis-lipreading must be balanced against the frustration and exhaustion that reading lips produces. As Gerald Shea demonstrates, reading "lyricals" through their various permutations is tiring work. But is it really "reading"? Or is it, in fact, another kind of hearing?

My topic in this chapter, mishearing, must include what hearing means for constituencies who hear visually rather than audibly. More specifically, we need some discussion of how reading implicates the face and body. A 2019 *PMLA* forum on the "Cultures of Reading" focuses on expanded notions of what (and where) it means to read. The organizers of the special issue of *PMLA* stress an interest in "broadening the range of textual objects available for study" and "the settings in which reading happens—namely, in a universe of 'books without borders'" (10). Essays in the volume discuss "reading pictures," reading habits in the nineteenth-century, "emotivism in close reading," Machiavelli's reading of Dante and Ovid, the geopolitics of reading, and many other topics. The essays cover numerous genres, historical periods, and geographical and architectural issues, but the common assumption in every essay is that "reading" means parsing words in texts, not only for the pleasure gained thereby but for knowledge formation, cultural solidarity, and national consolidation. The one culture of reading that is not discussed is the vast body of readers who because of deafness, sight impairment, or disability, read the body. The *PMLA* forum might have considered blind persons who read tactilely through Braille or read novels through audiobooks. What about persons with intellectual disabilities or who have aphasia and require more time to read or read through audible readers and text-to-voice platforms? And most important for my purposes, what about members of the deaf community who read through sign language?

In speaking of different contexts of readability, I may be conflating two very different concepts, one that involves reading printed material and one that more properly describes communication in general. But lipreading—my main focus here—would seem to fulfill the four categories I mentioned above: pleasure, knowledge formation, cultural solidarity, and national consolidation. For prelingually deaf persons, lipreading bears the stigma of its enforced usage in oralist pedagogies. One might say that the emergence of a historical Deaf culture was formed through its opposition to lipreading protocols advocated early on by Alexander Graham Bell and instituted in oralist residential schools for the deaf. But for persons who are hard of hearing or who are postlingually deaf, lipreading is an inevitable means of communicating with hearing persons. And as many commentators have noted, lipreading skills increase as we age so that it becomes a more pervasive activity within the general population. Reading lips is in some respects a textual activity involving the attempt to differentiate phonemes that appear the same—*p* from *b*. If reading for most people implies the silent perusal of a printed text, lipreading for the deaf or hard-of-hearing person translates "text" into "mouth." The "Cultures of Reading" forum stresses the spaces "both domestic and geopolitical" in which reading occurs, a fact of which deaf and hard-of-hearing persons know very well as we position ourselves in face-to-face environments, in rooms, and on screens.

The artist and theorist Joseph Grigely has been deaf since childhood and has made the task of reading and communicating in a hearing world a centerpiece of his visual and theoretical work. Many of his installations consist of conversation slips—paper fragments from dialogues with hearing people—that he arranges on tabletops, mantlepieces, or in large, wall-sized panels. The slips are not framed, giving the appearance of a rather carefully organized punchboard of different sized pages. Their rectilinear placement hints at the modernist grids of Agnes Martin or Sol Lewitt, but these grids have become unmoored from uniform size and color to create a varied surface. The individual slips may include a single word or phrase, the rest in the original conversation completed by gestures, lipreading, or ASL. He calls these works "Conversations with the Hearing" to emphasize the crossing of cultural and linguistic barriers that constitute his bicultural status. When the conversation slips are massed on a wall, they become an intimate babble of past but partial conversations over drinks or coffee.

As an artist and teacher who interacts daily with both deaf and hearing friends and colleagues, Grigely is particularly interested in the errors and mistakes that occur in lipreading that create what he calls "a meaningful kind of meaninglessness" (9). In his large choral work, *St Cecilia* (2007), he provides an operatic sense of how mis-lipreading can create an alternative kind of music. In terms I have discussed in this chapter, mis-lipreading is also a form of mishearing, since the errors that are produced become the material for a new text, full of surprises and mondegreens. In this case, the artist explored his own relationship to music, which he remembers from the period prior to losing his hearing at age ten. That interest includes a fascination with the physical production of sound, from the open mouths of the singer to the baton work of the conductor. In homage to St. Cecilia (the patron saint of music), Grigely interviewed sixty people of varying backgrounds and ages, asking them to lipread the lyrics to a series of songs silently mouthed by the artist's partner and artist, Amy Vogel. He tried to use songs that were known but whose lyrics would not necessarily be familiar (they were, significantly, songs he remembered from his hearing childhood). He then scrambled the lines, adding a "dummy song" to throw off easy identification and, as he says, created a "lipreading" test. Once he had a sample of mis-lipread lines, he mixed and recombined words and phrases to coincide with the original version. He then submitted the two versions, original and mis-lipread, to the Baltimore Choral Arts Society Chamber Choir and filmed its members singing both versions. The films were then shown on two adjacent screens so that the singers appeared to be singing the same song. By an exhaustive process of editing, Grigely and his staff were able to sync the two versions, one chorus singing the lines from "Jolly Old St. Nicholas"; "Johnny wants a pair of skates; Suzy wants a dolly" while the other sings "Johnny was a bastard child; Doosie wants a collie." In a sense, this is a double chorus work based on a lipreading error that is then distributed in two forms through the same labial shapes.

Grigely is quick to take issue with descriptions of him as a "deaf artist whose work is about [his] deafness," thereby reducing all of his work to personal testimony (10). The two examples I've mentioned, "Conversations with Humans" and *St. Cecilia*, are explorations of human communication and the varieties of misunderstanding that are inevitable byproducts. Against normative linguistic models—words conforming to syntactic and morphological patterns imposed by the brain—Grigely asks, "What happens when conventional patterns of human communication are subverted by neurological and physiological rupture to the system" (21). Mis-lipreading is one such rupture when the unexpected error—the mondegreen—reveals a secondary narrative. Freud calls such errors a "means of self-betrayal," but in Grigely's terms, "the private self, the one that speaks for all, betrays the public self, the one afraid to speak at all" (21). In his introduction to *St. Cecilia*, he provides an anecdote about a postal worker's slip of the pen in posting an explanation of the artist's flashing light doorbell: "Customer is Death!! Please Ring Door Bell; They have a Flashing Bell will come to door." Grigely's humorous retrieval of a graphic error speaks to what the graphic note hears otherwise, "written," as he says, "as if spoken" (21).

Conclusion: Hearing Caddie

> Luster came away from the flower tree and we went along the fence and they stopped and we stopped and I looked through the fence while Luster was hunting in the grass.
>
> "Here, caddie." He hit. They went away across the pasture. I held to the fence and watched them going away.
>
> "Listen at you, now," Luster said. "Aint yo something, thirty three years old, going on that way . . . Hush up that moaning."
>
> —William Faulkner, *The Sound and the Fury*

In the opening scene of William Faulkner's *Sound and the Fury*, Benjy Compson looks through the fence of his family home and watches golfers in the adjacent field. He mishears the term for the golfer's caddy as the name for his beloved sister, Caddie, and begins to moan. Benjy lives with an intellectual disability, and although he doesn't speak, he hears words, which are translated through Faulkner's internal monologue. Although there is no direct relationship between "caddy" and "Caddie," Benjy's misheard version of the former brings into focus the relationship between his property and family. It turns out that the golf course that Benjy observes is land that was to be his birthright, sold by the family to pay for his brother Quentin's Harvard education. When Benjy frightens a schoolgirl outside of the Compson property, his brother Jason sees this as a threat to society (and a door to his brother's inheritance) and has him castrated. Caddie, the sister, is the only nurturing figure in Benjy's life but is now banished from the family for giving birth to a child out of wedlock. When her name is repeated on the golf course, its affective charge summons memories of childhood and produces his inarticulate moans. As David Mitchell and Sharon Snyder say, Benjy is not a "symbolic representative of human tragedy." Rather he provides a focal point for addressing the variable meanings of cognitive disability. They note that "[all] of the Compson family members are explicitly judged in their relation to their ability to imagine Benjy's humanity" (167).

Mental disability, deafness, racial and gender difference, and queer identity all are players in the feedback loop of conversation, torquing, twisting, distorting language to mishear what others take for granted. By discussing hearing, hard-of-hearing, and deaf artists I want to suggest that mishearing occurs in various modalities, depending on what assumptions are brought to bear on the infinitive *to hear*. For most people, "I hear what you say" is synonymous with "I understand," testifying to the authority of hearing as a marker of intelligence and social awareness. Not to hear or to hear differently may mark the individual who mishears as deficient or, like Benjy Compson, less than human. The arts of creative misunderstanding usefully test what we mean by "cultures of reading" that presume a conduit joining equal participants.

The epistemological turn from sight to sound, embodied in Heidegger's late writings and a host of recent articles and books, is not much of a turn for many who rely on sight to access sound or who translate sound into text through a digital interface. In Joyce's *Ulysses*, Leopold Bloom, studying the deaf waiter, Pat, at the Ormond bar, notes that he "seehears lipspeech," condensing the twin modalities by which hearing and sight are joined; he hears by reading lips (232).[18] The feedback-loop model of communication with which I began must incorporate these interstitial communicational protocols. As Paul Carter says, when the ground rules for listening are not established, listening becomes "cultural work . . . vocalizations may or may not signify. They produce ambiguous auditory traces" (44). One may hone one's listening around better amplification or clearer sight lines, but the ambiguous auditory traces or misread lips or misheard words sometimes produce lyricals.

2

Siting Sound

Redistributing the Senses in Christine Sun Kim

After trying my animal noise
i break out with a man's cry
—Larry Eigner

O Say Can You See

At the 2020 Super Bowl in Miami, Christine Sun Kim was to perform the national anthem in ASL along with vocalists Yolanda Adams and Demi Lovato. It was a much-anticipated event for members of the Deaf community since Kim is a respected artist and advocate for Deaf culture. Unfortunately, Kim's eloquent signing was invisible to the television audience. After briefly showing her standing on the forty-yard line poised to begin her translation, the cameras switched to shots of football players and the two vocalists. The anthem's opening words, "O say can you see," resonated ironically for deaf viewers, who once again were denied the ability to "see" what she was "saying." As Kim asked in a *New York Times* opinion piece, "Why have a sign language performance that is not accessible to anyone who would like to see it?" ("I Performed")

The erasure of Christine Sun Kim's signed performance of the "Star-Spangled Banner" illustrates a problem of translation that coincides with an issue of citizenship. In her opinion piece Kim acknowledged her pride in being chosen to sign for this occasion. The opportunity recognized the privileges she and other deaf and disabled citizens have received through the Americans with Disabilities Act. But being granted rights does not necessarily mean that they will be exercised equally when one's language does not conform to the dominant (media) version. The NFL's decision to focus on the faces of football players and not on the signed anthem negated the league's attempt to make the Super Bowl accessible to its viewers. The question remains: If the Star-Spangled Banner can only be heard, what does it *say* to those who *see* through an alternative set of signs? Can the translation of those words accommodate the social stigma that continues to attend Americans who speak a different language?

Questions like these were raised at a 2005 conference at Ohio State University, where a group of deaf poets, sign-language interpreters, and deaf-studies scholars gathered to discuss issues of translation, culture, and aesthetics in ASL. Unlike traditional conferences where speakers sit on a dais facing an audience, the room was arranged in a V shape, poets sitting on one side and translators/scholars on the other side to facilitate visual contact.[1] It was one of numerous instances of how forums to discuss sensory or bodily difference require different spaces, schedules, and accommodations. In this specific case, a discussion about sign-language aesthetics required participants to consider the site of signing and equally the siting of sound as a visual as well as acoustic phenomenon. The felicitous phonic interplay of site, sight, and sign animates issues central to a poetics of disability and deafness.[2]

At the conference, participants were asked to engage with a number of questions, one of the most salient being how to define ASL literature if "literature" is presumed to be a textual or verbal phenomenon.[3] Discussion pursued possible alternative modes of translating and documenting signed storytelling or poetry, whether rendered into print, video, or some other medium. The poet Peter Cook suggested that perhaps holography might be the best format since it would more accurately represent the spatial character of signed performances.[4] Cook was no doubt thinking of his own collaborations with Kenny Lerner, many of whose performances as the Flying Words Project utilize the 360-degree field around the poet—Peter signing behind his back, he and Kenny dual-signing, Peter "throwing" a sign in an imagined circle around the pair, or the two of them passing a sign back and forth.

Cook's response suggests something fundamental about what happens when genre meets the body, when aesthetic categories encounter sensoria that defy what they are meant to contain. Classical generic divisions are often founded on the presence of a *different* body, one that inspires pity and terror, as in the case of *Oedipus*, where the hero's limp and subsequent self-blinding are the core of Aristotle's definition of tragedy. Among contemporary artists, as Tobin Siebers has written, the presence of disability, disfigurement, and bodily display calls attention to the centrality of embodiment and affective response in aesthetic discourse. Among the contemporary artists Siebers studies—both disabled and nondisabled—aesthetics is revealed not as a field of detached appreciation and evaluation but as "the domain in which the sensation of otherness is felt at its most powerful, strange, and frightening" (25). I would add that for artists who are disabled, that sensation of otherness manifests itself formally as well as thematically. The sculpture and installations of Corban Walker are framed, quite literally, according to his four-foot height and often require viewers to look up at objects or crouch down in order to enter a gallery space. The photography of blind photographer Evgen Bavkar incorporates the artist's tactile response to the object being photographed.[5] Contemporary dance movements like those of Alice Shepherd or the late Hector Avila are transformed when the artist uses a wheelchair or is missing a leg. The deaf drummer Evelyn Glennie claims, counterintuitively, that her job is to "listen," albeit through various sensory inputs ("How to Truly Listen"). She refers to the use of her whole body in performance as "touching the sound." Remembering her childhood music teacher's question about how she could possibly hear music, she says, "I hear it through here . . . through my hands, through my arms, cheekbones, my scalp, my tummy, my chest, my legs and so on" ("How to Truly Listen"). Rather than attempting to configure disability *to* a given genre (casting Lear or Hamlet by an actor in a wheelchair), we might think of how disability challenges traditional genres, forcing a reconsideration of the role of sensation in reception. Peter Cook's holographic suggestion goes beyond genres and formalist models to transgeneric modes of cultural production—to the specific capabilities (not limits) of different bodies.

The philosopher and theorist Jacques Rancière has provided a way to think about such matters by his influential definition of aesthetics as the "distribution [or partition] of the senses" (*Le Partage du sensible*). Although he does not mention disability, his emphasis on sensory experience over representational fidelity allows us to consider aesthetics from the standpoint of a sensate body. Instead of finding sensations appropriate to each genre, as have philosophers from Aristotle to Lessing,

Rancière's emphasis is on how art *distributes* sensations within a common world, determining what makes certain figures visible or invisible, heard and not heard. By thinking of aesthetics as foregrounding the visibility of sensate subjects, he introduces an important challenge to the usual formulation of a political art:

> Politics consists of reconfiguring the distribution of the sensible which defines the common of a community, to introduce into it subjects and objects to render visible, what had not been and to make heard as speakers those who had been perceived as mere noisy animals. (*Politics* 25)

His emphasis on the ways that art constitutes what is "common" has special applicability for deaf and disabled persons who are often dismissed as "mere noisy animals." The production of an alternative common requires cultural practices that broaden collaborative possibilities between artist, environment, and audience:

> In situ art practices, displacements of film toward the spatialized forms of museum installations, contemporary forms of spatializing music, and current theatre and dance practices—all these things head in the same direction, towards a despecification of the instruments, materials and apparatuses specific to different arts." (*Aesthetics* 22).

In what follows, I want to extend Rancière's idea that recent art distributes the senses to reveal a common body, both biological and social, and to think about how aesthetics also *redistributes* senses. My slight adjustment of Rancière's phrase emphasizes how an art that *distributes* the senses toward a new, inclusive public sphere must also *redistribute* or re-site social values assigned to each sense.[6] In the work of Christine Sun Kim, as I will point out, sound and speech have social currency that is felt acutely by deaf persons. Modes of perception are not value neutral, nor is a "common" common for persons who live in situations of interdependency, whose ways of walking and talking disturb social proprieties, whose mobility requires different forms of access and accommodation. In Kim's work, voice, as the presumed site of interiority and consciousness, must be distributed among its various platforms, prostheses, and producers. Rancière does speak of the ways that distributed sensations account for what (or who) is included and excluded, but we need to go further and think of how sensation itself has been a means of inclusion and exclusion. And, as I will develop the theme, redistributing and democratizing sensation occur in specific sites—a holographic projection, for example—in which that common can be imagined.

Recent technological advances in neurophysiology, robotics, and prosthetics have literalized this redistribution metaphor. Devices such as the BrainPort, which enables blind persons to "see" objects via the tongue, or vOICe, which turns visual information into sound, or various forms of AAC (augmentative and alternative communication) that deploy a communication board that the user manipulates with a laser pointer—such devices utilize the brain's ability to "process perceptual information in much the same way, no matter which organ delivers it" (Twilley). The expansion of voice-to-text software through natural language processing, as I explain in my last chapter, has made speech visible as text. Of course, such contemporary developments are extensions of much earlier prosthetic devices like Braille and the white cane, which substitute tactile sensation for sight. The telephone, after all, was developed by Alexander Graham Bell not as a device for hearing people to communicate across distances but to facilitate better communication among deaf people. As an oralist educator whose wife and mother were deaf, his technological innovations began as prostheses for deafness and deaf education and became foundational devices in sound reproduction.[7]

My subject will be the role of sound and voice in poetics, although I hope that my claim for a trans-sensory aesthetics will expand the study of genre in general. As I point out in chapter 6, a good place to begin thinking about the sonic and spatial redistribution of the senses is in avant garde music and sound art during the early 1960s and 1970s. The work of John Cage, David Tudor, Alvin Lucier, Iannis Xenakis, Luciano Berio, La Monte Young, Pauline Oliveros, and many others stressed the spatial and architectural environments in which sound is produced, the visual representation of sound in scores, signs, and sculpture, the audience as co-collaborators in producing sound, and in the case of Oliveros, the sound as haptic and ritual engagement. Cage's famous foregrounding of silence, both in his compositions and writings, queried both whether music is intended to be heard or, alternately, if silence exists at all.

A more recent example of this fusion of media and sensation is the artist Christian Marclay. In his various photographic, musical, and video projects, Marclay sustains an interest in the *site* as well as *sight* of sound. The urban environment in which a sound is heard, found, or represented is as interesting to him as the city's sounds. Graphic reference to noise or music, whether in musical notation or advertising logo, marks both the potential of sound and its absence—the residue of a person who has vacated a site, a musical staff advertising a record store. The material form in which sound is represented and produced—musical notation, tape cassette, LP record—becomes a component of the sound itself. Marclay quotes a remark made by Stravinsky, who said that he couldn't understand people closing their eyes at a concert; for Stravinsky, "the French-horn player gearing up for the big solo was almost an athletic event" (Interview).

Marclay's work fuses aural and visual materials in equal parts, and in his more recent photographic work, he foregrounds the *image* of sound as represented in advertising, street signage, posters, postcards graffiti, and other forms of vernacular visual media. He collects such memorabilia—photographs of street musicians, images of families making music, film clips of clocks, pictures of people dancing—which he combines in large photographic or video series. Although he does not read music himself, he was an active member of several punk rock groups in the 1970s. Long before hip-hop, Marclay saw the advantages of treating turntables as instruments in clubs and art venues in which the barriers between popular music, avant garde art, and performance were being broken down. As important as any aural element of his music was his visual presence on stage as he sampled and played records as part of the band. His musical antecedents, including musique concrète, Varese, Cage, and Tudor, inspired his use of vernacular materials, but punk encouraged him to see those materials as always already manipulated. Or as one reviewer notes, "The only thing better than a ready-made is a manipulated ready-made." (Smith, "Seeing").

Things I've Heard (2013) is an exhibit and catalogue consisting of photographs taken at random on city streets and urban spaces in numerous world cities. Their common thread is some reference to sound—a doorbell with a sign saying "ring," a partially erased image of an ear on a brick wall, a bin full of discarded speakers. Instead of sounds he has heard, these are "things" he could have heard. At first glance the photographs seem trivial, taken casually without much framing or editorializing. The camera, as he says, is more of a sketchbook to capture "interesting coincidences of things I find curious or funny" (81). Although the images are rather banal and flat, each is a node in a larger story. An open guitar case with coins and bills with the legs of two figures hints at the invisible buskers and their audience; a sign partially covered in snow reveals the image of a guitar beneath. "There's a potential for narrative," as Marclay says in an interview, an occasion to anticipate a story beyond the photo's frame. Marclay seldom features people in his photographs, allowing objects and signs to suggest an absent user or interpreter. A yellow payphone handle dangles from its cord in a payphone kiosk, referencing an earlier caller; a train or subway races past a sign advertising "Hotel Sound"; a wire coat hanger serves as a radio antenna on a car whose occupant is visible only by his legs. Each image projects a different sort of sound—a lost telephone conversation, a train's noise imitated by the hotel's logo, a car radio metonymically indicated by a makeshift antenna, a dog wearing a cone standing at a door. One particularly striking photo displays holes cut into a protective plastic barrier in an airport currency exchange booth, the holes standing both for communication that is in some way mediated by protective plastic. Through the plastic one can read the phrase "Global Value," adding an ironic commentary on the jet-setting cosmopolitans of globalization. These peopleless images suggest sites of interaction, communication, and mobility whose actors have disappeared.

My more extended example of sited sound—visual and installation artist Christine Sun Kim—is studied through a transgeneric or multimodal disability optic. Kim's deafness is an essential component of work that materializes sound beyond its communicational function. She redesigns sound through the difficulties that she experiences in a world that presumes hearing as a norm. Her work implicitly responds to the historical oppression of deaf persons as "dumb" or as having little or no relationship to sound. Hence the redistribution of sensate life to other forms of materiality accompanies the historical and social value of sound as it is marshaled into acceptable formats. And as my chapter title suggests, Kim both "sites" and "cites" sound. For Kim, the spatial representation of sounded materials—from urban street noise to studio

Figures 2.1 and 2.2. Christian Marclay, from *Things I've Heard* (2013)[8]

spaces to musical notation—shifts acoustic to visual and haptic information. For her to "cite" sound is to assume control over its social meaning and rearticulate its authority.

Wearing a Voice

Let's listen with our eyes and not just our ears.
—Christine Sun Kim, "Christine Sun Kim; A Selby Film"

One of the enduring legacies of the poetic renaissance of the 1950s and 1960s is the invention of a voice. I say invention rather than rediscovery since the voice that became prominent in postwar poetry was often the product of new technologies of tape recording, typewriting, and offset printing. This highly mediated voice took several forms. Charles Olson provided the best known description by stressing the poetic line as a "score for the voice" and the typewritten page as a record of physiological and affective responses ("Projective Verse"). The phenomenon of poetry readings at coffee houses and bars provided a second modality by taking the poem off the page and into an audience. That voice was then extended and disseminated through the portable reel-to-reel and later cassette tape recorders that produced what I have elsewhere called the "tapevoice" of postwar poetry that displaced the elocutionary inflected voices of Wallace Stevens or T. S. Eliot on early Caedmon recordings.[9] A third form that this voice assumed was a more phenomenological one, illustrated by the title of Hayden Carruth's 1970 anthology, *The Voice That Is Great within Us*. For Carruth and his contributors, poetry renders a subterranean, more authentic voice too deep for tears and presumably inaccessible to ears.

Poststructuralism notwithstanding, the "voice that is great within us" has been revealed as a product (not the source) of the textuality it is presumed to displace. Its revival of the oral tradition and its embodiment in the vatic and testamentary poetry of Allen Ginsberg, Robert Bly, or Robert Duncan brought the body back into poetics after a sojourn in impersonality and formalism. In its more cultural nationalist form, a poetics of voice or shout took on a collective potentiality that coincided with social movements of the period. In more recent poetry—language writing, flarf, digital poetics, conceptualism—that self-present interiorized voice has been subjected to considerable deformation and atomization. The collective voice of social movements becomes distributed among multiple idiolects (Harryette Mullen, Charles Bernstein, Douglas Kearney, Cathy Park Hong, Don Mee Choi), national languages (Albert Artiaga, Alurista, Myung Mi Kim), public discourse (Claudia Rankine, Jena Osman, M. NourbeSe Philip), and collectivities (stand-up, slams, conceptualist appropriation, the Four Horsemen). But within the longer trajectory since the New American Poetry of the 1950s and 1960s to the present, "voice" is presumed to be the acoustic property of a community of speakers.[10]

Enter Christine Sun Kim, deaf since birth, fluent user of ASL, whose project as a visual and installation artist has been to explore the materiality of voice and sound. Her drawings and installations make sound visible and tactile while enabling her hearing audience to listen through a deaf optic. Her work challenges the idea that the world of deaf persons is silent and, correlatively, that there is no voice in deafness. The voice that is great within Kim is neither inside nor outside but in a state of continual circulation and reinvention, complicating boundaries between sound and silence, deaf and hearing, language and space. By materializing sound, Kim exposes the social currency of hearing while enlarging the possibilities of a d/Deaf epistemology. We might describe the voice revealed in Kim's work as a form of distributed voicing to account for the intersubjective and prosthetic elements of communication.[11] For persons who are deaf or hard-of-hearing, the voice and its reception are distributed among hearing aids, interpreters, captioners, cochlear implants, computer software, and other interfaces that complicate the idea of a self-present, interiorized voice.[12] Of course, this phrase might as easily be called "distributed hearing," since distribution works in both directions, sending and receiving. The fact that the two terms are somewhat interchangeable testifies to the limitations of a unidirectional communicational model. I would add to this the fact that communication is inherently collaborative, a circuit of micro adjustments in understanding between sender and receiver. By stressing sound's materiality—as sound wave, scriptural representation, recording, and so on—Kim places the voice in the world, among other objects, constituencies and systems.

Or spaces. One prominent way that she materializes sound is by placing the various modalities through which sound is represented—musical notation, waveforms, recorded street sounds, conversation transcripts, movie captions—in new and unfamiliar spaces. As a consequence, sound is experienced through multiple sensory inputs, or what sound studies theorists call "multimodal" listening. Although her work is widely known in the world of visual arts, it should be better known in the field of poetry, since all of her projects enhance—and challenge—the presumptive auditory and textual basis of language. Whether transforming musical notations into crudely drawn concrete poems or asking audience members to access sound files on a magnetic tape through a prosthetic wand, each of her experiments subjects the textual and acoustic representation of language to spectacular deformation. I want to emphasize the spectacle aspect by which she situates and cites sound—spectacle regarded in the sense of visuality and performance (as in the phrase "she made a spectacle of herself"). She refers to what she calls the "ownership of sound," the audist assumption that speech and sound are the norms to which deaf people must adapt. Kim is acutely aware of the authority of sound in a hearing world and displays that awareness by creating installations and collaborative projects that attempt, as she says in her TED talk, to "unlearn sound" ("The Enchanting Music"). Voice is treated thus not only as an acoustic phenomenon but as a conceptual and performative frame, something, as my section title indicates, that you wear, not what you are.

In a documentary about her work, Kim is shown recording street sounds near her apartment on the Lower East Side of Manhattan. She then returns to her studio, where she plays those sounds through large subwoofer speakers.[13] She places colored powder, coated paintbrushes, and plastic objects on boards or paper attached to the speakers, whose volume and vibrations produce kaleidoscopic colored designs—what she calls "speaker drawings" or what Molly Hannon calls "seismic calligraphy." Hearing audience members who witnessed these performances were unnerved by the intensity of the sound produced by the speakers, often covering their ears or inserting earplugs. Amanda Cachia notes that "Kim's piercing noise through her voice and feedback 'violate[s]' sound because she consume[s] . . . and claim[s] it as her own, whilst simultaneously tormenting and playing with sound as though it [is], in fact, an invaluable commodity" ("Raw Sense" 192). As I have suggested, she makes a "spectacle" of sound by redistributing sensation, making noise visible and tactile, making pitch and dynamics colorful. Her more recent work explores the interface between words and signs, text and affect, exploiting the acoustic venues in which sound is normalized. "For me," as she says, "sound had always been an idea—an intangible space that separated me from others—so I was curious about how art could transcend sound and vice versa" (qtd. in Hannon).

When she was young, Kim's parents insisted that she "be quiet. Don't burp, drag your feet, make loud noises."[14] There was an etiquette to sound that she had to learn—and then *unlearn* in order to become an artist. There is, perhaps, a cultural aspect to this etiquette as the daughter of parents who immigrated to the United States from Korea. She became fluent in ASL and identifies as culturally Deaf (although she refuses to be regarded as a "disabled artist"), yet her forays into sound place her in an odd liminal relationship to Deaf culture.[15] For many deaf poets and artists, incorporating sound or speech in poetry is problematic since it implies a fatal alliance with hearing culture rather than producing new art through ASL.[16] Yet for Kim, the alliance with sound and voice generates work that brackets the privilege associated with sound by removing it from its auditory domain and communicational function. Moreover, it illustrates her bicultural identity as someone using twin language systems, ASL and English. Deafness is not synonymous with silence, as Carol Padden and Tom Humphries have written, but exists on a spectrum of multi-sensory experiences (*Deaf in America*).[17]

Figure 2.3. Christine Sun Kim, from *Game of Skill 2.0* (2015)[18]

That spectrum is explored in a work like *Game of Skill 2.0* (2015), in which audience members use a two-foot antenna to follow a magnetic strip covered in blue Velcro strung overhead in the gallery space. On the strip is a recording of a speech written by Kim and translated by a museum intern. To hear the speech through a speaker attached at the base of the antenna, each hearing participant must hold the device carefully against the tape while moving forward at a pace keyed to that of the overhead strip. Participants in *Game of Skill 2.0* have described the difficulties of walking continuously while keeping the raised antenna attached to the magnetic sensors.[19] As Kim says, the listener becomes a "human turntable," where "you are the needle" (Barry). *Game of Skill 2.0* places the hearing participant in the awkward position of a deaf person trying to access a spoken text that exists just out of reach, available through multiple interfaces—an interpreter, an architectural space, a tape recording, hearing aids. Hearing is difficult—a game of skill—that involves following a narrow path prescribed and designed not by the hearing world but the deaf artist.[20]

This exchange of roles between hearing and deaf persons becomes a key issue in many of her collaborative works in which she appropriates the voices of others. In *Fingertap Quartet* (2014), this appropriation involves adapting voice samples into sound files and submitting them to public review. Kim gave a list of twelve discrete sounds to the musician Dev Hynes, who then made voice samples based on her instructions. Using a combination of digital recorder, computer, and transducer, Kim then edited Hynes's voice samples into four sound files. In her performance, she first addressed the audience by typing her remarks that were projected onto a screen behind her. She then played the sound files at high volume while projecting a waveform representation on a screen accompanied by a running typewritten interpretation of those files. She also projected emojis that indicated her pleasure (thumbs up), displeasure (thumbs down), or ambivalence (one thumb up, one thumb down) with a given file. By having a combination of deaf and hearing persons in the audience, Kim was able to illustrate varying, often conflicting, evaluative criteria of a given sound, depending on whether it was heard or seen. For the deaf members of the audience, the visual representation of the sound file with its peaks and valleys offered a chance to evaluate a sound as a visual entity, beyond its acoustic properties; for the hearing audience, the loud representation of the file offered a different—perhaps subversive—response.

Speaking of Hynes's sound files, Kim says that she "leased his voice" (Packard). Leasing the voice of others means borrowing the means of vocal production for critical ends. Many of her collaborative works involve repurposing verbal or textual matter from a deaf vantage. In *Close Readings* (2015), she addresses the captioning of films in which diegetic sound is often reduced to a simple phrase: "music in background," "crowd noise," "sound of thunder." Kim asked four deaf friends to provide captions for expressive moments in film clips from five mainstream films, all involving some thematic treatment of vocalization. In her video installation, she blurred part of the image to emphasize the captioned text, placing the deaf caption in parentheses above the official version. In one image taken from Disney's *The Little Mermaid*, a movie in which our heroine, Ariel, relinquishes her voice (and her fins) for two legs so she can marry the prince. The official caption reads "whoa, whoa, careful easy" to describe the prince's words to the now upright, if unsteady, mermaid. The deaf caption of the scene, "the failure of gesture," places emphasis on another, equally relevant, aspect of the scene, since in it, Ariel attempts to communicate with the prince using sign language. Her awkward attempts are,

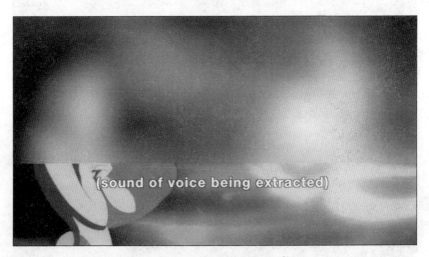

Figure 2.4. Christine Sun Kim, from *Close Readings* (2015)[21]

indeed, a failure of gesture, analogous in various ways to becoming, as it were, a fish out of water in an able-bodied world.

In another image from the same film, the deaf caption concerning the moment Ariel relinquishes her voice reads, "sound of voice being extracted," a phrase that captures the vertiginous implications of what it might mean for a deaf person to live in a world where the loss of voice is a tragic disability. The Disney company felt that the sound of Ariel's voice being extracted by the evil sea witch, Ursula, required no caption, and yet the scene's affective power for the deaf viewer is understandably powerful. Kim titles this series *Close Readings*, perhaps as a satire of formalist textual interpretation but also as a description of a more insurrectionary kind of deaf hermeneutics. By putting the captioning in the hands of a deaf viewer and not a hearing interpreter, the film's expressive content is expanded and enlarged.[22]

What I've described as a repurposing of sound's ownership is to some extent influenced by her reliance on and respect for her ASL interpreters:

> I work with many different ASL interpreters. And their voice becomes my voice and identity. They help me to be heard. And their voices hold value and currency. Ironically, by borrowing out their voices, I'm able to maintain a temporary form of currency, kind of like taking out a loan with a very high interest rate. ("The Enchanting Music of Sign Language")

At the same time, she recognizes that only a portion of ASL signing is accomplished by hand signs, the rest rendered through non-manual classifiers: facial expression, direction, location, and movement: "Grammar is on your face," as she says ("Signs of Friendship"). In her work *Face Opera* (2013), Kim directs a chorus of prelingually deaf friends who "sing" words presented to them on a tablet, using only facial expression. Each singer—including Kim—takes turns interpreting a word for some emotional state or physical condition—nudity, skepticism, sadness, excitement—which they articulate with facial expressions while keeping hands in their pockets. Not only does *Face Opera* enlarge and complicate the idea of a vocal chorus; it foregrounds the broader expressive potential within sign language beyond hand signs.

Figure 2.5. Christine Sun Kim, from *Face Opera* (2013)[23]

Kim often likens ASL to music, and in a series of drawings that she titles *Scores and Transcripts*, she provides an extended visual meditation on the relationship between two forms of language. She emphasizes that just as musical notations are approximate and variable, depending on the performer or conductor, so ASL allows for great variation depending on the speaker, interactive context, geographic origin, and historical generation. She exploits the visual features of performance marks for dynamics in a series of drawings that render the variable relationships of loudness. The drawings themselves embody this variability by their rather rough, off-center design and use of acrylic, charcoal, and pencil whose smudges and smears are the antithesis of a carefully printed musical score. In one of these drawings, *mezzo forte*, Kim, in Amanda Cachia's description, "has crudely described her rendition of [mezzo forte, *mf*] moderately loud as 'annoying like a loud mother fucker' while her moderately soft is 'soft enough to pass as loud silence'" (196).[24] The transformation of two letters that form the neutral *mf* into the expletive *motherfucker* vividly illustrates how "loud"—and disturbing—the representation of sound may be.

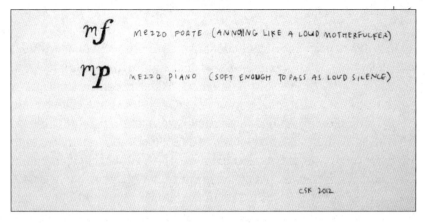

Figure 2.6. Christine Sun Kim, *mezzo forte*[25]

In *Pianoiss . . . issimo (worse finish)*, she creates what looks like a flow chart with *p* for piano (the dynamic notation for soft) at the top branching out into *pp* for pianissimo and further to *ppp* (pianississimo). Kim summarizes the design as demonstrating that "no matter how many thousands upon thousands of *p*'s there may be, you'll never reach complete silence. That's my current definition of silence—a very obscure sound" ("Signs of Friendship"). As a flow chart or family tree, she provides a graphic image of an endless withdrawal into silence, each stage marked by an increase of *p*s into a blurred red scribble.

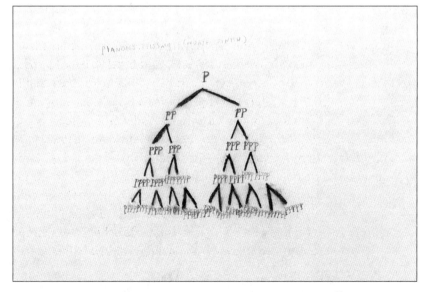

Figure 2.7. Christine Sun Kim, *Pianoiss . . . issimo (worse finish)* (2013)[26]

In another drawing, *How to Measure Loudness*, Kim uses a similar design using the forte dynamic mark (*f*) in a series of diminishing lines, each given a marginal interpretation according to its possible equivalence to an acoustic event, beginning with "Voice lost in oblivion," to "Blow Drier," to "Asian flute," and finally to mezzo forte (*mf*), "sleep." The title suggests that sounds are relative to specific affective states, each dynamic mark measured by its relationship to all others. In one respect, Kim updates John Cage's composition *4'33"* by "playing" silence as an infinitely deferred possibility, a musical Zeno's paradox.

American Sign Language lacks a widely accepted written system, leaving the graphic interpretation of signs ripe for reinvention. Kim asks, "What if I was to look at ASL through a musical lens?" ("Signs"). She answers by taking the sign for "all day," which involves the right arm pointing up at 12:00 and the elbow resting on the back of the left hand and then rotating down until it is flush with the horizontal left arm. Kim represents this visually as a roughly drawn half circle.

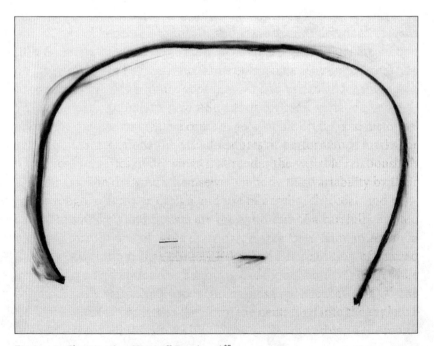

Figure 2.8. Christine Sun Kim, *All Day* (2013)[27]

And by a similar logic, in her rendering of the sign for "all night," in which the right arm rotates up from beneath the left arm, Kim inverts the arc. The sign for "future" involves the flat hand, fingers together, extending away from the head and pointing forward. In Kim's scriptural version, the future sign becomes a series of repeated arcs, as if to represent the concept's infinite extension. In this respect, she joins ASL poets like Clayton Valli, Peter Cook, and Debbie Rennie and the rapper Sean Forbes, whose playful variations on a given sign are standard features of their work.

"A Very Obscure Sound"

My subject thus far has been the "siting" and "sighting" of sound and the redistribution of sensation across several levels of reception. Kim's work offers a deaf-centered critique of this intersection by exposing the institutional and cultural meanings of sound. This aspect is vividly rendered in a recent exhibition in which the work addresses the public spaces in which art is seen and validated. In her installation at the 2019 Whitney Biennale, the artist submitted a series of panels containing charcoal drawings showing different degrees of what she calls "deaf rage." Each panel refers to institutional settings with inadequate accommodations for deaf and hard-of-hearing persons (DHOH): lack of adequate signage, interpreters, captioning or—most often—understanding. These drawings, heavily smudged and roughly drawn, show various plane geometric angles—acute, obtuse, reflex—that measure degrees of rage she feels as a deaf artist in art exhibits, airports, and public venues, in which access presumes a hearing population. One panel deals with dismissive attitudes toward DHOH persons in travel situations. She feels "straight up rage" at the lack of captioned movies on planes. She feels "acute rage" at the "Uber driver [who] calls instead of texting." Her "obtuse rage" is directed at airports where "important transit announcements are in spoken English only." And so forth. Each angle describes a degree of affective response to specific encounters with a hearing world. Her docent descriptions are sketched next to each angle—within the canvas—and serve, significantly enough, as her own captions. By using the basic elements of plane geometry, she draws attention to the building blocks of all structures, including paintings and drawings, yet her messy application of charcoal and pencil seems to contradict the pure formalism implied by Euclidean geometry.

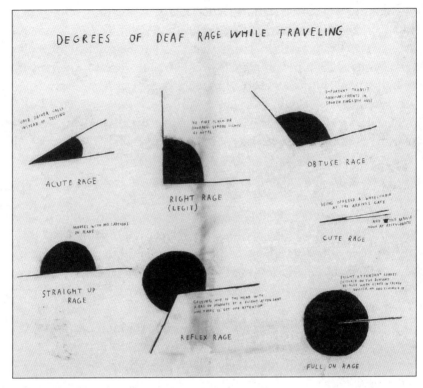

Figure 2.9. Christine Sun Kim, from *Deaf Rage* (2019)[28]

The issue of deaf rage is also a matter of aesthetics—of who is being represented and by what means. One of the panels focuses her anger at various institutions within the art world—museums without adequate deaf docents, curators who feel that it is fair to divide fees between artist and interpreters. One might feel that this is much ado about very little and that "rage" is a somewhat overdetermined descriptor of a deaf person's frustrations in public spaces. But the larger implication of these panels concerns how common sense assumptions about space, sound, and accessibility—not to mention what is displayed on museum walls—often exclude large populations. Instead of providing captions next to each panel, Kim incorporates her own versions within the work itself, seizing the artist's prerogative to define and explain her images. And since her panels lack images in the conventional sense, they speak to the discursive environment in which objects appear in a museum or public venue.

Earlier I invoked Rancière's theory of aesthetics as a distribution of sensations, which is elaborated in the work of Christine Sun Kim as a redistribution of the senses. The reference to distributive justice is intentional, economic disparities now mapped onto atypical bodies. Many of her comments about her process draw on economic metaphors—leasing the voice, social currency, "like taking out a loan"—to describe deaf appropriation of a hearing world. The economic implications of this phraseology are important, since for Kim, sound is a form of cultural capital that only by distributing its value among the senses can its authority be neutralized. By redistributing the senses among deaf and hearing audiences, she brings a new kind of common into being, one that does not exist within the narrow binary, hearing/deaf. And as I suggested in my opening remarks about the importance of the voice invented by Cold War technologies of orality, Kim uses multiple forms of electronic reproduction and digital interfaces to blur the boundaries between poetry and other arts, between lyric voice and manual sign. Heard melodies may be sweet, but those unheard, in the work of Christine Sun Kim, are louder.

3

Misspeaking Poetics

"A nice derangement of epitaphs"

We now know that Saddam has resumed his efforts to acquire nuclear weapons.

There is no doubt that Saddam Hussein now has weapons of mass destruction.

We know he's reconstituted these programs since the Gulf War.

We believe he has, in fact, reconstituted nuclear weapons.
—Derrick Z. Jackson

We now know (believe, assert, confirm) that former US vice president Dick Cheney's various claims for Saddam Hussein's possession of weapons of mass destruction were false. They were based partly on bad intelligence and Pentagon advocacy—and no doubt wishful thinking—but their performative impact has had dire consequences for civilian populations in the Middle East from the early 2000s to today. Asked by Tim Russert on "Meet the Press" about whether he misspoke in these instances, Cheney replied, "Yeah, I did misspeak. I said repeatedly . . . 'weapons capability.' We never had any evidence that he had acquired a nuclear weapon" (Jackson). Cheney's diversion of "we know" to "I did misspeak" turned a slip of the tongue into a plausible justification for global catastrophe.[1]

Cheney's revisionist statement differs substantially from Freud's famous account of what it means to misspeak. He describes slips of the tongue (parapraxes) as intentional if unconscious acts, rooted in repressed psychic material. The misspoken word or phrase always contains what he calls the "disturbed intention" to say otherwise. One of his examples concerns a female patient who, speaking of her uncle, says that "nowadays I only see him *in flagranti.*" The next day, embarrassed by her mistake, she apologizes for her slip (she had intended the French *en passant*), but in the ensuing session, she remembers a scene "in which the chief role was played by being caught *in flagranti.*" Freud concludes that the "slip of the tongue of the day before therefore anticipated the memory which at the time had not yet become conscious" (64). The repressed sexual content manifests itself by a remark that is quickly withdrawn as a mistake, one prompted by reference to the uncle who may or may not (Freud doesn't elaborate) be connected with the woman's being caught in a compromising situation. This is a far cry from Dick Cheney's misspeaking, yet both suggest that verbal error always reveals a subterranean level of truth. Cheney's misspoken claim about WMD belies a wish for it to be true and thus justifies intervening in Iraq. One wonders whether Cheney's "slip" is in his original claim that Saddam has WMD or in his subsequent claim to Russert that in saying so he misspoke. In a sense, both reinforce Freud's contention that slips of the tongue are both unconscious and motivated.

David Sachs argues, contra Freud, that slips of the tongue or pen cannot be intentional; the two are mutually exclusive. For Freud, an intention to speak is thwarted by the unconscious substitution of another term or phrase. Intentionality rests not in the slip but in the slip's registration of an original intention to say this or that. For Sachs, however, this is nonsense. If one is unaware of what one is saying, then it cannot be intended. His example: if you scratch an itch, you are not aware you are doing it; if it is unconscious, then it is not intentional. In the case of the literary examples I study in this chapter, however, slips of the tongue produced by brain lesions, strokes, political coercion, or aphasia reveal *both* the intention to speak *and* the failure to fulfill that intention. The art of error resides in a work's toggling back and forth between these two positions. One observes the poet's struggling to "get it right" and in the process observes the power that rightness claims over individual speakers. In this case, misspeaking or misspelling is not error but the expression of an internally distanced relationship to an ideology of embodied wholeness and verbal clarity.[2]

Misspeaking has a venerable literary heritage, from Mistress Quickly and Constable Dogberry in Shakespeare to Mrs. Malaprop in Richard

Brinsley Sheridan's 1775 play *The Rivals*. The latter features the character whose verbal misprision is enshrined in the term derived from her name. In act 3, she declares to Captain Absolute, "Sure, if I reprehend any thing in this world it is the use of my oracular tongue, and a nice derangement of epitaphs!" which may be a variation on "If I apprehend anything in this world, it is thanks to the use of my vernacular tongue and a nice arrangement of epithets" (80). It would probably be a sacrilege to subject Mrs. Malaprop's mal-appropriate usage to Freudian analysis. More recently, Mrs. Malaprop has appeared as Yogi Berra ("It ain't the heat it's the humility"), Archie Bunker ("We need a few laughs to break up the monogamy"), and Texas governor Rick Perry, who described states as "lavatories of innovation and democracy." Such verbal faux pas become the stuff of legend, turning Berra's verbal confusions into pop philosophy or, when used by Perry's opponents, into evidence of his incompetence.

Modern poets have long enlisted misspeaking in their arsenal of strategies designed to unseat or satirize normative discourse, Lewis Carroll's "Jabberwocky" and a good deal of *Alice in Wonderland*, Christian Morgenstern's *Galgenlieder*, Russian Futurist *zaum* poetry, Hugo Ball's "Karawane" and contemporary sound poetry being the exemplary cases. An expanded definition of literary misspeaking could include the wordplay in Gertrude Stein's *Tender Buttons* or the homonymic translations of David Melnick's *Men in Aida* or Louis Zukofsky's *Catullus*. Such examples deliberately exploit sonic variations from a norm, either by providing verbal equivalents or by placing nonconventional words in conventional syntax. Although these examples do not foreground speech per se, they exploit textual conventions of which speech is a component.

Misspeaking needn't necessarily involve improper usage; it may involve socially inappropriate conversational pragmatics. A recent media example is that of the Swedish homicide detective Saga Norén (Sofia Helin) in the Scandinavian noir television series *The Bridge*, whose blunt, often offensive questioning of suspects and frank answers to personal questions reveal someone on the autism spectrum. She does not misspeak in an inappropriate manner but offends the speech-act protocols of everyday conversation by being brutally honest. To her colleagues on the police force, her lack of social decorum and blank affect are objects of ridicule, but her dogged pursuit of justice and attention to details ultimately win her grudging praise. Here, misspeaking is a product of a neurodiverse condition that proves an advantage in getting answers and solving crimes. She misspeaks by speaking plainly and frontally where others misspeak by indirection and obfuscation.

William Cheng notes that "sounding good" usually means sounding authoritative, rational, competitive," values that may "impress people, win arguments, and elevate one's status" (8). Sounding bad, on the other hand—or what I am calling misspeaking—may require some reparative regime or therapy that would restore speech to some putative standard. Misspeaking reveals the fragile basis on which social acceptability is based and measured:

> Literate societies put huge stock in rhetorical ability—yet for reasons of alterity, disability, or disenfranchisement, some people do not speak well (by societal conventions), some are admonished for speaking too much (oversharing and making noise), some do not speak frequently (due, to, say, shyness), some speak unusually (slowly, with a stutter, or via conspicuous technological assistance), some do not speak at all (from injury or trauma), and some speak but nevertheless go unheard. (8–9)

What Cheng introduces into our discussion of verbal error is the role of disability in producing socially acceptable speech. For persons for whom speech is physically difficult or rendered in alternative forms such as manual sign language or for whom cognitive disabilities make speaking difficult, sounding good is a moving target.

On that note, consider the following:

> Coca-Cola tonic krill
> gill baleen
> dream wrenched
> Kleenex smack
> Baltic Pyrex
> megahertz humpback
> kickback: flex
> nukes flub
> blubber sexy
> plankton number

This segment from Jordan Scott's *Blert* (37) consists of phrases that are challenging for him to vocalize while being sonically rich and semantically complex. Scott, who lives with a stammer, has turned what most would regard as embarrassing blurts into "blerts," diverting misspeaking into new and often sensuous combinations. Speech impediments are by definition forms of misspeaking, yet as Scott illustrates, his errors often reveal alternate associations and connections among words at both a phonic and philological level. The poem above is threaded through by references to whales and associations with their physical nature (blubber, gill, baleen), and in his larger book project, *Blert*, these elements contribute to an ecopoetics that links environmental and vocal barriers. I will develop the ecopolitical implications of his work later in this chapter, but I want here to complicate the definition of misspeaking as an attempt at rationalizing a falsehood (Cheney) or diverting subconscious intentions (Freud).

Speech Production

constellation
stardust
nuclear glow train, Yucca, Nevada
rotate the exhaust
on second thought

Did you *make* that: the sheep, yarn, afghan? birds, feathers, pillows, bookshelves, (trees, nails etc.) the books on them, the slides (yes), their glass mounts, tray, projector? lamps, record player, records (vinyl!), occasional tables, desk, chair, papers? their colors and weights, sizes, like that candy wrapper? notes (perhaps), postcards, newspapers, my cane, myself?[3]

— Norma Cole, "Speech Production: Themes and Variations"

What initially looks like one of Gertrude Stein's list poems, Norma Cole's "Speech Production: Themes and Variations" derives from a very different source. Cole experienced a stroke in 2002 that impacted her speech and mobility. In this example, misspeaking becomes an occasion for verbal exercise and, as her title indicates, a theme upon which variations are played. In the first half of this segment, Cole condenses cultural materials from postwar US history—bomb testing in Nevada, glass mounted slides, vinyl records, record players, projectors—that provide mnemonic resources while posing verbal challenges for oral delivery. In the second half, she creates variations on this thematic material that move from the historical period invoked to the present circumstance of living with, as she says, "my cane, myself." Cole collects fragments drawn from her disability and from contemporary conversations. Speech coincides with a neurological condition that she rearticulates—quite literally—into new work, and in the process, she discovers an aesthetic pleasure in words removed from their communicational function.

"Speech Production" is also part of an installation, *Collective Memory*, that was housed within the California Historical Society in San Francisco's Mission district from December 2004 to April 2005. The installation was itself part of a larger exhibition, *Poetry and its Arts: Bay Area Interactions 1954–2004*, curated by the San Francisco State University Poetry Center. In *Collective Memory*, Cole acknowledged her debts to San Francisco's literary past by setting up a writing space, circa 1960, filled with furniture, books, record players, rugs, and images inspired to some extent by her close friendship with Robert Duncan and Jess, who lived not far from the gallery space.[4] Cole spent each day in what she called the "Living Room," entertaining visitors, friends and neighbors who dropped in whose conversations are included ("Did you *make* that?"). The room or salon was, as she says, "designed to be an open, permeable space that encouraged and relied on interaction with its audience."[5] The space was indeed a "living" room. While occupying the space, sitting at her desk, Cole composed poems and prose poems whose title, "Speech Production," emphasizes not only her difficulty in producing speech but the actual, material site where speech was produced as a poem. The line quoted above, "Did you *make* that?," may have come from one of the visitors to the gallery, but its larger meaning may refer to the making of this poem and producing it as speech. In one version of the installation at the Museum of Contemporary Art, she read the poem with Caroline Bergvall, the two poets speaking simultaneously, Cole reading "Speech Production" and Bergvall improvising (producing) her own speech.

Summarizing a reading by Norma Cole at the Bowery Poetry Club in 2005, Jennifer Bartlett notes that because of her stroke, "Cole lost and regained her ability to speak. Now, she used her temporary aphasia and slurred speech to compose a poem that noted a list of words she could no longer enunciate."[6] Cole's use of lists containing words with similar sounds would seem to test her ability to manage aphasia by finding synonyms or by subjecting words to atypical syntactic structures. But her larger purpose is to link qualities of aesthetic production based on distressing language and the defamiliarizing physical effects of disability:

> Why do I like it under the trees in autumn when everything is half dead? Why would I like the word moving like a cripple among the leaves and why would I like to repeat the words without meaning? (261)

Cole acknowledges the pleasure of wandering among errant words just as she enjoys wandering among autumnal leaves. Restricted movement, in her account, becomes a corollary to her verbal pleasure in repetition.

Dyslexia is a textual or graphic cousin to aphasia, involving difficulties in reading, spelling, and pronouncing words when reading aloud. While not exactly a speech disorder, it derives from similar wiring problems. The poet Charles Bernstein lives with cognitive dyslexia and, like Cole, has used it to structure a number of his poems. His verbal dexterity and skill at managing social idiolects (literary theory, stand-up comedy, cartoons, vernacular culture) may in fact extend from his dyslexia and its tendency to substitute an alternate for the target word. In his poem "A Defence of Poetry," he debates the critic Brian McHale, who in an essay that includes another of Bernstein's poems discusses the role of nonsense in difficult postmodern poems (McHale). In the spirit of Shelley's "Defense of Poetry"—also written as a response to a critic, Thomas Love Peacock—Bernstein provides his own witty riposte to McHale but in terms that include making nonsense out of his writing impediment as a response to McHale's use of nonsense in literate prose. Here is the first part of the poem:

> My problem with deploying a term liek
> nonelen
> in these cases is acutually similar to
> your
> cirtique of the term ideopigical

unamlsing as a too-broad unanuajce
interprestive proacdeure.
You say too musch lie a steamroller when
we need dental (I;d say jeweller's)
tools.
(I thin youy misinterpret the natuer of
some of the political claims go; not
themaic
interpretatiomn of evey
evey detail in every peim
but an oeitnetation towatd a kind of
texutal practice
that you prefer to call "nknsesne" but
for *poltical* purpses I prepfer to call
ideological!
, say Hupty Dumpty) (213)

Bernstein may not be misspeaking in the vocal sense, but his misspelled words and typos are a textual version—perhaps a miswriting—of the same phenomenon. He has specified that he is "trying to rescue 'misspeaking' from its Freudian interpretations and locate it as a basis for understanding."[7] In "Defence," we recognize the familiar tone of scholarly debate, undermined by misspellings and typos. The poem's argument concerns whether McHale's use of nonsense is adequate to describe difficult postmodern poems—including Bernstein's—or whether *ideological* might be a more accurate term. McHale, in his essay, rejects ideology as being too broad to describe the way that poetry refuses conventional sense-making, a "steam roller" where "dental tools" would particularize. McHale feels that the value of nonsense is its dialectical relationship to "common sense," an idea that he derives from yet another critic, Susan Stewart.[8] Nonsense, for McHale, "should be valued for itself" rather than as a "critique and demystification of current language practices" (25). Bernstein counters, in his pose as Humpty Dumpty, by observing that nonsense is not the antithesis of sense, "but perhps, in some / cases, the simulation of sense-making: decitfullness, manifpulation, the / mediaization of language, etc."[9] By writing out his defense (or as he spells it, "defence") while leaving in his typographical errors, Bernstein argues that such binaries as nonsense/sense do not take into account cognitive and neurological factors that make nonsense of nonsense—or rather, make a different kind of sense than what we would usually call ambiguity. There is a certain vertigo that attends this "defense"—an epistle in verse in response to an essay that responds to an earlier poem of Bernstein's ("Dysraphism") discussed in an essay by Marjorie Perloff, who first uses the term *nonsense* in the context of Bernstein's essay on "Absorption." Bernstein exploits the hermeneutic vortex of poem and commentary by distressing his own language in shamelessly unedited fashion. The poem is multistable, making an argument on theoretical grounds but making another argument on . . . it's hard to say what the other grounds are, but I would argue that they are cognitive and embodied grounds.

Most of the lines in "Defence of Poetry" contain verbal or textual errors, except for the last three that quote Karl Kraus: "the closer we / look at a word the greater the distance / from which it stares back." Given the poem's refusal of readable language, this quote is rather jarring, as though Bernstein has thrown off the mask of dyslexia to reveal the "real typist" beneath. But by this time, we must distrust any attempt at resolution, since the poem wittily proves the impossibility of any deeper revelation. The poem "looks back" at its putative readers to render inoperative the particular form of misspeaking through which the gaze is constituted. To some extent, "Defence" is a version of the classical verse epistle or philosophical poem—Ben Jonson's *The Forest*, Pope's "Essay on Man," any number of Wallace Stevens's poems that are addressed to a friend or a fellow poet ("Ramon Fernandez, tell me, if you know" [Stevens]). In many of Bernstein's poems, the addressee is often a critic or critical position whose language and tone are both adapted and satirized. His poetry often engages the rhetoric of critical debate, its theoretical terminology and academic jargon, to debunk its authoritative role in discussing poetry. "Artifice of Absorption," to take his best known version, is an essay in verse that in attacking the poetry of transparency and assimilation (absorption) deploys the authoritative voice of the critic to celebrate work that is anti-absorptive, recalcitrant, and improvisatory. Like "Defence of Poetry," the rhetoric of authority is qualified by turning that authority back on itself.

My references to Norma Cole and Charles Bernstein concern the productive possibilities of speech or lexical impediments on aesthetic practices. These are not outliers among contemporary poets but symptomatic of work that courts error and even failure as a structuring device. As I said in my previous chapter, the psychologically deep voice of 1960s mainstream poetry now may emerge in broken, slurred, nongrammatical, or misspelled forms, a challenge to vocalize and an obstacle to traditional hermeneutic protocols. These forms of misspeaking are neither intentional nor unintentional but arise out of an aesthetic confrontation with bodily and social limits. One might say that poetry is itself a form of misspeaking since it subverts communicational norms and subjects language to deformation, whether through rhetorical, or formalist constraints, or minimalist economy. In the case of Norma Cole's variations, her slurred speech and aphasia (unintentional misspeaking) led her to investigate associative possibilities that intentional acts must repudiate. In the work of Jordan Scott, his lifelong stammer is the occasion for building on misspoken phrases new and startling "blerts." For Paul Celan and Carolyn Bergvall, as I will develop it, the shibboleth is a form of misspeaking with mortal consequences. We have come a long way from Dick Cheney's politically expedient "misspeaking" to generative verbal error.

Saying Shibboleth

To speak becomes a give-away. Are you one of us, not one of us? How you speak will be used against you.
—Caroline Bergvall, "Overview" to Say, "Parsley"[10]

There are certain language situations which are historically repressive. People talk of language as a means of expression, but it is also evidently a means of selection. In certain social—historical circumstances, there are things which could not be said, and therefore, in any connecting way, not thought
—Raymond Williams, Politics and Letters

The origins of the biblical shibboleth appear in a passage in Judges (12:5–6) that describes a battle between two Semitic tribes in which the warriors of Gilead defeat the tribe of Ephraim. When the Ephraimites flee to their homeland across the river Jordan, the Gileadites, knowing that the people of Ephraim have difficulty pronouncing the digraph phoneme *sh*, ask any stranger to pronounce the word *shibboleth* (a Hebrew word referring to grain or corn). Since the Ephraimite dialect pronounced the word with the first syllable "si-bboleth," they were revealed as the enemy and were slaughtered on the spot. The word has come to refer to any password that permits entry for some and denies entry for others.[11] The mispronounced word is not an error but a difference that the class in power exploits. In its more conventional applications, a shibboleth refers to any use of status or cultural appurtenance (clothing, adornment, appearance) that marks one as an outsider. Recently, the American Civil Liberties Union filed a lawsuit against the US Customs and Border Protection on behalf of two women stopped and detained at a small town in Montana near the Canadian border. The border agent asked for their identification and detained them for speaking Spanish. Both women are American citizens of Spanish descent, but the border agent's justification for detaining them was as follows: "The reason I asked you for your ID is I came in here and I saw you guys are speaking Spanish, which is vary unheard-of up here."[12] This incident typifies the shibboleth's flexibility in weaponizing language against the stranger, enforcing what Sarah Dowling calls "settler monolingualism" (3). Her term "aims to account for the new meanings monolingualist ideologies accrue in settler colonial contexts. This term highlights the ways in which English is understood as the most natural and appropriate way to '#SpeakAmerican' or to participate in the mainstream society of Anglophone Canada" (3). In our current xenophobic moment, typified by my example above, such incidents suggest that the shibboleth continues to be deployed around linguistic nationalism.

In Paul Celan's 1954 poem "Shibboleth," the poet signals his own estrangement as a Romanian born, German-speaking Jew, now exiled in Paris:

Mitsamt meinen Steinen,	Together with my stones
den grossgeweinten	wept large
hinter den Gittern,	behind the bars,
schleiften sie mich	they dragged me
in die Mitte des Marktes,	into the market's midst,
dorthin,	there
wo die Fahne sich aufrollt, der ich	where the flag I never swore
keinerlei Eid schwor.	allegiance to unfurls. (145)

This could describe any loyalty trial that demands fealty to flag and fatherland. But Celan is not alone in the market square; he remembers the Viennese workers who were slaughtered by Nazis in 1934 and the partisans in Madrid whose Republican banners read *"no pasarán"* against Franco's Phalange and Hitler's Condor Legion. Celan cries out:

Herz:	Heart:
gib dich auch hier zu erkennen,	reveal yourself here too,
hier, in der Mitte des Marktes.	here in the market's midst.
Ruf's, das Schibboleth, hinaus	Cry out the shibboleth
in die Fremde der Heimat:	into your homeland's alienness.
Februar. No pasarán.	February. No pasarán. (144)

For Celan, speaking the Hebrew word *shibboleth* in a poem written in German marks his minority status as a Jew, estranged from his homeland and his family who were killed in labor camps during the war. He writes in a "minor literature," in the terms developed by Deleuze and Guattari, that characterizes his use of a language tainted by the Holocaust. Yet writing in a language not one's own permits one to live within and beyond an oppressive society. By pronouncing the Spanish word *pasarán,* he marks his solidarity with other strangers, exiles, and subalterns. Since the shibboleth is a password that allows passage, Celan's quotation of the famous Republican motto becomes, as John Felstiner says, "a password for the poet himself; can he pass into the realm of Goethe and Schiller by proving his identity with a Biblical password?" (82).[13]

But the passage into official German culture was not easy, as Celan's suicide testifies. Writing after Auschwitz and within an alien language create fissures in personal and national belonging. This fissure is literalized in Doris Salcedo's 2007 installation at the Tate Modern, *Shibboleth.* It consisted of a long crack or channel running the entire length of the museum's Turbine Hall, stark in its simplicity yet complex in its implications for the work of art in an age of global migrations. Salcedo describes her work as "a piece about people who have been exposed to extreme experience of racial hatred and subjected to inhuman conditions in the first world . . . I wanted a piece that intrudes in the space, that it is unwelcome like an immigrant that just intrudes." ("Transcription"). Not only was *Shibboleth* a stark reminder of racial tensions in the current period,

Figure 3.1. Doris Salcedo, *Shibboleth*, Tate Gallery, London (2007)[14]

but it left a literal scar when the crack was filled in, "a commemoration of all this life that we don't recognize" ("Transcription").

Salcedo, as Mieke Bal observes, is engaged with an act of mourning, attempting to speak to loss without providing an objective correlative. If we think of the shibboleth as an unpronounceable word, then the crack or fissure in the floor of the museum represents that flaw in speech that marks the foreigner, the migrant, the native. We think of sculpture as something imposed on a space, but Salcedo negates the object, creating a rupture in the Tate's massive gallery. In her installation, the shibboleth is a cenotaph for those who have disappeared and fallen through the cracks of the national and human condition. Other works by Salcedo similarly treat such absences. Her 1992 work *Atrabiliarios* (worn shoes) consists of shoes, mostly women's, worn by actual disappeared persons, *desaparecidos*, through political violence. The shoes are placed in niches dug into the museum wall covered by a layer of animal fiber and attached to the wall with medical sutures. Like *Shibboleth*, *Atrabiliarios* explores negative space, persons as ghosts remembered only by the article of clothing that touches the earth. We see the trace of the human, the migrant who is landless, the political victim who has been erased.

Her shoe is the sign of the person who once wore it. In both *Atrabiliarios* and *Shibboleth*, the trace marks a disparity between the subaltern and the ability to "pronounce" national and cultural identity. For the migrant seeking asylum in a homogenous Europe or America, crossing the border exposes a cut or break in that homogeneity. As a symbol of cultural continuity and privilege, the museum is invaded, broken open, its depths exposed. And that exposure distressed visitors to the exhibition who feared tripping or falling into the gap. According to the *New York Times*, "Fifteen people suffered minor injuries in the first eight weeks after 'Shibboleth' opened" (Lyall).

The spatial and museal implications of the shibboleth are elaborated in Caroline Bergvall's *Say, "Parsley,"* a series of sound and language installations that she created in collaboration with the composer Ciarán Maher. The title refers to the 1937 massacre of Haitian creoles by members of the Dominican Army under Rafael Trujillo. Deemed "thieves" and "revolutionaries," twenty thousand Haitians were slaughtered under Trujillo's authoritarian, US-supported regime. Since many of the Haitians could not be distinguished from dark-skinned Dominicans, the former were singled out by being shown a sprig of parsley and asked

Figure 3.2. Carolyn Bergvall, from *Say "Parsley,"* Arnolfini Gallery, Bristol, UK (2010). Photo credit: Jamie Woodley

what it was. If the individual did not pronounce the word *perejil* by trilling the *r* in the Spanish manner, their Haitian identity was revealed, and they could be killed. What has come to be known as the Parsley Massacre has been treated in a number of literary works, including Edwidge Danticat's novel *The Farming of Bones*, Rita Dove's poem "Parsley," and Junot Diaz's *The Brief Wondrous Life of Oscar Wao*.

Bergvall's installation emphasizes the *imperative* of the shibboleth, the authoritative demand to pronounce the word correctly and thus identify its user.[15] Using the historic massacre as her backdrop, she created an initial installation at the Spacex Gallery in Exeter that consisted of a soundscape based on recordings of various British speakers pronouncing words that reflect a wide spectrum of class and regional inflections of British English. After recording fifty different voices, she and Maher placed loudspeakers around the space, each projecting the phrase *rolling hills* as spoken by speakers chosen from different regions. In the middle of the room were suspended a series of plumb lines with anchoring balls at the bottom that could be moved by gallery visitors—or perhaps that served as interruptions to easy passage. Listeners, according to Bergvall, "caught in their own ears, created their own sense of what they heard, moved around the room, piercing together the pairings only to discover more words in the recesses of their hearing, their memory ear."[16] On the wall in the entrance were four stenciled white *R*s on the white wall, announcing perhaps the vulnerable *r* in *perejil* or the repeated *r* in *rolling hills*. On the wall at the far end of the warehouse space was the following text:

> speech mirrors ghosts [speak] as if
> appeased by the evidence of this
> when [I speak] I hold at least two
> or as if intensely preoccupied
> when [I speak up] I am held to one (56)

The repetition of *speak* in brackets signals the gatekeeper function of the shibboleth in which speaking interpellates oneself as other. The mispronunciation of the shibboleth creates a ghost that responds to the imperative "speak: or "speak up." The "I" who speaks is in brackets, a specter, both there and not there.

The list poem that accompanies Bergvall's installation consists of a series of commands in which one and two-syllable words are arranged in a vertical column that were projected through facing speakers in the gallery:

> Say: "pig"
> Say: "fig"
> Say: "fag"
> Say: "fog"
> Say: "frog" (58)

Despite its more ominous associations with forced interrogation, the list resembles an audiological exam where one is asked to repeat a series of simple words broadcast through earphones. Having one's hearing tested is hardly the same as the shibboleth, but it shares an uncanny resemblance to more sinister exams and interrogations that chart and categorize.

Over the years, the term *shibboleth* has moved from a word that isolates and marginalizes to a term for some outmoded or old-fashioned idea: "don't use musty old shibboleths" or "there is no place today for outworn shibboleths." This more recent usage transforms a word "used as a test for detecting foreigners" (*OED*) to one simply referring to some belief we no longer hold. This new usage hides the word's violent history that continues to erupt in current debates about black English in courtrooms and classrooms, bilingual education, and class and gender-inflected discrimination practices. As Marjorie Perloff says of Bergvall's installation, "One language's shibboleth is another's everyday speech," although I might amend this to emphasize that one language's shibboleth *denies* the other language's everyday speech (131).

From Blurt to *Blert*: Jordan Scott

In Tom Hooper's 2010 film *The King's Speech*, Colin Firth plays King George VI, thrust uncomfortably into the monarchy by the sudden abdication of his brother, Edward (Bertie), to marry his American mistress. The film concerns George's attempt at overcoming a lifelong stammer with the help of an Australian speech therapist, Lionel Logue (Geoffrey Rush). We witness the hapless king struggling to pronounce tongue-twisters or engage in operatic bouts of swearing at full volume. Although Firth does not have a stammer, the film's screenwriter, David Seidler, does, and he presumably based much of the script on his own speech difficulties. As is so often the case with mainstream movies about disability, our protagonist overcomes his impediment, and in the film's climactic scene, George delivers his famous 1939 speech declaring war on Germany with only the faintest of pauses and hesitations. The film cuts to images of British citizens, sitting tensely by their radios, showing the impact of this radio-distributed voice as a voice of national resolve.

Robert McRuer reads the film through a disability perspective that acknowledges the importance of films like *The King's Speech* in making disability visible. But he is critical of the triumphalist character of such films in which a disabled character overcomes an impediment to speak "normally" again—and in this case, to serve as England's commanding monarch on the eve of war. McRuer also sees the historical appearance of *The King's Speech* as a sign of neoliberal politics in the United Kingdom during a period of enforced austerity following the worldwide recession of the late 2000s. He asks, "What does the applause for *The King's Speech* obfuscate? And what might it mean that in 'austere times,' or 'times of adversity,' a disabled figure is not only deployed to represent a feel-good national unity, but even pedagogically offered up to the current House of Windsor, which . . . might 'earn itself a generation of ovations' if it walks the walk and talks the talk like Bertie?" (43).

What alternatives might there be, then, to this overcoming narrative that would materialize disability along a different axis than that of cure, redemption, and speech? How could the king's speech be turned, in McRuer's terms, to the "crip's speech"? One answer is provided by the Canadian poet Jordan Scott, who transforms his own stammering blurts into "blerts." The word *blurt* originally referred to a physiological expulsion, "a sudden discharge of breath or fluid from the mouth after an attempt to retain it" (*OED*). Another version explains the term as "to utter abruptly and if by a sudden impulse; to ejaculate impulsively; to burst out with" (*OED*). As an onomatopoeic word, *blurt* imitates evacuations of bodily material. It has come to mean a sudden, unreflective and unplanned remark, laying no claim to truth value but rather to its performative potential in affecting an audience.

Scott also blurts, although to very different ends. The title to his 2008 book *Blert* returns, as he says, "to the fact of my mouth" and its tendency to halt, repeat, delay, and defer as a result of a lifelong stammer. As he says, he is a "parasite of metaphors, so easily am I carried away by the first simile that comes along. Having been carried away, I have to find my difficult way back, and slowly return, to the fact of my mouth" (7). Scott's portmanteau variation *blert* emphasizes the stutterer's common practice of substituting for an intended word a variant version while maintaining the performative force of "blurting out," or what Marc Shell calls "compensatory verbal substitution" (6).[17] Such substitutions and variations do not compensate for a correct utterance so much as generate new, sensuous and associative possibilities. Scott's blerts enlist processes inherent in the physiological, lexical, and philological sources of language itself. At one level, he continues a distinguished tradition in sound poetry from Dadaists and Russian futurists to contemporary figures such as Henri Chopin, Christian Bök, and the Four Horsemen (B. P. Nichol, Steve McCaffery, Paul Dutton, Rafael Barreto-Rivera). In Scott's case, there is an additional pedagogical component to his vocal pyrotechnics, one that challenges him to tune his voice around a score of complex verbal elements, a text, as he says, "written to be as difficult as possible for [him] to read" (64).[18] In the book's afterword, he figures its composition as "a spelunk into the mouth of a stutterer . . . a trek across labial regions, a navigation of tracheal rills, and as full bore squirm inside the mouth's wear and tear" (64). References to geology, travel, and natural flora and fauna abound in the book as if to emphasize the vocal apparatus as a geological landscape he must negotiate. He consistently links terms for the musculature and physiology of speech with geological formations and natural life. As with Christine Kim's *Game of Skill 2.0*, he makes "voice" a problem, not a transparent vehicle.

Blert could be seen as Scott's ars poetica in which the sound-producing cavities of the body are linked to the biological and geological growth of the planet. In a YouTube interview, he says, "All my existence as a stutterer was perhaps preparing me to be a poet because . . . you want to treat language delicately, really get into the granular sensation of words in your mouth" (Interview). Scott warps the usual understanding of an utterance as a unit of meaning and sees it as a repository of sounds, mis-pronunciations and associations that vie for expression. His siting of sound occurs through three interlinked thematic elements: species, spaces, and speech that complicate boundaries between human and non-human nature.

Scott's interest in the natural world is reflected in passages that concern the formation of organic life:

> *What is the utterance?*
> Phonemes flounder briquette warmth. Tethered to seven mollusks, an osteoblast chomps into the burger of kelp's wreck; an osteoclast nibbles a puffin's scapula in mid-afternoon weight. Each webbed foot tussles, the soft hum of slipper on hardwood floors. (11)

The repeated question of this opening section, "*What is the utterance?*," is answered by a series of alliterative non sequiturs that evoke a littoral landscape. Osteoblasts are the basic cellular material of bone. They participate in the formation of endochondral ossification or bone growth. Scott fuses bone matter, meat and kelp in a sequence referring to natural growth and decay. Recent research has shown that marine life—kelp, algae, mollusks—contribute important chemicals to bone preservation. Hence it is not absurd to say that osteo*blast* eats a "burger of kelp's wreck" or that an osteo*plast* "nibbles a puffin's scapula in mid-afternoon weight." Osteo*clasts*, on the other hand, are cells that contribute to bone repair so that for one to "nibble a puffin's scapula" could suggest reconstitution of or therapeutic use of a puffin's shoulder blade. Such a literal reading sidesteps the sonic properties of Scott's sensuous language. Scott works at several verbal levels at once: imagery of natural life, phonemic equilibrations, imagistic associations. The answer to the question "What is the utterance?" partakes of the speaker's particular impediment (to utter with difficulty) as well as his associative senses as words pile up, frustrate expression, and resolve a clause. He is, as he says, a "parasite of metaphors" (7). The imagery of bones, their growth and decay, the building and decaying of cellular matter, approximates on the organic plane what goes on linguistically in the formation of an utterance.

In this same introductory section, Scott confronts the stutterer's verbal anxiety:

My mouth drew the swallow's panic. Chew pteryla. The spaces between them chomp apterium; gizzard beat Broca, broca. Chirped electrode. Sing *fuming*. Sing *furious*. Now, open your mouth and speak. Incisive fossa in labial turbulence, sing *fuming*, sing *furious*. In nejroimaging, filoplumes blitz. Now open your mouth and speak. Sing *frumious*. (11)

The previous section's avian references continue here. "Pteryla" are the feather tracks on birds; the "swallow's panic" may refer to the bird's characteristic chirps, chatters, and gurgles that have often been compared to stuttering. Apterium refers to the spaces between a bird's feathers. Injuries to the Broca area of the brain often cause forms of aphasia—including stuttering. The repetition of *f*-initial words (fuming, furious, frumious) seems part of a speech therapy exercise. *frumious* is of course a portmanteau word in Lewis Carroll's (also a stutterer) "Jabberwocky" (the "frumious Bandersnatch"). When Scott concludes his tour of these avian and neurological paths, the utterance "Now open your mouth and speak" has been displayed as a phonological labyrinth. "My mouth drew the swallow's panic" describes both Scott's own anxiety in public speaking yet, perhaps, projects his own mediated speech onto that of the swallow.[19]

My second category, "spaces," refers to Scott's interest in geography and geology. Scott often refers to his verbal detours as spelunking, an exploration of the resonant caves of the body's vocal apparatus. In a section titled "Spelunk," he descends into the inner recesses of the mouth:

Buccal slinks into hoodoo. The dawn clots oort. Bruise syllabic upon upturned halibut, welded to sky curve. We watch, in a book toss, the yap blip, and in careful, clasp to each blurt, clug clug the sherbet angles of vowel's echolalia Trash lip, lisp smudge: July, mucus, raspberry. Inside, a toothful jujube purls comma. We'll all meet on the tongue. We'll all meet in the tongue. Pickaxe plosive bloat and say: *b is for* by the mouth's slight erosions. (12)

Here, Scott foregrounds the muscular (buccal) production of sound within the mouth and extends it through sequences of sensuous non-sequiturs, held together by alliterative and associative patterns, "a full bore squirm inside the mouth's wear and tear" (64). If the passage is a challenge for Scott to repeat, it is no less an attempt to give physical form to speech, to embody words as obstacles, barriers, and bridges. "The dawn clots oort" merges an image of planetary time (dawn) with barrier (clots) and space (the Oort Cloud is a ring of icy crystals at the edges of our solar system). These lines do not imitate the stammer (although at times blank spaces between passages reflect the stutterer's pauses) so much as project an auditory landscape that the stammer produces. It also provides a concise image of what happens when the first light of day eclipses the vast darkness of the solar system. As a challenge, the work tests Scott's vocal abilities, but its function is not to serve as an exercise. Rather, it maps the poet's associational patterns.

Scott's emphasis on the physiological, material condition of the utterance also contributes to the work's interest in geological formations:

> Skookumchuck narrows, puckers waka waka against the rush of river. A
> haboob burst in your pharynx, technoed badunkadunk in zgomaticus
> major The cochlear yawn centipedes tattletale in buckthorn orange. Each
> maxilliped bongos, fresh cornflakes suplex atop enamel. (41)

Here, First Nation words from British Columbia (Skookumchuck River), black argot (badunkadunk), scientific jargon (zgomaticus), meteorology (haboob, a wind or dust storm) jam up against each other in a rich verbal stew. What often appear to be nonsense words or non-sequiturs turn out to be highly specific technical terms.[20] For postwar poets who are urged to "find their voice," Scott's stammer poses a distinct obstacle, one that in *Blert* he seems happy to exploit. The obstacle is that of the confusion of a metaphysical subject with an embodied technology. The poetic voice of the romantics or the Beats speaks through a prediscursive, adamic language revealed through open-throated confession. Jordan Scott's voice is first and foremost physical. Or to adapt Robert Creeley's terms, "Speech / is a mouth" (283).

Unfaithful to the Original

> Open paragraph   It was the first day   period
> She had come from   a far   period   tonight at dinner
> comma   the families would ask   comma   open
> quotation marks   How was the first day   interroga-
> tion mark   close quotation marks   at least to say
> the least of it possible   comma   the answer would be
> open quotation marks   there is but one thing   period
> There is someone   period   From   a far   period
> close quotation marks
> —Teresa Hak Kyung Cha, *Dictee*

The opening page of Teresa Hak Kyung Cha's *Dictee* features a dictation exercise in which a French passage is translated by the non-native
speaker whose first language is Korean into the above version. The immigrant translates the speaker's unvoiced punctuation marks as part of the
verbal sample spoken by the teacher (*"Aller a la ligne. C'etait le premiere
jour point"*) marking in print the faithful, if misunderstood, rendering
of the dictation exercise. The book's title, *Dictee*, stresses the degree to
which the immigrant subject is dictated into national identity by learning how to speak properly. Just as she must learn the dominant (in this
case French) language, so she must "submit to prohibitions against what
cannot be said and to consent to closures which eliminate the unsayable
and which refuse the indeterminate and inadmissible" (133). Lisa Lowe's
summary of the national imperative of dictation in Cha's work refers
to Cha's experience under French Catholic missionary schooling. "The
French grammar lesson dramatizes not only the indoctrination of the
Korean narrator within a 'foreign' Western language, but the dictée—as
a paradigmatic instance of French educational influence on the Korean
subject" (132). Elsewhere in the poem, Cha describes her subjection to
the new language: "She would take on their punctuation. She waits to
service this. Theirs. Punctuation. She would become, herself, demarcations" (4). Such subjects are, in Lowe's terms, "unfaithful to the original,"
and as a consequence are marked as always misspeaking the official language. Cha's use of the third person here testifies to the bracketed nature
of self-identity under the condition of national dictation.

In a similar vein, the Jordanian-Lebanese artist Lawrence Abu Hamdan's work in acoustic technologies and surveillance investigates the political implications of speech and mis-speech. As a self-declared "private ear" and forensic linguist, he studies soundscapes of urban life for what they tell us about the ways that sounds contribute to spatial and geographic phenomena. Like Cha, he is interested in how speech creates "the other" both within and without Western societies. He uses the technologies of speech analysis to map the complexity of geographic and national origins of asylum seekers and migrants crossing borders.

In his documentary audio essay *The Freedom of Speech* (2012), Hamdan satirizes the impossibility of locating the origins of one's "native tongue":

> —So, where are you from?
> —I'm from Hackney.
> —But you're Danish, aren't you?
> —No, I'm Palestinian.
> —So where are you from in Palestine?
> —I'm not from Palestine.
> —So where are you from
> —We're Palestinians from a refugee camp in Lebanon.
> —So you were born in Lebanon?
> —No, I was born in Dubai.
> —Why do you have an American accent?
> —What do you mean?
> —You speak English with an American twang.
> —It's because, you know, because of Eddie Murphy, Stallone.
> —So you're from Hollywood?
> —No, no, I'm from Hackney. (qtd. in Apter, "Shibboleth" 143–44)

Emily Apter asks, "Where is the shibboleth in this no-man's land of language histories and errant identification? How could his consonants and vowels be held legally accountable as testaments to his origins?" (144). As Hamdan says in *The Freedom of Speech*, "We are not free to choose the ways we are being heard" (Apter 144). The liberal humanist belief in free speech is qualified by submitting private speech to public scrutiny.

Figure 3.3. Lawrence Abu Hamdan, from *Conflicted Phonemes* (2012)[21]

In his 2012 installation *Conflicted Phonemes*, Hamdan created voice maps based on audio tests given to Somali asylum seekers by the Dutch immigration authorities. Their applications were denied because their dialects and pronunciations marked them as members of specific "safe" communities of northern Somalia unscathed by political violence farther south. These linguistic maps, tracing phonemic differences across geographic spaces, complicate the idea of "place of birth" by considering patterns of migration, cultural exchange and education. The maps provide material evidence of how people describe the "volatile history and geography of Somalia over the last forty years as a product of continual migration and crisis. Its complexity is a testimony to the irreducibility of the voice to a passport, namely its inapplicability to fix people in space." In their various installations around the world, the maps offered the denied asylum seeker "an alternative and nonvocal mode of contestation" by showing the rhizomatic pattern of speech patterns over the life course.

In a series of black-and-white diagrams, designed by Hamdan's collaborator, the graphic designer Janna Ullrich, each individual Somali applicant's verbal status is described in clinical detail. At the top of each form are individual words that the applicant was asked to pronounce. At the bottom of the page are the three categories into which they may be placed—ACCEPTED, REJECTED, and WAITING—in large capital letters. In one, Abdirahman is WAITING and is described as "definitely not traceable to the speech community of South Somalia." At the same time, his origin suggests that he was "socialized in South Somalia" (131). Another applicant, Jama, is REJECTED because his accent "is definitely traceable to the speech community in North Somalia" (133). On another wall of the installation, Hamden has created large blue vinyl wall prints or "coding circuits "of language competence and cultures of linguistic exposure that . . . dismantle the presumption of a one-to-one correspondence between digital voice recognition and identity" (145). The clinical quality of the speech interpreter's diagrams helps to illustrate how individuals seeking asylum are reduced to formulas and "data" that do not take into account patterns of migrations, locations of education and socialization, and diasporic citizenship.

I conclude with Cha and Hamdan to suggest that misspeaking, mistranslating, and misunderstanding are formative in creating the nonidentical subject—turning, in the case of Cha, the Korean into the American or in the case of Hamdan, the Somali asylum seeker into an unqualified subject. It is in such works that a speech impediment meets national citizenship, where a mispronounced word becomes a test of social identity. When the body stutters, mispronounces a word, fails a dictation exercise, speech produces exclusion—but also, as in the case of Jordan Scott, poetry. Poets and artists who have made misspeaking a form of critical expression have tapped into what it means to be "unfaithful to the original" where the original is the language spoken by power. At the same time, they have used the condition of misspeaking to permit access to untraveled linguistic byways and philological detours.

These detours are what we call speech. Or to put it even more succinctly, misspeaking is speaking. At one level, all speech is subject to deformation, whether from memory lapses, slips of the tongue, fatigue, neurological damage. But there is a more fundamental sense in which misspeaking is speech. What I have called distributive voicing describes speech as always already filtered through various modalities of transmission, some electronic but some, as in the case of Cha and Hamden, cultural. As Amanda Weidman says in her entry on "Voice" in *Keywords in*

Sound, "Sonic and material experiences of voice are never independent of the cultural meanings attributed to sound, to the body, and particularly to the voice itself" (232). All these "sonic and material" elements conspire to produce a fiction of speech as unmediated expression. As much as poets have been enjoined to "find your own voice," that imperative is a ventriloquism of the phonocentric. When Donald Trump accepted the nomination for president at the 2016 Republican Convention and assured his constituents that he would "give a voice to those who don't have one. I am your voice," we heard how wildly distributed that voice can be. By an ironic inversion, to speak with a stammer or with an accent or, like Cordelia, to refuse to speak—these are perhaps the most valid forms of expression, since they display the fractures and fissures implicit in every speech act, revealing, as Wallace Stevens says, "ghostlier demarcations" out of "keener sounds."[22]

4

"Tongue-tied and / muscle / bound"

Doing Time with Eigner

> a poem is a
>   characteristic
>   length of time
>
> —Larry Eigner

The phrase *disability poetics* encompasses a wide range of possible meanings. In its simplest form, it implies the representation of disability in poetry—the appearance of a blind soothsayer in *The Waste Land* or the "idiot boy" in Wordsworth's titular poem. As disability scholars have observed, disabled figures in literature are ubiquitous, and thus to create a separate subgenre around their appearance is somewhat arbitrary, turning a physiological or cognitive condition into a metaphor. As important as this usage has been for a disability hermeneutics, it leaves the body as a rather inert support for the poem's larger concerns. As David Mitchell and Sharon Snyder observe, the use of disability as a "narrative prosthesis" in literature emphasizes how a disabled figure often serves as a "crutch" for a work's formal and thematic coherence without attending to the specifics of an individual's condition (49).

A more complex meaning would refer to disability's foundational role in poetics itself, the ways that bodily impairment or physical difference are used to define the aesthetic function. In *Invalid Modernism*, I argue that an autonomy aesthetics requires a grotesque or impaired body upon which to erect formal criteria of organic unity and evaluative criteria of detachment and disinterestedness. Edgar Allan Poe's famous reiteration of Bacon, "There is no exquisite beauty without some strangeness in the proportions," anticipates a disability aesthetics by conflating the affective level of reception with formal production. Debates about prosody in the early modern period are often framed by references to disability and debility.

George Puttenham in his *Arte of English Poesie* (1589) notes that stanzas are like a "bearer or supporter of a song or ballad not unlike the old weake bodie that is stayed up by his staff, and were not otherwise able to walke or to stand upright" (qtd. in Smith II: 68). The Elizabethan poet Samuel Daniel argues that attempting to configure English verse to Greek and Latin meters is "but a confused deliverer of their excellent conceits, whose scattered limbs we are faine to looke out and joyne together" (Smith II: 364). Roger Ascham counters by speaking of verse based on patterned stresses rather than classical quantities as having "feet without joints" that are "born deformed, unnatural, and lame" (Smith I: 32–33). A more recent version of this by Jim Ferris and others is to look for ableist terms in prosody—limping meters, eye rhymes, enjambment—in which the poem is regarded as a body whose individual elements may, at times become crippled, broken, deaf or blind.[1] A disability poetics, as I've written elsewhere, "theorizes the ways that poetry defamiliarizes not only language but the body normalized *within* language" (*Concerto* 118).

A third form that disability takes is its use as a descriptor for poetry produced by poets living with disabilities. While this has been a rich resource for many coming out as members of a community (represented generously in Jennifer Bartlett, Sheila Black, and Michael Northern's *Beauty Is a Verb* anthology), it still leaves untouched the question of *poetry* since the various forms it takes—with the possible exception of sign language poetry—tend to reflect the dominant practices across the aesthetic spectrum. It also implicitly treats disability as a discrete category of poetry rather than an intersectional component of a poet's multiple identities, reducing Audre Lorde, to take one example, to a cancer survivor instead of, as she asserts in *The Cancer Journals*, a "woman, a black lesbian feminist mother lover poet, all I am" (25).

My *insight* into this issue is to *see* whether disability doesn't *revision* significant *sites* of poetics in the first place. What *appears* when we *look* at poetry—and indeed, literature in general—through a disability *optic*. As my phrasing here demonstrates, it is hard to escape an ocularcentric rhetoric that takes sightedness for granted and uses that vantage like a better pair of glasses. This revisionist imperative—what some are calling "cripistemology"—asks what kinds of knowledge are produced—or envisioned—through what Rosemarie Garland-Thomson calls the "extraordinary" body?"[2] A crip poetics would study the ways that poetry produces—not reflects—different ways of thinking about the spectrum of human variation and about the contingent relationship of bodies to other bodies. It would also redirect generic categories based on their presumed appropriateness to specific sensory regimes. The pity and terror produced by Oedipus's self-blinding that, for Aristotle, is central to tragedy may mean something quite different for the sight-impaired poet; the voice presumed necessary for lyric may mean something different for a deaf poet who uses sign language. And as I will suggest with reference to Larry Eigner, the classical unities of time, place, and action signify differently for a poet whose mobility is impaired by cerebral palsy.

I have intentionally begun by speaking of disability poetics in terms of its ocularcentrism, its emphasis on staring and scopic regimes by which nontraditional bodies and minds are isolated and marginalized. But a disability poetics also crips speech and sound by interrogating what it means to speak clearly. As I suggest in my previous chapter, "sounding good" often marks the horizon of what constitutes a national subject. What happens to rhetorical emphasis on clarity and grace when speech is impaired, stammered, or delayed? As Melanie Yergeau asks in *Authoring Autism*, what is rhetoric for autistic persons who are deemed unable to be rhetorical? Or as the neurodiversity activist and author, Amanda Baggs says in her video *In My Language*, "It is only when I type something in your language that you refer to me as having communication."

Speaking improperly may, in the case of the biblical shibboleth, marginalize the other, the subaltern, the immigrant, and in extreme cases, it may lead to imprisonment and death. It may also marginalize the person whose speech is contorted from neurological damage or who speaks through voice-activated software or who may not speak at all. In this context, I want to focus on Larry Eigner's voice as a form of distressed and distressing language. Raphael Allison observes that critical studies of Eigner have tended to focus on his use of the typewritten page—what he calls "page fetishism"—as a register of physical hesitations and neurological difficulties of the disabled body (178).[3] Allison argues that William Carlos Williams's late work, following a series of strokes that left him with aphasic slurring, must be read in terms of changes to his speaking voice—its hesitation, false starts, and distortions. The same goes for Eigner, whose neurologically mediated speech embodies a distinct challenge to the privilege accorded voice and orality among his contemporaries.

Eigner's voice was difficult to understand, and when he gave readings, organizers developed creative ways of representing his poems by projecting them on walls or screens or on handouts. Referring to the importance of voice in postwar poetry, Allison asks, "What happens . . . when the speaker himself *can't* speak? How does vocal authenticity matter differently to one for whom motor speech has become a challenge?" (150). The distressing voice challenges the image of the poet as "solitary singer" or open-throated bard and, more significantly, the authority that subtends authorship. If voice for Charles Olson is the unmediated, embodied presence of the poet, is the fractured or un-hearable voice then denied subjecthood? Olson admired Eigner's poetry a good deal, which suggests that his emphasis on the oral was less about delivery and more about rendering the physiology of the poet in the poetic line.[4] But many persons encountering an individual with a severe speech impediment may find the question of subjecthood problematic. Prelingually deaf persons often speak with a lateral lisp or other vocal variants of what is presumed to be normal speech. Hence, the derogatory description of such persons as "deaf and dumb" links their inability to hear with their presumed inability to speak or think. As William Cheng asks, "If some people seem to lack rational faculties and rhetorical virtuosity where do their voices fit in the chorus of just debate?" (10).

The first time I heard Larry Eigner speak was in the middle of a presentation I was giving at a Modern Language Association panel on contemporary poetry. He was there in the audience with several other poets—Ron Silliman, Robert Grenier, David Bromige—and halfway through my talk, Larry began to speak. Cerebral palsy from birth affected his speech, making it hard to decipher. Nor was he reticent about speaking, as I found to my dismay. As confused as I was at being interrupted, I was also interested in this detour in that most characteristic academic ritual: a panel of professors professing. It was all the more important that the panel topic concerned a generation of contemporary poets for whom orality was paramount. There was Larry Eigner, one of the most important figures in the postwar poetry movement commenting in the *midst* of the event, not in the Q&A that followed. Nothing could have been more appropriate, given the topic, than to have the actual poet present in the room, interrupting the presentation and speaking in an indecipherable manner—indecipherable, at least to me. As I remember, I asked Larry to repeat his comment, but it was no use, and so I stumbled and flailed until my time was up.[5]

In retrospect, what I have learned from this experience is what "my time" means in a disability context. Academic conferences, with their short breaks between sessions, multiple, overlapping schedules, and over-caffeinated presenters are a model of intellectual entropy; the more you cram into a day of presentations and lectures the less you are able to process. Eigner's interruption of my talk offered another way to think about the performance of knowledge, a reparative version that requires diversions and surprises rather than the completion of a prepared speech. And it is an awareness that contemporary poets, often with Eigner as model, have put to good use in interrupting thought, allowing for asides and distractions, delaying closure, and jettisoning conventional rhetorical markers of time, place, and person. Lytle Shaw has characterized these features as a "slow poetics" on the analogy of slow food.[6] The time of speaking and speaking in time may be two very different things as persons who require more time intervene in the chronometric dependency syndrome in which we live. If you speak with a stutter, thick accent, or verbal tic, time takes its time.

Eigner's distressing speech is linked not only to temporal matters but also to his longstanding environmental concerns. The two issues are joined when we think of the multiple temporalities of nonhuman animals and organisms, plants and weather patterns. To speak well, to "sound good," is to be human. Not sounding good links one to the non-human or animal world, a fact that Eigner thematized in an early poem:

```
I have felt it as they've said
   there is nothing to say

there is everything to speak of
  but the words are words

when you speak that is a sound
What have you done, when you have spoken

  of nothing
  or something I will remember

After trying my animal noise
i break out with a man's cry (140)
```

The poem acknowledges the impact of speech by others ("I have felt it as they've said") and reflects on the claim that "there is nothing to say" when, in fact, "there is everything to speak of." He tests the inertness of words in their materiality ("When you speak that is a sound") against the "something" that gives it voice in memory. He recognizes that "to speak" is a speech act ("what have you done, when you have spoken") that performs as much as represents. The recalcitrance of words to say "something" is an auditory limit for Eigner that he captures in the final couplet: "After trying my animal noise / i break out with a man's cry." Although the line breaks make parsing Eigner's intent difficult, he speaks of a barrier between what his words "sound like" to others—a kind of "animal noise"—and what they represent for him—a "man's cry." The poem refuses to side with either animal noise or human speech but rather sees them, in Mel Chen's terms, as sites on an "animacy continuum" (Chen). The ambiguities of agreement and modification that characterize this and many of his poems are evidence of his multistable perspective, a recognition that he inhabits a bodymind defined by others while, at the same time, living beyond it. In becoming animal or by regarding his utterance as "animal noise" Eigner establishes both his presence as a speaking subject while acknowledging a temporal and epistemological distance from the Subject, capital *S*.

"the endless / Room at the center"

As I have indicated, cripistemological distance is especially concerned with issues of time and what it means to be in and on time. To be interrupted by incomprehensible speech is to lose one's place in time, to take time to renegotiate the speech-act situation. What Alison Kafer, Margaret Price, Robert McRuer, and others have defined as "crip time" is the way that disability challenges the temporal terms by which bodily difference is defined: chronic fatigue, cure, intermittent symptoms, temporary injury, frequency, incidence, occurrence, relapse, remission, prognosis, delay, recurrence, and the triumphalist rhetoric of "overcoming" and "transcending." Each term imagines a body in a state of transition from normative health to possible negative futures or to the reoccurrence of prior conditions. Jasbir Puar and Sarah Lochlann Jain have used the phrase *prognosis time* to describe the *long durée* of diagnosis and anticipation imposed by a biomedical regime. To "crip" time is to recognize the variable times required by persons who because of physical or cognitive impairment have trouble arriving on time, who need more time to take exams, who require more time to obtain captioners or interpreters.[7]

I want to adapt the biomedical uses of temporality to the aesthetic and see how disability in poetry upsets the regimes of prognosis, cure, and rehabilitation—and audition. Eigner, despite, or perhaps because of, physical restrictions, composed a vast body of work and maintained an active epistolary communication with a larger literary community. His work is encrusted with fragmentary quotations from various forms of media, newspapers, conversations, and literature, often without quotes or explanatory context. He seldom mentioned his physical condition, and when he did, he diverted the focus from the personal to the social: "I took to aiming for normalcy—of course, being self-sufficient is good" (*Areas* 163). Without foregrounding disability, as more recent disabled poets have, he thus provides us with an opportunity to consider bodily difference where least represented:

> When, wandering, I look from my page
>
> I say nothing
>
> when asked
>
> I am, finally, an incompetent, after all (87)

Such lines suggest how Eigner treated his disability as what Heidegger calls a "mood" or "attunement" (*stimmung*) within which the world is revealed (172–79). His rueful admission of "incompetence" redirects his condition onto social expectations of what it means to "say nothing." Eigner reflected on the lived experience of limit to reimagine what it means to "wander" both as a physical and phenomenological fact. He asks what it means to be "competent" in a compulsorily able-bodied world where doing or saying "nothing" is regarded as being "incompetent." Foregrounding that expectation defines a new interpretation of competence that is not underwritten by narratives of overcoming.

The short segment on Eigner in the *United States of Poetry* documentary shows him pulling a page from a box full of paper in his Berkeley home, inserting it in his typewriter, and beginning a poem. That room on McGee Street in Berkeley, like the one on Bates Ave. in Swampscott, Massachusetts, where he spent the first fifty-one years of his life, could be called, as he says in one poem, "the endless / Room at the center." It is an oxymoronic description of both the condition of limit and the extensiveness of perception that were his daily condition (51). Every surface of his home in Berkeley was covered with papers, books, and magazines that he could easily access from his wheelchair. He was careful to organize poems by number and date, filing them in folders that could be found on window ledges, tables, and shelves. Eigner was by no means house-bound, especially once he moved to Berkeley in 1978—attending readings, visiting a local community center, meeting other friends and poets—but his point of view, necessarily constricted, gave him an almost preternatural ability to focus and refine what he saw out the window, heard on the radio, and as I will suggest, lived in the durations of disability.

It is worth thinking of this poetics of limit as a variant of a more familiar trope in Romanticism. For Coleridge, this lime-tree bower is a prison yet a confinement that, paradoxically permits a form of transcendence:

> Well, they are gone, and here must I remain,
> This lime-tree bower my prison! I have lost
> Beauties and feelings, such as would have been
> Most sweet to my remembrance even when age
> Had dimm'd mine eyes to blindness! (178)

According to a note Coleridge appended to this poem, an accident that "disabled him from walking during the entire time of their stay" prevented him from joining his friends, yet his disability allows him a moment of introspection that projects him beyond his lime-tree bower into his friends' peripatetic journey: "A delight / Comes sudden on my heart, and I am glad / As I myself were there!" It is the qualifying "as if" that distinguishes Coleridge's perspective from Eigner's, a rhetorical diversion of his disabled present state to a promised future of participation and communion. The Romantic poet uses his loss of that communion to imagine what the experience might have provided "as would have been / Most sweet to my remembrance" in later life, when his eyes are "dimm'd . . . to blindness." By an odd circumlocution, Coleridge imagines a future sight within blindness foreclosed by a disabled present.

In the latter half of the poem, Coleridge reconsiders his limited state and worries that by mourning his loss of participation with his friends, Charles and Mary Lamb, walking on the heath, he disavows the pleasures of his immediate situation, the "broad and sunny leaf" and "solitary humble-bee [that] Sings in the bean-flower!" (181). He observes that in his lime-tree bower, he has "not mark'd / Much that has sooth'd me" and recognizes that "nature ne'er deserts the wise and pure" (180). The rook that he spies overhead flies out of sight, to be seen by his friends on the heath, thus joining local and distant perspectives. He begins in dejection but ultimately chastens his prison metaphor into a kind of qualified transcendence.

In what could be a variation on this theme, Eigner collapses the space in which he writes and the temporality it occasions:

```
the knowledge of death, and now
   knowledge of the stars


     there is one end
                        and the endless


   Room at the center


     passage / in no time


   a rail  thickets  hills  grass (370)
```

Eigner draws out the "now" in "knowledge" to suggest the importance of lived time through which knowledge of both mortality and universe is understood. He does not mourn lost time that would have redeemed a future blindness but *does time* as an ongoing activity. Hillary Gravendyk refers to this phenomenology of time as Eigner's "chronic poetics" that "acknowledges simultaneity, chronicity, duration, and other forms of embodied perception" (7). The double entendre in Gravendyk's use of "chronic" synthesizes Eigner's chronic physical condition with the "no time" that it produces. As perhaps an illustration of what a "passage / in no time" might mean, Eigner provides a condensed list of objects—"a rail thickets hills grass"—that can be seen (or imagined) from his room. Such lists are everywhere in Eigner's work—birds, clouds, sounds, radio chatter, news items, car horns, smells—that mark sensory reception of temporal moments. The stochastic nature of these substantives refuses any subordination one to the next and allows them to map a phenomenological field. Eigner's entire oeuvre, now massively contained in the Stanford University Press four-volume edition, might be defined as a single "passage / in no time."

In these lines, connectives between words have been eliminated, dependent elements juxtaposed without rhetorical bridges. There is no single point of view or vantage, no shifters that position a speaker. As Barrett Watten, using speech-act theory, and Jessica Luck, using phenomenology, have pointed out, Eigner's poetry is multistable, constantly shifting focus and perspective, leaving reference open to multiple readings, the "uncertain limits / of the simultaneous" (704).[8] Eigner's uncharacteristic capitalization of "Room" allows that word to shift back and forth between its function as the concluding term of the previous clause ("endless / Room") and the initial word of a new clause ("Room at the center"), providing a vivid instance of that multistable rhetorical perspective. The spatiotemporal metaphor that Coleridge establishes between his isolate state and his desired communion is eliminated in Eigner in favor of a temporality of the poem itself, one that Robert Duncan observed by saying that his phrases "are suspended in their own time within the time of the poem."[9]

The video segment from *United States of Poetry* illustrates another aspect of Eigner's crip time. We witness the poet's deliberative, slow placement of each letter of the poem on the page, the click of the key, a grunt of satisfaction with each word. In a marginal comment in one poem he writes "slow / is / the poem," marking through enjambment the slow process of typing one letter at a time (609). When he was in his thirties, cryosurgery provided a degree of control over his flailing hands, but he still relied on a succession of portable manual typewriters on which he could organize lineation and position of the platen. His "slow" composition might seem to contrast with the poetics of immediacy and spontaneity that we associate with his Black Mountain peers, yet this slowness oddly enhances the intensity of thought. He elaborates on this issue in his *Stony Hills* interview. Asked about the density of letters on his page, Eigner responds:

> Well, letters get crowded just from my attempt to save time, i.e., cover less space, avoid putting another sheet in the typewriter for a few more words as I at last hope there will only be. There's always been so many things to do. For instance, with only my right index finger to type with I never could write very fast—to say what I want to when I think of it, before

I forget it or how to say it; I sometimes say 2 things at about the same time, in two columns. It'll be from not deciding or being unable to decide quickly anyway what to say first, or next. (*Areas* 149)

The materiality of the page here is directly tied to the material body; typing registers the immediacy of affective and cognitive states, double columns permitting him to say "2 things at about the same time." Raphael Allison qualifies the importance of the typewritten page, feeling that in his public readings, Eigner's voice permits him to "untype" his poems, allowing them to "sound different," and returning them to the body (174). Allison feels that the taped or live voice of the poet offers a literal form of embodiment as opposed to the "trace" of the voice marked by the text. George Hart disputes this claim, noting that Allison "returns to the logic of representationalism and logocentrism, reinstituting physical sound as the natural bond between speech and language" (*Finding* 23). Both these approaches have the advantage of foregrounding embodiment in Eigner's poetry, but Hart allows for a slippage between the two positions: "Eigner never privileged speech over writing, or vice versa, but was always interested in the differential relationship between the two" (23).

We can see this condition of "slow immediacy" in the few poems that refer to disability:

```
Tongue-tied and
    muscle
       bound


      years
        or the seasons
           leaves
              and
             snow  (1272)
```

Eigner decisively does *not* say, "Since I am tongue-tied and muscle bound, I experience years and seasons by observing the changing leaves and the arrival of snow." By leaving out relevant connectives, he correlates relationships between physical limits and seasonal change, between his physical voice and natural growth, between "muscle bound" as a definition of athletic ability and as muscular constriction. If he is tongue-tied, the very fact of the poem belies speechlessness. The lack of completed periods or parallel rhetorical features permits each element of the poem to fuse with all others. One could imagine, for instance, that "years" is modified by the opening phrase as if to collapse the experiencing subject "tongue-tied and muscle bound" with the seasons he experiences.

Hart calls this indirect linkage of disability and slow time an example of "embodied ecopolitics." Eigner's disability "is a material condition that daily made him confront 'the radical tragedy of nature' in a way that [an Emersonian] compensation doesn't solve" (153). To illustrate Hart's point, we might consider Eigner's naturalism through his numerous references to birds seen out the window and that serve as a measure of the present space and time, but they also serve as a trigger for his own precarity:

```
birds the
    warmest blood in the world

   keeps hopping

      powerful breath a ground

         target while brooding

                     the
                 positions

           man's
        growth precarious birth
           to soar in the mind

         so big to the earth

                whole  parting

           active  wake

     all the dimensions

           a great head of (945)
```

The lines deal in various ways with vulnerability, "all the dimensions" that measure normative growth and inevitable decline. Perhaps influenced by a nature program or his extensive reading in environmental literature, Eigner begins by noting that birds have "the warmest blood in the world," allowing them constant movement against the threat of becoming a stationary "target." While brooding on the mortality of birds, he switches to human vulnerability, alluding, obliquely, to his own "precarious birth" in which a forceps injury during delivery led to his cerebral palsy. Precarity joins vulnerable birds to humans, links material head to imagination ("to soar in the mind"). This mobile-like structure of the poem permits the two realms—avian and anthropomorphic—to reflect (on) each other. The poem is not about the onset of the poet's disability so much as the degree to which a different "head" permits identification with other species (birds) and spaces ("so big to the earth").

Eigner's ecopolitical concerns often record the passage of time, showing how "the shadow of slow / day" moves across his awareness. Light, weather, objects swarm in a "blizzard" of sensations in this first part of the poem:

```
    the dead
     light
    the walls
      no stream but
    the union
       things are
         the wonder
           tree

    thing see now
              pole corner
        front moon sliced
            sun

      catch light shadow

    a screen flopped
             loose

       it was one of those blizzards, one
    on another

               the shadow of slow
                     day
                  passes  (460)
```

In this sequence, Eigner records the slow movement of a day through images of light and dark, sun and shadow. The "things" that he sees (a window screen, a "pole corner," the moon) do not form a "union" but rather exist as discrete events. Or rather, they achieve a union by sheer propinquity. The one independent clause in the poem, "it was one of those blizzards," seems to summarize, in addition to weather, the accretional movement of the poem, a blizzard of associations: "thing see now / pole corner / front moon sliced / sun / catch light shadow." We can never tell whether "pole" modifies "corner" or whether a pole is *on* the corner. Does "sliced" modify sun or moon? What about the non-agreement between subject and verb in the phrase "thing see now" unless it is a way of emphasizing the "thingness" upon which individual perceptions are based? To adapt Leslie Scalapino's collection of essays, *The Public World/ Syntactically Impermanence* (although not about Eigner), her title nicely captures the quality of Eigner's poetic language.

By the end of the poem the materiality of his environment merges with his subjective apprehension:

```
a broken-up plane     there is
          touch     sea


                  there is
              the wind


    I was disappearing   into the sunshine

      you live the

        hopeful
               life


        to see
      depth to the moon (460)
```

These extraordinary concluding lines embody, through their heavy enjambment and spacing the "broken-up plane" that has been the poem's major focus. As Jessica Luck has observed, drawing on Merleau-Ponty's writings on Cézanne, Eigner spatializes his perceptual field by facets or planes. I would add that for the poet, these facets occur as temporal markers of an ongoing "inner speech." The "shadow of slow / day" that focalizes the sun's movement is experienced as a "broken-up plane" of disparate sensations. To disappear "into the sunshine" is to live the "hopeful / life" by seeing depths in the flat orb of the moon.

"Between typing and mind's voice"

George Hart quotes a letter in which Eigner remarks on his characteristic gaps and blank spaces as lacunae that reflect a "coordination between typing and mind's voice" (*Finding* 175). In the interest of expanding the meaning of Eigner's voice, I want to return to the question of speech and pursue what "mind's voice" might mean. In the debate over whether Eigner's more "authentic" voice is textual or vocal the question of authenticity seems too narrowly drawn around a Derridean opposition between a self-present voice and a textual trace or supplement. In this dyad, "voice" becomes a strictly acoustic phenomenon, linked to the vocal chords, larynx and tongue as prostheses to presence. Another way of thinking about Eigner's poetic voice would be to understand it in terms of what Denise Riley calls "inner speech."[10] She is referring to the ongoing, unedited quality of speech that continues nonstop, as we say, "in the head." Riley, drawing on V. N. Volosinov and Lev Vygotsky, speaks of inner speech as a kind of autoventriloquism in which we become both the speaker but also the one spoken *through*. Her definition is worth quoting at length:

> For inner speech is no limpid stream of consciousness, crystalline from its uncontaminated source in Mind, but a sludgy thing, thickened with reiterated quotation, choked with the rubble of the overheard, the strenuously sifted and hoarded, the periodically dusted down then crammed with slogans and jingles, with mutterings of remembered accusations, irrepressible puns, insistent spirits of ancient exchanges, monotonous citation, the embarrassing detritus of advertising, archaic injunctions from hymns, and the pastel snatches of old song lyrics. (73)

Inner speech is not a private language, separate from social idiolect, but rather the dense mesh of heard and overheard languages repeating themselves, "a voice without a mouth," as Riley titles her essay. The effect of autoventriloquy "disposes or arranges me to speak as if I myself were their source" (73). Far from denying agency, inner speech may more accurately account for the multiple agents through which one speaks.[11]

We might debate whether the various terms here apply to Eigner, but the implications of Riley's thesis for poetry are worth pondering as a way of describing the kind of voice that animates writing in real time. And to continue our theme, the time of the inner voice is constant, unending, nonperiodic whereas verbalization occurs in time and over time. Furthermore, inner speech, in Volosinov's terms, is always already ideological, reflecting opinions and attitudes, received wisdom and cant. Eigner's ability to focus on what he sees and hears is accompanied by what he remembers and thinks, how received wisdom is subjected to lived experience.[12]

Take, for example, two poems written around Christmas, 1971:

```
                                   (December 24, 1971)

    the proper arm's-length
      for a spastic

                                   (December 25-6, 1971)

    it's obvious

    but how I forget

    If thy right arm of-
    fend o
          waters

          Jerusalem (1070)
```

In these two closely related poems, Eigner reflects on two biblical passages that fuse his identities as a person with a disability and as a Jew. The first passage is from Matthew 5:29:

> And if thy right eye offend thee, pluck it out,
> and cast it from thee: for it is profitable for
> thee that one of thy members should perish, and
> not that thy whole body should be cast into hell.

In the second poem, written the day after the first, Eigner transposes "eye" with "arm," bringing Christ's lesson on adultery in the Sermon on the Mount into line with his own reflections on disability (Eigner only had the use of one finger of his right hand). Jesus is saying that if something offends ("causes you to stumble" in the original Greek), it is better to pluck out one's eye than live in sin—better not to see than to see through an eye of lust. Eigner is less interested in the moral lesson than in a hypostacized other who is offended or distressed by a palsied arm that doesn't "measure up" to some bodily ideal. In the first poem he muses on the absurd notion that there is a "the proper arm's-length / for a spastic." He then subjects the idea of embodied difference to cultural and racial difference, fusing disabled and ethnic identity by invoking the Jews captive in Babylon.

The second poem shifts from New to Old Testament, invoking famous lines from Psalm 137 about the Jews in exile—"By the waters of Babylon, there we sat down and when we remembered Zion"—and adapts short passages from verses five and six:

> If I forget you, O Jerusalem, let my right hand wither!
> Let my tongue cleave to the roof of my mouth if I do not remember you;
> if I do not set Jerusalem above my highest joy. (Oxford University Press 761)

It is difficult to know what is "obvious" in the first line of Eigner's poem, but as we move through his adaptation of biblical verses, it becomes clear that he is identifying his physical with his ethnic difference. "How could I forget that?" he seems to say. He inverts the passage's emphasis on the one who sees himself ("if thy eye offend") to one who is seen differently. In these short poems, both written around a Christian holiday, we watch Eigner musing on the obvious and the hidden, the spoken and unspoken assumptions in scripture with special application to himself. As a disabled Jew, he is doubly exiled in a religious context that measures bodies by a golden mean, that identifies difference and apostasy by metaphors of blindness and withering limbs. The poems are somewhat anomalous in Eigner's oeuvre by their specific reference to doctrinal example. They provide, however, a clear example of how the so-called inner speech is conducted through several platforms, public and private. Exiled in audism, Eigner remembers Zion.

Conclusion

During the 2020 Democratic presidential debates, a good deal of attention was focused on the leading candidate, Joe Biden, whose verbal missteps, gaffs, and delays were regarded as worrisome signs of mental disorder. During the debate in late July in Detroit, Biden was asked about his primary topic, health care. "We f-f-f-f-further support— . . . The uh-uh-uh-uh . . . the uh ability to buy into the Obamacare plan." John Hendrickson, himself a stutterer, records that the conservative media seized on these stammered delays as marking Biden's disqualification from candidacy:

> Fox News edited these moments into a mini montage. Stifling laughter, the host Steve Hilton narrated: "As the right words struggled to make that perilous journey from Joe Biden's brain to Joe Biden's mouth, half the time he just seemed to give up with this somewhat tragic and limp admission of defeat."[13]

Biden is a lifelong stutterer who has managed to get past words and syllables that cause his voice to pause, repeat, and stumble. Hilton's interpretation of these vocal features as "tragic" and "limp admission of defeat" reflect troubling stereotypes of verbal difference. The idea that Biden's candidacy should be dismissed because of his speech impediment is one more example of the debilitating social effects of distressing speech. And time is of the essence. Stutterers "take time" to create a complete utterance. Interlocutors become impatient with having to wait for the final period, but it is a good example of the close proximity of speech and time that disability foregrounds. Larry Eigner's difficult oral delivery may have been distressing for his auditors, but his poems register acutely the clarity of his inner speech.

I began by speaking of Eigner's "distressed" and "distressing voice" as cripping the authority of voice and the normative temporality implied by "sounding good." Crip time must include crip speech, the durations of speaking and hearing, the delays produced by a stammer, the recalibrations in captioning, the feedback loop of utterance and confirmation. And as with much avant garde art and language, hearing or speaking differently poses new ways of understanding what language does and means for others. Eigner's poetry, although deeply introspective, is always a sustained dialogue with voices he internalizes as interlocutors. Whether it is a biblical verse, a news program, or a piece of received wisdom ("it's obvious"), he is in constant dialogue with persons who may not be listening. If he is "Tongue-tied / and / muscle bound," he uses his lime-tree bower not as a prison but as a window.

5

Diverting Language

Jena Osman's Corporate Subject

"The question is," said Humpty Dumpty, "which is to be master—that's all."
—Lewis Carroll

Difficult Matters

A recurrent theme in many of the works discussed in this book is the instability of semantic and discursive frames—the shifting of an expected meaning or context onto another realm, crossing lexical and generic fields and diverting one idiolect onto another. If this is distressing for the literalist, it is diverting for readers of poetry who continue to value indirection and uncertainty. Such diversion makes for difficulty in recent poetry in ways that differ from modernist models of complexity and ambiguity. But is difficulty the same as ambiguity? The latter has a noble pedigree in literary study, canonized famously in the New Criticism and through William Empson's *Seven Types of Ambiguity*, where the term refers to "any verbal nuance, however slight, which gives room for alternative reactions to the same piece of language" (1). To this extent, ambiguity is a characteristic of all literary language insofar as words function beyond the level of denotation. Henry James's late prose is ambiguous as a result of its long, heavily subordinated sentences, complex deictics, and parentheticals that thwart forward movement. Ambiguity here lies less in equivocal semantics than in the way James's sentences displace or defer meaning in pursuit of the novel's often absent cause: the figure in the carpet, the beast in the jungle, the crack in the golden bowl.

Difficulty, on the other hand, is associated with the hermeneutic labor involved in decoding a work's ambiguity. As the *OED* stipulates, difficulty is "not easy; requiring effort or labor; occasioning or attended with trouble." One might say that the "trouble" with individual phrases in James—or in Gertrude Stein or John Ashbery—is not in ambiguities in their denotative meaning but in their creation of a rhythm of affect that, like Whitman's rolling cadences or Robert Creeley's heightened enjambment, instantiates a particular voice or mood. The hermeneutic labor involved in decoding difficult modern poetry, for which James is an essential antecedent, often requires understanding the function of a given allusion or idiolect in a work's larger cultural project. When Ezra Pound invokes James in canto 7 ("the old voice lifts itself / weaving an endless sentence"), it is through an imitation of the novelist's style:

> We also made ghostly visits, and the stair
> That knew us, found us again on the turn of it,
> Knocking at empty rooms, seeking for buried beauty (25)

Possibly referring to the late story "The Jolly Corner," in which the protagonist, Spencer Brydon, encounters a ghostly apparition while descending a staircase, Pound appropriates James's characteristic references to houses and rooms, but he also uses these lines as one stage in the canto's larger portrayal of cultural decline, for which Jamesian realism ("the house of fiction") becomes a diagnostic tool. Invoking James in this canto terminates a sequence of quotations, from Homer and Ovid through Provençal poets and Dante to Flaubert, each one embodying virtues of verbal clarity in contrast to the "Beer bottle on the statue's pediment!" that marks the decline of culture in the modern era. The Jamesian description of bourgeois rooms and houses is less important than its cultural meaning as a historical stage in mimesis.

When it comes to postwar poetry, difficulty is less about obscure allusions or odd juxtapositions of dissimilar materials than qualities of tone and voice. The desultory movement of lines chronicling the poet's associations, observations, and hesitations is an index of psychological response. When Frank O'Hara refers to Bill or Grace or Mike or the Ziegfeld theater, he doesn't really care if one knows who these people or places are; his references do not shore fragments against cultural ruin but enact moments of attentiveness that create a constellation of value. Meaning lies not in an individual line or group of lines so much as in the cumulative effect of tone and voice. Anyone applying New Critical standards to work found in Donald Allen's anthology *The New American Poetry* would find such informality disturbing precisely because its ambiguity could not be located in the poem but in the verbal nimbus created by the poem.

Language poetry said goodbye to all that by attacking voice as a register of value. The flatness of *Ketjak* or *My Life* or "China" is difficult not by any ambiguity in its language so much as by its refusal to organize disparate elements into any recognizable voice or cultural thematic. Procedural methods, appropriation, collaboration, parataxis are deployed to remove words from speakers and return them to the social idiolects, class inflections, and media heteroglossia that reinforce social identity. The point is to retrieve language from the "predatory intent" of more confessional modes while making visible the sensuous particularity of language as a complex system.[1] If, to adapt Adorno, "what is considered to be intelligible to all is what has become unintelligible," language poetry by making work unintelligible as poetry curiously redeems what is most familiar (Adorno 183). Lest this sound like a revision of Russian formalist *ostranenie*, I would add that the familiar includes the systems and institutions that guarantee clarity: classrooms, boardrooms, and, significantly for my purposes here, courtrooms.

One of the salient practices of poetic difficulty represented in *Distressing Language* involves techniques of appropriation that draw on another cultural text or rhetorical frame to produce new work. Either the work erases an original (Rauschenberg's erasure of deKooning's drawing would be one version) or finds a new text in the interstices of another. In Srikanth Reddy's *Voyager*, the poet's language is entirely based on passages from the former UN secretary general Kurt Waldheim's autobiography. By erasing portions of the memoir, Reddy creates a new text, one that contrasts the public voice of the UN secretary general against the hidden voice of his Nazi past. Those two roles, as Langdon Hammer says, "and the discourses proper to them, no matter how distant from each other in style and function, are joined in the moral history of one man's voice" (33).

We encounter the aesthetics of appropriation in several works discussed in this book—Harryette Mullen's "recyclopedia" of black vernacular, Carolyn Lazard's recaptioning of Julia Child's cooking show,

Kenneth Goldsmith's variations on popular song lyrics. Such works divert material from one realm (or medium) to another in order to call attention to elements elided in the original or to reinforce sonic and associational elements otherwise unrecognizable. When Laurie Anderson diverts Longfellow's "Hiawatha" ("By the shores of Gitchee Gumee / By the shining Big-Sea-Water" on her *Strange Angels* album) to country western blues ("Hello Operator / Get me Memphis Tennessee"), she fuses two wildly opposed versions of the west in a common rhythm.[2] M. NourbeSe Philip's *Zong!*'s fragmentation of language from an eighteenth-century court case concerning slavery brings to the surface actuarial precedents for dealing with the treatment of slaves as cargo during the Middle Passage. In my next chapter, I discuss Alison O'Daniel's restaging of John Cage's *4'33"* that reproduces a central work of late modernism while adding a soundtrack and filmic narrative that extend possibilities inspired by the earlier work. The implications of such appropriations are not only aesthetic; they raise questions about the authenticity of speech (or, in O'Daniel's case, the aura of originality), who controls it, and for whom it is intended. The question is a matter of power, or as Humpty Dumpty says to Alice, "which is to be master—that is all."

Diverting language is also diverting in a pleasurable sense by bringing together multiple discourses into a common frame. *Finnegans Wake* is almost entirely constructed out of language from a vast linguistic archive of quotations, simulations of public rhetoric, imitations of literary styles, and cross-linguistic, multilingual puns. In its mashup of various languages and argots, the *Wake* creates alliances across cultures, subverts official rhetoric, and vaunts demotic sources. As I have suggested in earlier chapters, the pleasures of mondegreens, malapropisms, and paronomasia are precisely a result of the conjunction of two signifiers occupying the same semantic space. But the politics of appropriation is always fraught when the use of one discourse—the autopsy report for a black man killed by a police officer read by a performance artist—is seen as a racist violation of the black body for aesthetic ends. I am referring to Kenneth Goldsmith's reading of the autopsy of an African American male, Michael Brown, in a 2015 performance that became a catalyst for protest by members of minority communities. Brown was killed by a white police officer, Darren Wilson, in Ferguson, Missouri. His death and the court's exoneration of Wilson incited more public protests and demonstrations. The performance was part of Goldsmith's conceptualist project *Seven Deaths*, which included copies of television reports on the deaths of major public figures, including Michael Jackson and John F. Kennedy. But it was his addition of an "Eighth Death" to the series, featuring a direct copy of Brown's autopsy report that incited a ferocious response. By opening up Michael Brown's autopsy, Goldsmith seemed to violate Brown's body a second time, disappearing the racialized body for aesthetic ends. To this extent, diverting language may also be a form of cultural theft. The pleasures and dangers of appropriation, then, go hand in hand by forcing attention on affective elements of reception—who is pleased and who distressed by seeing a familiar phrase in an unfamiliar position.

Although in this chapter I move rather far from issues of disability and deafness, I want to extend forms of distressing language to other fields of aesthetic endeavor concerned with the precarious body. How are different bodies disqualified from human diversity and what institutions and social protocols participate in this erasure? When personhood is defined by progress, privatization, and profit, the body, as Jasbir Puar says, "is always debilitated in relation to its ever-expanding potentiality" (*The Right to Maim* 13). Aesthetic disqualification, in Tobin Siebers's terms, is a "symbolic process [that] removes individuals from the ranks of quality human beings, putting them at risk of unequal treatment, bodily harm, and death" (23). In what follows, I look at how one poem exposes that removal process by appropriating and diverting the language of legal jurisprudence onto the lyric. In this case, a poem not overtly about disability provides another way of thinking about how bodies under capitalist expansion become members of what Viet Thanh Nguyen calls "the precariat" (Nguyen 10–11).

Legal Subjects

The diversion of one text to suit another end has particular relevance for recent court cases involving corporate personhood where the individual corpus is diverted onto the corporate body. This issue animates Jena Osman's *Corporate Relations* (2014), in which she draws on—diverts—the language of legal jurisprudence to expose how laws designed to protect individuals ultimately make them disappear. Here is the opening poem from that book, "The Beautiful Life of Persona Ficta":

a corporation is to a person as a person is to a machine
  friends of the court we know them as good and bad, they too are sheep
  and goats ventriloquizing the ghostly fiction.

a corporation is to a body as a body is to a puppet
  putting it in caricature, if there are natural persons then there are those
  who are not that, buying candidates. there are those who are strong on
  the ground and then weak in the air. weight shifts to the left leg while
  the propaganda arm extends.

a corporation is to an individual as an individual is to an uncanny valley
  the separation of individual wills from collective wills, magic words. they
  create an eminent body that is different from their own selves. reach over
  with the open palm of the left and force to the right while pamphlets
  disengage.

a corporation has convictions as a person has mechanical parts
  making a hash of this statute, the state is a body. Dobson Hobson and
  Jobson are masquerading under an alias. push off with the right foot, and
  at the same time step forward with the left foot. childlike voice
  complements visual cues and contributes to cuteness factor of the
  contestational robot.

a corporation has likes and dislikes as a body has shareholders
  bound by precedents the spectral then showed himself for what he was,
  a blotch to public discourse. the right foot is immediately brought
  forward. the body flattens toward the deck rather than leap into the air.
  it is not a hop. subversive literature engaged.

a corporation gives birth as a natural human births profit margins
  some really weird interpretations fully panoplied for war, a myth, torso
  breaks slightly forward. the hand is not entirely supine, but sloping from
  the thumb about thirty degrees. head rotation and sonar sensing
  technologies are employed to create believable movement, while allowing
  for only the most limited interaction.

a corporation has an enthusiasm for ethical behavior as a creature has
  economic interests only
  facial challenges. this person which is not a human being. not a physical
  personality of mankind. custom built from aluminum stock.

a corporation is we the people as a person is a cog
  a funny kind of thing, naïve shareholders. where there is property there is
  no personality. take off in full stride. lead leg exaggerates the knee lift of
  a normal stride. cordless microphones, remote control systems, hidden
  tape recorders.

a corporation has a conscience as a body has a human likeness
  forceful lily; so difficult to tell the two apart. paralyze the wheels of
  industry. an insatiable monster, soulless and conscienceless, a fund.

a corporation says hey I'm talking to you, as an individual speaks through a
  spokesperson
  they wear a scarlet letter that says "C" rejecting a century of history. the
  strong over the weak. better armed. supernatural. richer. more
  numerous. these are the facts.

a corporation admires you from afar and then has the guts to approach you
and ask you for your number, as a being activates a cognitive mechanism
for selecting mates
  it is a nightmare that congress endorsed. mega-corporation as human
  group, the realm of hypothesis.

a corporation warms the bed and wraps its arms around you and just wants
to spoon as a natural human wants to organize profits
  it's overbroad, a glittering generality, a fiction to justify the power of the
  strong invented by prophets of force. there were narrower paths to
  incorporeal rights.

a corporation has upstanding character as a body has photorealistic texture
  the absorptive powers of some prehistoric sponge. there are good fictions
  and bad fictions. can the fiction ever disappear? (11–12)

In "The Beautiful Life of Persona Ficta," Osman sustains language poetry's interest in social idiolects and the pragmatics of speech acts but engages in a documentary endeavor that subjects poems to an investigative project for which the individual poem is one component. Difficulty in this poem stems from the particular function that a specific rhetorical device—analogy—serves in a juridical and institutional context. The poem's quotations from legal language offer a recognizable verbal surface to the poem but also permit Osman to suggest links between aesthetic and social validity. As my title suggests, she *diverts* the language of legal jurisprudence onto a lyric frame in order to explore the ways that the legal subject—*persona ficta*—replaces the one who speaks.

"The Beautiful Life of Persona Ficta" is *a* poem, but it is not *the* poem. The distinction between indefinite and definite article is one between two definitions of poetry, one that designates an integral language unit and another that recognizes integral units beyond the single poem. For Osman the distinction matters, since her poetry often consists of large, exploratory works in which individual components contribute to a speculative endeavor—what Brian Reed calls the "poem as project" (64–65). I have chosen "The Beautiful Life of Persona Ficta" as characteristic of her poetics generally, but it is only one element in a densely textured documentary work, *Corporate Relations*, constructed out of multiple registers, voices, and found materials. While it is possible to read this individual poem on its own terms—as I will attempt to do here—to do so violates its participation in the larger book specifically and in Osman's poetics generally. And this is a problem that vexes the readings of much contemporary poetry whose integral structure is tied to factors beyond the individual poem.

Corporate Relations consists of a set of five variations on US constitutional amendments that protect rights of speech, religion, and citizenship. Since the industrial revolution, these amendments—the first, fourth, fifth, sixth, seventh, and fourteenth—have increasingly been used to grant rights of personhood to collective entities such as corporations. Each section is based on foundational court cases that have contributed to corporate personhood. Osman appropriates language from court transcripts and breaks them into fragments, scattering phrases across the page in a seemingly discontinuous manner (more on "seemingly" in a moment). Each section includes a prose summary of the case in question and a short lyric that extends the local terms of the case into more general issues of social justice and personal agency. The book is thus composed of several layers that blur the boundaries between poem and essay, lyric and document, private and public voice. Osman's intent is to expose the close proximity of legal and aesthetic judgment without aestheticizing its language. A document that protects free speech may, in fact, contain the spectral residue of corporate entities that benefit from such protection; a poem that speaks through the voice of legal authority makes visible the agency ghosted by that authority.

"The Beautiful Life of Persona Ficta" appears at the beginning of *Corporate Relations* as prelude to what follows, condensing the book's exploration of what Osman calls a "shaky analogy: If corporations are persons, are persons machines?"[3] The courts recognize two sorts of persons, natural and juridical, the first of which refers to biological, historical individuals and the second to collective units—corporations, partnerships, sovereign states—that may be treated as persons in certain cases. The latter definition of personhood has governed several recent Supreme Court decisions—*Citizens United v. Federal Elections Commission* and, more recently, *Burwell v. Hobby Lobby*—that declare corporations to have the same constitutional rights as persons. The former case involved a conservative group's interest in distributing a film critical of Hillary Clinton during the 2010 presidential race. *Citizens United* sought injunctive relief from the Bipartisan Campaign Reform Act (McCain-Feingold) that prohibited "electioneering communication" for purposes of political fundraising. Arguing for the majority, Justice Kennedy declared that the First Amendment protects *associations* of individuals as well as individuals and does not prohibit speech based on the identity of the speaker. By this reasoning, corporations have speech rights as individuals, and those rights may be enlisted in the pursuit of political advantage. To prohibit "electioneering communication" would be tantamount, in the majority's opinion, to the banning of books or restrictions on religious freedom. Of course, the court's majority decision went far beyond whether a political entity could produce an on-demand video during an election season; it rewrote the rules on campaign financing that gutted all previous finance reform legislation, including McCain-Feingold. Perhaps more ominously, the ruling in favor of non-profit organizations paved the way for subsequent rulings for for-profit corporations, most recently that involving a chain of hobby stores, Hobby Lobby. In this case, the court majority argued that for-profit "closely held" organizations may refuse to provide contraceptive devices through its health-care plan if it violates the owner's religious beliefs. Here, a for-profit entity was granted rights under freedom of religion principles established in the First Amendment.

What does any of this have to do with poetry? How are finance reform, political documentaries, contraception, or health-care appropriate topics for poetry? Which is a little like asking, What do sovereignty, political intrigue, or Deism have to do with Shakespeare's plays, Swift's satires, or Blake's prophecies? More importantly for our topic, how do Osman's formal strategies contribute, as the editors to a recent volume on poetic difficulty ask, to "the imaginative power of the work" (Altieri and Nace)?[4] Osman provides one answer in a passage in her 1999 book, *The Character*:

> Someone tells me that according to a poetics of difference, there is a need to leave the experimental behind: writers not privileged by the dominant discourse 'cannot leave judgment to 'chance.'" but what if the nature of judgment itself is a matter of chance? (64)

If one of the key components of poetry is the issue of voice, what happens when that feature is mediated by legal rhetoric? And to extend the analogy, if one of the key components of Kantian aesthetics is the issue of judgment, what happens when disinterestedness is revealed to be the product of gendered, classed, and political interests? In *Citizens United*, disinterested legal judgment was used to divert agency from the individual to the corporation, speech from the individual to the marketplace. Osman observes that a poetics of difference that does not account for the nature of judgment by which such categories are created and sustained does not go to the structural forces that legitimate such categories. Legal judgment and aesthetic practice are linked insofar as they create criteria of value—as in civil rights legislation—by which persons may be granted civil visibility. Despite the blindfold on the female figure of Justice, interested parties make interested judgments. As commentators pointed out, the *Hobby Lobby* decision was made by an all-Catholic, all-male majority in a case involving women's reproductive health. Osman's idiosyncratic textual techniques—documentary, visual, cartographic, archival, performative, digital—permit her to explore fissures in the presumed neutrality of judgment through the means and rhetorics by which policy is secured. In all her work, she deploys what Joan Retallack calls a "poethics," in which poetry asserts its claim to imagine new ways to live and work. Osman plunders newspapers, encyclopedias, science texts, media images as sources to probe social realties that those texts cannot imagine. She implicitly asks how poetry can do political work by exploring and framing the productive means that create social identities.

Osman's poem can be read through several poetic subgenres. The tradition that her work most easily resembles is the documentary imperative manifested in such works as Charles Reznikoff's *Testimony*, Muriel Rukeyser's *Book of the Dead*, Teresa Hak Kyung Cha's *Dictee*, Mark Nowak's *Shut Up! Shut Down!*, and any number of works by Susan Howe. The poem also contributes to a longer tradition of legal poetry that would include several of Shakespeare's sonnets (35, 49, and 134), John Donne's satires (2 and 5), Emily Dickinson's "I read my Sentence steadily," Edna St. Vincent Millay's "Justice Denied in Massachusetts," and, as I have already noted, M. NourbeSe Philip's *Zong!* But whereas many poems in this latter tradition use legal rhetoric as metaphor (*Zong!* is the exception), Osman draws on the specifics of the court case to study how legal doctrine contributes to the reifying effects of capitalism. In the case of *Corporate Relations*, her focus is on how private speech becomes ventriloquized through forms of public media, producing in the process a puppet or automaton. Her focus on the uncanny speech of this figure has immediate application to poetics, obviously, but she realizes that to claim lyric interiority—or vatic transcendence—does not strike at the heart of how voice is imbricated in social factors that produce it.

Osman's previous work offers a series of variations on the theme of mediation, whether verbal or social. The poems in *The Character, An Essay in Asterisks, The Network,* and *Public Figures* use research-based and procedural strategies that complicate the usual terms for poetry. These hybrid texts draw on multiple visual and textual realms, often incorporating technical data from science journals, Supreme Court cases, etymological dictionaries, cartography, urban history. In *Character* (1999), she uses the periodic table of elements to generate a hypertext work in which each element leads to a short lyric poem based on its source. In the title poem, footnotes at the end of stanzas lead to commentaries or quotations that offer a cryptic response to the source text. In *Essay in Asterisks* (2004), a series of stage directions for boxing ("Force the opponent's left and lead to the right with the left glove") are interrupted by prose passages dealing with forms of political resistance and critique. In *Network* (2010), Osman studies the twin trajectories of history and etymology by subjecting the names of streets in lower Manhattan to their sources in mercantilism and the slave trade. In *Public Figures* (2012), she photographs public monuments around Philadelphia and then follows the trajectories of their subjects' eyes back to the world they see. Because the statues she photographs are often of military figures, she suggests the close relationship between public memorials and military might. These books are, as I have indicated, also projects, based on a balance of historical and archival research and speculation.

Persona Ficta

Thus far, I have focused largely on contextual matters rather than text, hoping to frame some of the historical, generic, and political issues that underlie and frame "The Beautiful Life of Persona Ficta." Osman's poem is haunted by what lies outside the text, both within the book it inaugurates and in the world to which it refers. Perhaps it would be better to say that she attempts to render inadequate the putative border between text and context, poem and history. "The Beautiful Life" is about who (or what) speaks and by what agency. Its anaphoric structure, appropriated legal rhetoric, analogical development mediate between the distributed and unitary voice. If *Citizens United* grants speech to a corporation, then it sets a precedent for agency that impacts many forms of communication.[5]

The title, "The Beautiful Life of Persona Ficta," establishes the main premise of the book: if a fictive person such as a corporation can have a life, then criteria of beauty are passed from Kant's subjective judgment to public consensus. The poem's thirteen strophes or stanzas outline what that "beautiful" life might resemble, for as fictive person its beautiful life can only exist as resemblance to something else. As the book's title suggests, it is a corporate relation. Each strophe begins with an analogy, A is to B as X is to Y, which could be described as the skeletal structure of legal precedent: "A corporation is to a person as a person is to a machine"; "A corporation is to a body as a body is to a puppet." Osman extends these analogies to absurd lengths ("A corporation admires you from afar and then has the guts to approach you and ask you for your number") in order to expose the generative potential of the analogy itself. Since the court in *Citizens United* generalized from corporeal personhood to corporate personhood, based on legal precedent, Osman takes the next step and analogizes a non-human body into a human. Although her reference is contemporary, she looks back through an avant garde tradition that extends from the futurist metalized body and Duchamp's bachelor machines to Donna Haraway's cyborg. In such cases, as Dziga Vertov says in Osman's epigraph, "Our path leads through the poetry of machines, from the bungling citizen to the perfect electric man." But unlike avant garde utopian versions of the machinic human, Osman sees them more as puppets or automatons, manipulated by a master ventriloquist called Capital.

In earlier books, Osman expresses fascination with the inanimate become human, and at the end of *Corporate Relations*, she lists a number of classic versions: "Pygmalion's Galatea, Dr. Frankenstein's monster, Olympia in E. T. A. Hoffman's 'The Sandman,' Delibes' Coppelia, Pinocchio . . . etc." Paraphrasing Freud's essay on "The Uncanny," Osman writes:

> We are simultaneously attracted and repelled by the cognitive autonomy of our own creations: their immortality, their limited accountability, the impossibility of their imprisonment, their tendency to change citizenship overnight. (73)

Freud described the uncanny quality of such figures whose terror derives not from their strangeness or otherness but from their familiarity. The automaton that speaks, the unexpected appearance of oneself in a mirror, the replicant—all are unsettling when human agency is diverted onto a non-human object. We witness the return of repressed desires in another that resembles ourselves. For it *is* ourselves that we encounter, a latent version of childhood libido and, socially, an atavistic, polytheistic social identity that we have suppressed. In Osman's poem, this uncanny replicant appears as a puppet, doll and robot:

> A corporation is to a body as a body is to a puppet
>> putting it in caricature, if there are natural persons then there are those who are not that, buying candidates. there are those who are strong on the ground and then weak in the air. weight shifts to the left leg while the propaganda extends. (11)

. . . .

> a corporation has convictions as a person has mechanical parts
>> making a hash of this statute, the state is a body. Dobson Hobson and Jobson are masquerading under an alias. push off with the right foot, and at the same time step forward with the left foot. childlike voice complements visual cues and contributes to cuteness factor of the contestational robot. (11)

The analogy that begins each strophe is unpacked in the subsequent prose as a series of variations on the analogy proposed. Each phrase, separated by periods, is prosthetic to the fictive body—puppet, robot, automaton, Dobson, Hobson, and Jobson. The phrases are discontinuous like the mechanical parts that make up the machine, yet there are repeated figures—such as the dance instructions above or the various references to robots—that offer a through-line in the poem. Osman wedges her paratactic sequence within her analogical structure as if to show two incompatible forms of logic battling for supremacy. If analogy is the formula by which corporations may be converted into private bodies, parataxis renders the components as discrete inert parts. To this extent, Osman's experimental techniques are in direct, if oppositional, conversation with the structure of legal argument.

Osman suggests that legal definitions of corporate personhood have an interpellative function in producing the subjects they presume to represent. To respond to the siren call of Capital produces the Subject as subject to its power:

> a corporation says hey I'm talking to you, as an individual speaks through a spokesperson
>> they wear a scarlet letter that says "C" rejecting a century of history. the strong over the weak. better armed. supernatural. richer. more numerous. these are the facts. (12)

Osman's variation on Althusser's theory of ideological interpellation is to suggest that if a corporation can be granted agency, it asserts its authority by hailing Subjects, never speaking through itself but through a "spokesperson" or representative. Her prose elaboration refers to a latter-day Hester Prynne who wears not the scarlet letter of adultery and agency but the *C* of Corporate Capital. And indeed, there is a relationship between the erotics of the agent and that of the commodity fetish that seduces:

> a corporation warms the bed and wraps its arms around you and just wants
>   to spoon as a natural human wants to organize profits
>   it's overbroad, a glittering generality, a fiction to justify the power of the
>   strong invented by prophets of force. there were narrower paths to
>   incorporeal rights. (12)

Attended with Trouble

Gertrude Stein's famous observation that "Nothing changes from generation to generation except the thing seen and that makes a composition" has been used to explain why one era's aesthetic difficulty is the next generation's retrospective viewpoint (520). Innovative writers create the conditions by which their works will be read, but this hermeneutic circle leaves out the history within which writers themselves are created and which they address. Jena Osman commits herself to the historicity of her creative act so much so that in all of her books, she places herself literally "in the picture," photographing, as she does in *Public Figures*, not only the mounted hero in the public park but the citizens whom he would see from his plinth.[6] This dual vision, this testing of history for what is said about it and what it produces, is characteristic of Osman's investigative poetics.

Corporate Relations is deeply invested in the links between modern jurisprudence and the production of a new Subject. The *persona iuris*—legal person—that is Osman's focus achieves a special resonance when juxtaposed to other aspects of modern normalization— Taylorism, Fordism, Eugenics, racial science—that we associate with modernization. Marx's model of base and superstructure hardly accommodates the latter-day forms that these biopolitical regimes represent. By seizing on the analogical structure of legal argument, Osman suggests that there can be no neat separation of economic reality from the structures of legitimation that keep it in place.

To read Osman's difficulty adequately, we must read across it for its inseminating force in the rest of the book. In the process, we are encouraged to look more closely at the Bill of Rights, the structure of legal argument, psychological theories of the uncanny, modernism's cult of the machine, and a dozen other topics. What Osman does that the Supreme Court does not is weave these various discursive realms together as intersectional elements in the formation of the modern Subject. Analogy, the rhetorical basis of "The Beautiful Life," allows one element to be compared to something different, the "bearing across" that is the basis of metaphor. By creating a poem based on spurious analogies, Osman makes visible the links between modernist discontinuity and legal authority.

6

Missing Music

The Theft of Sound in Alison O'Daniel's The Tuba Thieves

My work internalizes and studies the details of what it means
not to have total access to sound.
—Alison O'Daniel

I was once told about a woman living in Paris—a descen-
dant of Scriabin—who spent her entire life writing music
not meant to be heard. What it is, and how she does it, is not
very clear; but I have always envied this woman. I envy her
insanity, her impracticality.
—Morton Feldman, "The Anxiety of Art," *Give my Regards
to Eighth Street* 25.

Without Music

Writing to fellow composer Alexander Zemlinsky, Arnold Schönberg
remarked on the listener: "I have as few [concerns] for him as he has for
me. I know only that he exists and that, to the extent that he is not 'indis-
pensable' for acoustic reasons (since an empty hall does not resound
well) he disturbs me."[1] What disturbs Schönberg, presumably, is the
assumption that musical value must be based on the listener rather than
elements in the compositional field itself. The compositional field may
include intervallic and mathematical relationships within a composition, the vibratory variations within individual instruments, musical
quotations, the cultural authority of certain sounds and motifs—and, as
Schönberg suggests, the acoustic effects of the concert hall. When John
Cage scored a composition in which a pianist sits at a piano without
playing a note for four minutes and thirty-three seconds, it is as much an

exploration of audience expectations as a musical composition. When Beethoven composed his late quartets and piano sonatas while being almost totally deaf, was he *hearing* his music or *remembering* it? What about musical notation, a silent mark that nevertheless is "played" by the musician? In the work of Christine Sun Kim or Christian Marclay, the visual representation of dynamic markings or musical notes refers to the graphic markers of music without their correlative function in producing amplitude or pitch in a given composition. It may be only a thought experiment to ask what exists beyond the sonic elements of music, but asking it raises the question of what makes music music.

My title is autobiographical; I miss music. As someone who can no longer hear, I ponder these questions to understand, in adaptive counterpoint to Morton Feldman's *The Viola in My Life*, the music in mine. I played piano from the time I was five throughout my life; my mother was a superb pianist who sang in church choirs and taught music; my wife is a flutist who plays in several chamber groups; my son is a skilled jazz pianist; I have written about music in a number of essays and books and have written program notes for a local chamber music series. Much of my life has been spent attending concerts, operas, and chamber recitals and obsessively collecting records and CDs. When I began to lose my hearing, music was one of the first things to go. I could no longer distinguish among pitches, and timbre was neutralized to a single monotonous drone, making it difficult to discriminate among instruments.[2] Most disturbing was the fact that something that had been so central to my experience was now painful to hear. Mahler's big orchestral sound was cacophonous—or as some people say, "deafening"—and the lightest Haydn piano sonata unbearable. I felt that music had been stolen from me, a metaphor I will pursue with regard to Alison O'Daniel's work, but its loss forced me to ask the questions above: Must music be heard to be music?

Nina Sun Eidsheim has written thoughtfully about these issues in *Sensing Sound*. She observes that music is not a fixed entity based on aurality but rather an "empty concept" that forces us to confront how we think about sound, listening, space, and culture. Although Eidsheim does not take deafness into account, her emphasis on elements beyond the acoustic addresses many of the ways that deaf and hard-of-hearing persons experience (and make) music. In her reading, music has been

"sonically reduced" to a set of discrete entities—qualities of "pitch, durational schemes, forms, genres"—that delimit our experience to a single
set of values (2). Regarded as a multistable, multisensory element, music
is open to experiential aspects where, to apply Eidsheim's title, we "sense
sound" in all of its cultural, environmental, and performative aspects.
She posits a vibrational theory of music that draws on the materialities of
wavelength and frequency, transmission and transduction, to specify the
way that, say, the guitar or piano string vibrates within the body of the
instrument but also within the body of the listener and ultimately within
the space of the room or auditorium in which it is played. "Vibrational
practice" does not refer strictly to sound waves but, in a larger context,
to the transfer of energies that travel, in Jessica Holmes's paraphrase,
"across time, space, and bodies, and for their relational and affective dynamics of musical experience" (189). As a classically trained vocalist,
Eidsheim is interested in the particular relationship of the vocal instrument's body to the sounds thus produced—what it means for a vocalist
like Juliana Snapper to sing underwater where the conducting element
of sound is not air but water. She wonders about Meredith Monk's *Songs
of Ascension*, which utilizes the spatial properties of a circular staircase
to think of space as an element of composition. Or what about Christopher Cerrone's 2013 *Invisible Cities*, in which listeners hear a composition through headphones while it is performed in the middle of Los
Angeles's Union Station. Such examples stretch the "figure of music" to
new levels involving the body, space, technology, and affective response.

Purists might argue that this denies the obvious: that of course, music
is meant to be heard, and to deny this fact is to engage in a specious
form of relativism or worse—cultural analysis. The examples of Monk,
Snapper, and Cerrone do include sounded elements, after all, so why
focus only on these ephemeral matters? But by understanding music as
a thick event, in Geertzian terms, Eidsheim is able to shift the focus from
acoustics to the figure of sound as it brings into play social and material
interrelationships. Her general argument about the need to expand the
discussion of music to account for "music's material dependency," as she
titles one chapter, is an important intervention into the issues that are
particularly relevant to any number of contemporary sound artists.

The issues Eidsheim raises are not new. Wagner debated the question
of soundless music in his various writings on Beethoven. Reflecting on

the composer's deafness allowed Wagner to think beyond the physical production of music to more philosophical issues:

> A musician without hearing! Is a blind painter to be imagined?
>
> But we have heard of a blind *Seer*. Like Tiresias, from whom the phenomenal world was withdrawn, and who, in its stead discovered the basis of all phenomenality, the deaf Musician, undisturbed by the bustle of life, now heard only the harmonies of his soul and woke from its depths to that world which to him—had nothing more to say. (qtd. in Szendi 121)

Peter Szendy refers to Wagner's analysis as Beethoven's "clairaudience," his ability to eliminate the "bustle of life" and produce music based on the "harmonies of his soul." Against critics who faulted Beethoven's late works for their incoherence and imperfections, Wagner viewed the work composed under deafness as reflecting the composer's genius, "the clairvoyant idea of the divine seer" (121). Deafness, in Szendy's terms, is the obverse of *total listening*, which is subject to the "structural law of the work," a formulation that anticipates aspects of serialism in Schönberg or Webern (121). But Szendy wonders whether the reverse is equally true: that *total listening* is a form of deafness since it requires shutting out the noises of life and committing oneself to the work. When listening is so totalizing, can it be called listening? "Shouldn't a *responsible* listening (which can account for itself as well as *for* the work rather than simply respond *to* an authoritative law) always be *wavering*?" (122). As Szendy points out, Wagner was to reverse his opinion of the late works, feeling that the composer of the Ninth Symphony had lost touch with the orchestra and had scored his music increasingly toward the lower registers, which were easier for him to hear, while subverting melody to endless repetition. Wagner tempered these problems by rearranging Beethoven's scores so as to bring out the salient qualities of instruments, drawing on Liszt's piano transcription of the symphony as his model. Thus a new symphony was born out of a piano transcription of a deaf composer's unheard symphony. The hearing person listens to the listenings of previous composers, but by extension, the late-deafened composer listens to his previous listenings.

This layering of listenings raises a related issue concerning the musical object, whether music is a discrete composition or a process, the product of individual endeavor or a collaborative project. Christopher Small has argued that music "is not a thing at all but an activity, something that people do"—what he calls "musicking."[3] He gives examples of the varying ways that music is experienced: heard in the quiet of a salon or physically felt in a giant rock concert, intoned by the householder folding laundry or performed by a pianist, danced in a tribal ritual or remembered. Although I can no longer hear music, I can summon up remembrance of performances past, specific compositions, their venues and audience response. My memory of the Beethoven Fourth Piano Concerto is indelibly affixed to seeing Glenn Gould playing the solo opening bars with the Oakland Symphony after first adjusting the piano stool so low that his large arms and hands were raised high above the keyboard. I can't help imagining Mussorgsky's *Pictures at an Exhibition* without hearing Sviatoslav Richter's famous missed note in the opening theme at the 1958 Sofia concert. And what about the score? To what extent is music a textual experience for the performer or musicologist? What music does the conductor play, if not the score? Small quotes an anecdote about Brahms, who was invited to a performance of Mozart's *Don Giovanni* but who said he "would sooner stay home and read it" (5). Jessica Holmes has discussed the multiple meanings of music within the deaf community, from culturally deaf members who eschew the very idea of music to those who accommodate song signing, Deaf jam rap, dance, and other forms into their cultural milieu.[4] Musicologists like Holmes, Small, Eidsheim, Jeanette DiBernardo Jones, Seth Kim-Cohen, Joseph Strauss, and others have opened the issue of music's hearability to include cultural issues beyond the sonic reception of sound. I might rephrase my initial question "What is music without music?" to read "What is the expanded field of music and for whom it is a value?"[5]

The Aeolian Harp

Make me thy lyre, even as the forest is.
—Percy Bysshe Shelley, "Ode to the West Wind"

Music loss, like hearing loss, occasions anxiety about a world devoid of noise and therefore without the sounds of human intercourse. Jacques Attali offers a capsule summary of what most people imagine living without music might mean:

Our science has always desired to monitor, measure, abstract, and castrate meaning, forgetting that life is full of noise and that death alone is silent: work noise, noise of man, and noise of beast. Noise bought, sold, or prohibited. Nothing essential happens in the absence of noise. (3)

He imagines silence as a kind of (masculine) death, the "castration" of complex meaning by calculation and rationalization; noise is life, labor, love. In his assertion that "nothing essential happens in the absence of noise" he may be invoking information theory's emphasis on noise as the messy and intrusive data that must be eliminated if a message is to be decoded. Apparently, Attali never communicated with a deaf person or reflected on what this remark implies about the requirements for agency or capability. He goes on to speak of music as a form of power:

With noise is born disorder and its opposite: the world. With music is born power and its opposite: subversion. In noise can be read the codes of life, the relations among men. . . . Everywhere codes analyze, mark, restrain, train, repress, and channel the primitive sounds of language, of the body, of tools, of objects, of the relations to self and others. (6)

Framed as an attack on the ocularcentric epistemologies from the Enlightenment to the modern period, Attali's *Noise* could be seen as part of an attempt among contemporary theorists to re-center Western knowledge around what is audible rather than legible. Drawing on Raymond Williams, Attali describes music as "a structure of feeling" around emergent systems of knowledge; it is a "herald of things to come." Music is interpretive, "an instrument of understanding. It prompts us to decipher a sound form of knowledge" (4). Its ubiquity in contemporary society inspires revolutionary change (he mentions Bob Dylan and Jimi Hendrix) as well as reinforces bourgeois mores, what Herbert Marcuse calls "affirmative culture." In 1977, when his book was first published, Attali could not anticipate the degree to which the technologies of sound would become digitized and vocal sound transformed into text. Voice-recognition software and captioning reorient the acoustic to a digital realm. The Cold War acoustic surveillance technologies Attali mentions—spies "listening in" on conversations, phone taps, and so forth—go the way of the long-playing record, the reel-to-reel tape recorder, and perhaps the telephone itself. Is there, then, a music that exists in the interstices of noise and silence? The aeolian harp might be one version.

Attali's view of music as a "herald of things to come" reminds us of earlier formulations of this figure in Romanticism. In "Ode to the West Wind," Shelley apostrophizes the wind as "trumpet of a prophecy," imploring it to "Make me thy lyre, even as the forest is" (300). Coleridge provides another version of this figure in his 1795 poem "The Eolian Harp." The title refers to a small stringed instrument described by Athanasius Kircher in the seventeenth century whose sound is produced by the wind blowing across the strings.[6] Sitting comfortably in his domestic "cot" with his wife, Sara, he meditates on the sound of this instrument, "that simplest Lute, / Placed length-ways in the clasping casement." Coleridge listens to the "desultory breeze" of the harp and reflects on his bucolic surroundings at Clevedon, Somerset, where the poem was composed. What Wordsworth called a "correspondent breeze" that stirs his fancy inspires a vision of "the one Life within us and abroad, / Which meets all motion and becomes its soul" (101). Here, music offers a potential synthesis of subject and object, of natural world and human consciousness. Lulled by this ethereal music and warmed by domestic bliss, he relates his indolent receptivity to nature itself:

> And what if all of animated nature
> Be but organic Harps diversely fram'd,
> That tremble into thought, as o'er them sweeps
> Plastic and vast, one intellectual breeze,
> At once the Soul of each, and God of all? (102)

As the poem proceeds, the poet moves further and further from literal lyre and domestic bliss to a more philosophical speculation on the "intellectual breeze" that links individual and God. In the process, however, he loses track of the idyllic natural surroundings that inspired his reverie and is brought up short by his wife and interlocutor. In the final section of the poem, Sara intrudes to add a "mild reproof" and remind him of herself and her Christian faith against the "idle flitting phantasies" of his "indolent and passive brain" (102). Whatever correspondent breeze Coleridge may have discovered through the sounds of nature played on the harp, it is felt only when he acknowledges the correspondence with the person who inspires his poem in the first place. But Sara's reproof is perhaps undercut by Coleridge's rhapsodic ode, suggesting the poet's impatience with her attempt to theologize natural harmonies.

Music produced by nature was a powerful trope among Romantic poets, and it marks an ecological imperative to join human and non-human forces through an idea of animate nature. What marks poems like "Eolian Harp," "Dejection, an Ode," "This Lime-Tree Bower My Prison," or "Ode to the West Wind" and many poems by John Clare and James Thomson is their dedication to place and locale where the poet stages a transition from solitary dejection to revelation, from local instrument to "intellectual breeze." If music is invoked as a herald or trumpet of things to come—modernity, modernization, social alienation—in these poems, it derives from the breeze and breath of the poet in his lime-tree bower. The almost unhearable music of the harp produces an internalized music of sublime participation and identification. As Thomas Hankins and Robert Silverman say, the aeolian harp, for Romantic poets, was an "instrument of inspiration, strung between the mirror of mimesis and the lamp of imagination" (88).

Coleridge's poem is as much about his rural environs—his "Cot o'ergrown / With white-flowered Jasmine, and the broad-leaved Myrtle," as it is about the sound of the harp. His emphasis on the silence that permits him to hear melodies otherwise unheard is defined by the harp's liminal location in a window casement, half in and half outside the house. It is this siting of sound that animates more recent manifestations of the aeolian harp. Contemporary variations often appear as site specific sculptural installations that focus on a local landscape or setting. This would include Aristides Demetrios's *Wind Harp* in an industrial park in San Francisco or Giuseppe Ferlengas's six-meter-tall aeolian harp in Negar, Verona, Italy, among many others. John Luther Adams's *The Wind Garden* at the University of California, San Diego (2017) uses the wind and changing light patterns of the nearby ocean to produce shifting atmospheres of sound, depending on the season and the weather. In each case, the installation registers the sounds of its locale that might otherwise be ignored or drowned out by passing cars, airplanes, or machines. One also might mention the work of Croatian architect Nikola Bašić, whose 230-foot *morse orgulje* (sea organ) uses the rhythm of the

Adriatic's waves to play a melody. As the shifting tides and lapping waves of Zadar ebb and flow, air is forced through openings at the sea's littoral which, in turn, connect to giant organ pipes under the ground, producing different pitches. Whether the harp is placed on a remote location, on a cliff overlooking the sea, in the middle of an industrial park, or in the sea itself, its strings sing its location, suspended between an increasingly lost natural world and an industrialized soundscape.

One of the more interesting variations on this theme is Catherine Yass's 2017 film *Aeolian Piano*, which takes this trope, literally, into the heavens. In her film, an industrial crane lifts a grand piano slowly out of the vacant site of the BBC Television Center to float high above the building. The image of a large black concert grand being pulled out of the center's court, hung by thin cables, is an uncanny sight, producing, at least for this viewer, conflicting emotions of anxiety and awe.[7] Yass's contemporary version expands the scale of the stringed instrument to that of a concert grand piano whose bulk seems to contradict the intimacy implied by the harp. It is out of place in every sense, freed from the concert hall and lifted into wind and weather. The faint soundtrack first records the sounds of tension in the cables holding the piano. When the piano rises above the building and begins to circle in the wind, the wind sounds diminish and the music of the strings can be heard. Yass says that at the end of the film, "The sound of the strings is cut off from all other sound and feels more internalized, coming as it does from successive re-recordings made inside the piano."[8]

Here, the location at the BBC is of foundational importance: a state sponsored broadcasting company whose cultural programming is beamed across the same winds that produce the piano's ethereal music. The fact that the BBC was being moved from its circular building in west London to a new location heightens the film's focus on urban development and mobility. Many of Yass's works deal with urban environmental and architectural issues, but here the so-called natural music produced by the wind is composed in a highly corporatized landscape. The modern piano itself is a product of that corporate, industrial economy, and so to place it in this awkward environment is to illustrate—by means of a thin cable—the difficult tension between the aesthetics and production. Yass may not have had Romantic poetry in mind when she conceived her work, but she certainly builds on the Romantic idea of natural af-

Figure 6.1. Catherine Yass, from *Aeolian Harp* (2017)[9]

finities between local and cosmic, human mind and non-human nature. Her use of a grand piano slowly hoisted above a broadcasting center in the middle of London turns the romantic metaphor into a reflection on "broadcasting" and music being played on a very different instrument than the one in Coleridge's window casement.

I am sitting in a room

Yass's films and installations are all about the redesign of space, the human impact on the built environment. In this respect, she continues a tradition of sound art that begins in the 1960s. The work of La Monte Young, David Tudor, Jackson MacLow, Pauline Oliveros, Michael Asher, Robert Morris, Alvin Lucier, and the Fluxus movement, with John Cage as tutelary genius, placed auditory arts at the center of installations and performances. Collaborations among visual artists, composers, dancers, and performers augmented the meaning of musical information and placed renewed emphasis on space, architecture, and design. At the same time, music was divorced from its presumed auditory role and explored as a spatial and temporal medium. In 2017, I was able to visit the Lyon Biennial, where a room was devoted to a recreation of David Tudor's 1973 sound installation *Rainforest IV*. The gallery was filled with various found objects (toilet seats, garbage cans, funnels, a tennis racket), many of which were hanging from the ceiling. Contact mikes and speakers attached to each object produced sounds based on the resonant character of the physical materials and the proximity of the auditor. People circulated around, under, and through the various objects, adding to the mobile-like structure of the gallery and often speaking *to* the objects. Referring in 1984 to *Rainforest*, Tudor remarked that "the object was to make the sculptures sound in the space themselves. Part of that process is that you are actually creating an environment. The contact mikes on the objects pick up the resonant frequencies which one hears when very close to the object, and then are amplified through a loudspeaker as an enhancement" ("An Interview"). In the case of La Monte Young, light and sound performances lasting for several days took place in the Dream House, located in lower Manhattan, where Young with his partner, Marion Zazeela, and others staged listening experiences over long—often very long—periods of time. Central to sound art experimentation like Young's is the importance of music generated outside of traditional harmonic relationships, tempi, and durations. The fourth wall of the concert is broken by events that last for hours or even days, allowing audiences the opportunity to come and go at their leisure. Seth Kim-Cohen, building on Duchamp's critique of non-retinal art, characterizes practices like Young's as "non-cochlear" music that does not require listening (136–37). According to Kim-Cohen, music is a conceptual frame for thinking about the conditions of its own possibility. This is a rather aestheticized definition, but it has the advantage of rethinking the acoustic basis of music and opening the possibility of other sensory processes and institutional factors. Of course, Young's durational drones were "heard" by listeners, but in Kim-Cohen's terms, their reception is secondary to their exploration of sound produced in a spatiotemporal context: "If an ear is required for Young's music, it is not the receiving ear but the producing ear" (137).

One obvious example of what it means to "site sound" through different senses would be Alvin Lucier's 1969 composition *I am sitting in a room*. In this work, Lucier, who has a severe stammer, reads a text that he records, the original then re-taped multiple times until the words are gradually effaced into an electronic drone. The text Lucier reads describes the composition's spatial environment:

I am sitting in a room different from the one you are in now. I am recording the sound of my speaking voice and I am going to play it back
into the room again and again until the resonant frequencies of the room
reinforce themselves so that any semblance of my speech, with perhaps
the exception of rhythm, is destroyed. What you will hear then, are the
natural resonant frequencies of the room articulated by speech. I regard
this activity not so much as a demonstration of a physical fact, but more
as a way to smooth out any irregularities my speech might have. (qtd. in
LaBelle 125)

Whatever auratic associations one might have with a singer's voice evap-
orate in the presence of a taped and gradually distressed voice. In its 1969
realization, each new recording gradually retards the composer's voice
until in the final iteration, one can hear only a single tone. For Lucier,
the degradation of sound into a drone may be an entirely appropriate
representation of his conflicted relationship to speech. As Brandon
LaBelle suggests, "The stutter . . . is a form of controlled feedback: it
comes back to haunt Lucier, yet to a point of comfort and composition,
where the composer may reside, take up home, within his own somatic
tick" (129). The work's title emphasizes the local nature of the performance; he is not in a concert hall or recording studio but in his home in
Middletown, Connecticut—as if to stress the important role of spatial
and architectural features in the composition. As with the poet Jordan
Scott, who creates sound poems as virtuoso triggers for his stammer, the
decomposition of speech inspired by a stutter does not imply a loss of
meaning but, rather, a discovery of new linguistic and sonic possibilities.

   One final observation about Lucier's project and that of many of his
contemporaries is to think of composition as an ongoing, fluid process
rather than an object. Eidsheim's emphasis on multisensory elements
in music challenges the notion of a work's fixity, embalmed in a printed
score: "Hence, music's ontological status can be changed from an exter-
nal, knowable object to an unfolding phenomenon that arises through
complex material interactions" (2). Long works such as those of La
Monte Young, or Morton Feldman's six-hour Second String Quartet, or
Stockhausen's seven-day-long music drama *aus Licht*, or, for that matter,
Wagner's seventeen-hour *Ring* cycle introduce duration into the musical
mix as a challenge to the idea of an isolated work, divided into discrete

tempi, measures, and movements. And equally, the passive listener that so troubled Schönberg is now a coconspirator in the musical experience. As we will see with regard to Alison O'Daniel's ongoing (and equally long) *Tuba Thieves* project, the idea of a soundless music enlists the audience into an alternate sonic reality.

The Aural Tradition

In 2012, thieves broke into several Los Angeles area high schools and stole a series of tubas from cabinets in band rooms. This rash of thefts, covered extensively in the *Los Angeles Times*, became the focal point for artist Alison O'Daniel's ongoing film and sculpture installation, *The Tuba Thieves*. For O'Daniel, who is binaurally hard-of-hearing and who reads lips and uses sign language, the theft of these large instruments becomes at one level a metaphor for hearing loss. But the thefts also provide her with an occasion to investigate how sound is subject to an auditory social contract: the presumption that communication is a function of listening.[10] When this pact is broken, when one can no longer rely on one's sensory "instrument," understanding must be sounded anew. One of O'Daniel's more subtle points is to emphasize the impact that the loss of these large, expensive instruments had on underfunded inner-city schools and the racially diverse student populations that play them.[11] The fact that the tubas were not replaced, due to scant funds and austerity measure, suggests that this loss continues to exert an impact.[12]

With this story as backdrop, O'Daniel began to make a series of short films that tell, in a rather discontinuous manner, a story about a deaf drummer, her hearing boyfriend, and her father, who manages an ice rink. Her protagonist, Nyke Prince, is an actual drummer and performer who lives in Los Angeles. She is flanked by fictional characters that include her boyfriend, Nature Boy, who is studying botany and works as a furniture mover, and her father, Arcey, who drives a Zamboni machine that smooths the ice. We meet them in piecemeal fashion, often via partial signs: a pair of ice skates, succulent plants, the looping pattern that the Zamboni makes on the ice, a skyscape full of brightly colored kites. As she says of her characters, "Their stories unfold quietly in a din of stolen sound, purposeful silence, and alternative communication in Los Angeles late 2012." The oxymoron—a "din of silence"—encapsulates the way that her narrative reconsiders conventional associations with auditory information. To say that *Tuba Thieves* "tells a story" is to impose a rather schematic frame around a very fragmented narrative. In one installation at the Hammer Museum in Los Angeles, the films occurred in the following sequence: a restaging of the actual theft of tubas followed by a revision of John Cage's 1952 "silent" composition *4'33"*, which then morphs into a reenactment of a punk concert in 1979 at a San Francisco deaf club then back to the present with a high school band at a football game. The films were projected onto facing walls so that the viewer was surrounded by shifting images. These spatial and temporal shifts reinforce O'Daniel's idea that interrupted or misheard speech/sound creates narrative disruptions as well. At present, the artist imagines that there will be fifty individual films plus sculptures and performances, each component of which will consist of elements from the others.

The impact of deafness on bodily and social coherence is implicit in the artist's procedure. She began *The Tuba Thieves* backward, commissioning the work of three artists to compose scores that then informed the direction and structure of the films. Instead of imposing musical scores on completed films—sound as prosthetic to narrative—she allowed the scores to suggest events and determine images and associations. The scores were themselves motivated by elements in her personal life that she used as cues for her composers. She asked artist Christine Sun Kim to meditate on a photo of sculptor Louise Nevelson and a letter sent to the Russian director Andrei Tarkovsky; she asked the composer Steve Roden to think about the zigzag patterns that the Zamboni machine makes on the ice. She enlists the help of friends and non-professionals to act in or advise on various elements of each film. High school students, deaf skateboarders, musicians, and members of the deaf community are her primary actors, but their participation often shapes the direction of a given film. She likens her procedure to a surrealist "exquisite corpse" in which a work is developed discontinuously, context redefined with each new element. Through collaboration with other artists and composers, O'Daniel interrupts artisanal authority and distributes it among a varied community of artists and musicians on a deaf/hearing continuum.

Working with her collaborators inspired her to create sculptures that accompany the films in their various installations. These sculptures ini-

MISSING MUSIC | 147

tially seem to have little bearing on the films until one realizes that they build on motifs established within the various chapters of the narrative. A wall-sized gray sculpture made of soundproofing material imitates the work of Louise Nevelson, whose photograph inspired one of the scores; a lattice-like sculpture against a wall, with arrows pointing up and down, was inspired by the pattern the Zamboni machine makes in its sweep of the ice rink. The fact that O'Daniel was a competitive ice skater adds another, more autobiographical, level to this motif. Each stage of *The Tuba Thieves* expands incrementally into other images and narratives, a procedure that reinforces my earlier reference to communication as a feedback system. The associative links between original impulse and final product are connected, in her mind, with mishearing, "showing the infinite ways that I could create new objects through the transformation that occurs in not hearing properly" ("Generative Misunderstanding"). Mishearing grants a kind of permission to follow divergent cues to see where they lead. By ceding certain artisanal labor to others, she reinforces the possibility of a more collaborative, speculative process.

In her installation settings, films are projected on various walls of a museum or gallery using split screens, a feature that contributes to the fragmentary character of the narrative. Visual and acoustic disorientation functions to mirror the experience of persons on a d/Deaf spectrum and their fraught relationship to the hearing world. Disorientation also functions to address different audiences who may experience the installation through varying sensory portals. Hearing visitors to the museum are exposed to a barrage of diegetic sound—band members tuning up, a truck shifting gears, wind blowing, waves crashing, people talking. Very little verbal dialogue occurs in the films that might provide context for the hearing audience. Deaf audience members may feel more at home since a good deal of the actual dialogue is signed. However disorienting the installation is, the brightly lit, sensuous cinematography, as I can testify from seeing her work in a variety of venues, is dazzling in itself.

What I described above as O'Daniel's rhyming of discontinuous materials is abundantly evident in the second film, *Hearing 4'33"*. Using a split screen, the film reenacts John Cage's epochal "silent" composition in the original Maverick Concert Hall in Woodstock, New York, where David Tudor first performed it in 1952. The opening sequence depicts the lush greenery around the building on one screen while on the other,

Figure 6.2. Alison O'Daniel, *Hearing 4′ 33″*, from *The Tuba Thieves (2013 and ongoing)*[13]

the camera pans slowly up the weathered shingles and windows of the auditorium. The sound of clapping interrupts the silence while the camera is still focused on green foliage. The next sequence shows David Tudor, played here by an actor (who bears a slight resemblance to the composer) sitting at the piano, closing the keyboard cover, and starting a stopwatch. A reverse shot shows the audience waiting expectantly for the concert to begin. The audience consists mostly of middle-aged white adults in pastel summer clothing, not, presumably avant garde hipsters conversant with Cage's aesthetics. We watch Tudor being watched by audience members who express, at times, slight discomfort but maintain respectful concert-going decorum.

Halfway through the sequence, an older man toward the back of the audience gets up and leaves the hall, moving out into the forest behind the building. We watch his progress through both split screens from different vantages, occasionally returning to the pianist and audience. As the pianist finishes his silent performance, the audience claps politely (but not enthusiastically) while on the other screen, the man moves farther into the forest, walking almost daintily over the leaves and fallen branches. He carefully removes his shoes and places them on the forest floor and then walks tentatively over the leaves. The gentle crackle of leaves is the only sound. He looks up at the trees, and the right-hand frame returns to Maverick Hall and its weathered shingles.

Cagean aesthetics is developed in O'Daniel's film in several forms—his claim, for example, that there is no such thing as silence or that music is a dialogic relationship between event and audience. This latter context hints at the social implication of *4′33″* insofar as a silent composition redirects emphasis from the acoustic event to expectations of what that event will consist.[14] O'Daniel materializes this fact by filming the audience from the pianist's standpoint and especially by having one of its members leave the concert space. That gesture—whether reflecting irritation with Cage's pretense or recognizing its aesthetic implications— foregrounds the important dialectic between event and reception. Far from aestheticizing silence, Cage's piece and O'Daniel's "hearing" of it validate the public nature of music, its material impact within and beyond performance. Salomé Voegelin summarizes this interplay as follows: "In the concert hall Cage's *4'33"* is musical silence, and as such any sound heard is practiced in relation to the expectations and conventions of musical performance and musical listening. When we have not heard it but only heard about it, as is the case for many, no doubt *4'33"* becomes a conceptual work" (81). In similar fashion, O'Daniel creates a "silent" film in which audience noises, however muted, and the sonic features of the natural world create a soundscape. Hence her title, *Hearing 4'33"*, refers to the critical aspect of her gesture; she "hears" (or steals) the work's silences and extends knowledge gained by this act beyond the printed score into new forms and spaces. I emphasize the idea that her gesture is a kind of theft since by removing *4'33"* from its original score, O'Daniel adds drama to what is, after all, a stage direction. And by adding sound to silence, she violates the purity of Cage's conception by incorporating the faint sounds of trees, leaves, audience, and wind. The man who leaves the concert validates this aesthetic theft by stressing its haptic (he feels the ground), visual (he sees trees), spatial (he moves in and out of the hall), and acoustic (he hears birds) elements. At the same time, fluid camera movements, often slightly out of sync between the two screens, create a corresponding visual rhythm.

If Cage is an inspiration for O'Daniel, the composer Pauline Oliveros occupies a similar position through her concept of "deep listening." Oliveros distinguishes between hearing and listening as two different modes of perception. For Oliveros, hearing is physiological and embodied, the reception of sound waves in the cochlea; listening is active cognitive engagement with sound.[15] For Oliveros, deep listening was an important compositional aspect of her work of the 1970s and 1980s, with vocal performances involving sustained tunings around a single tone. Deep listening emphasizes music that remains open to the total environment within which it is produced and the body for bodies from which it is produced.[16] One might say that O'Daniel engages her own form of deep listening by listening to listening, treating sounded elements—a band tuning up, wind in trees, a stopwatch ticking—in Brandon La-Belle's terms as a "field of sound, a partner in the unfolding of time and space, acting upon and being acted upon in a mutual intensity" (159).

Hearing 4'33" resonates with many other scenes in *The Tuba Thieves* in its emphasis on audience and reception. The presence (or presumption) of an audience is foregrounded in segments set at a deaf club, a high school football field, a practice room where Nyke Prince practices drumming, a trumpet player playing next to an empty culvert. In these instances, the idea of an audience or interlocutor, however implicit, re-directs sound from the performer to the would-be listener, from the source of sound to the environment in which it is heard (or not heard). In the deaf club segment, young deaf members of the audience dance enthusiastically to a punk band while older members play cards and gossip, aware of the raucous sound around them (one woman waves her finger in time to the music) yet remaining engrossed in their game and conversation. In *Away Game*, a high school band travels on a bus to play at a night football game. The latter episode is less about the music to be played (of which we hear only snippets) than about the social environment of youthful exuberance and conversations of the band members on the bus to the game. They are, after all, the figures most impacted by the theft of musical instruments. One amazing moment in this film consists of a lengthy shot of Geovanny, a young drum major from Centennial High School Marching Band in Compton, practicing for his baton-twirling moment at halftime. He performs behind the stands, matching his moves brilliantly to the band's music being played on the opposite side of the bleachers. Although he technically has no audience, we become his stand-in viewers. The band's invisibility and the youth's virtuosic routines blend the film's twin concerns with the visible and the invisible audience, the anticipated performance in front of a crowd and the actual performance before us.

Displaced Landscapes

There is an ecopolitical element to *Tuba Thieves* that extends the displacement of sound to the displacement of spaces in an urban environment. In one film in the series, *The Plants Are Protected*, O'Daniel quotes from a letter to the Russian director Andrei Tarkovsky about his film *The Mirror*. The correspondent writes that one must "watch this film simply; watch it as one watches the stars, or the sea, as one admires a landscape." This remark describes a kind of openness to viewing without preconceptions or anticipations. It also rhymes with specific scenes of figures looking and gazing at stars, oceans, or cityscapes. Social and cultural conventions supported by sight and sound are displaced from sensory organs. Eyes and ears are now freed from their interpretive role in organizing perception, redirected onto the social protocols they support. O'Daniel asks how it is possible to get outside of those protocols while recognizing their imperative force. How to render displacement as a site of innovation?

Salomé Voeglin studies the presumption among hearing persons that when we observe something visually and notice a concurrent sound, we likely

> . . . subsume that heard into the appreciation of the seen; sound fleshes out the visual and renders it real; it gives the image its spatial dimension and temporal dynamic. . . . Sound's ephemeral invisibility obstructs critical engagement, while the apparent stability of the image invites criticism. (xi)

O'Daniel challenges this subordination of sound to image by seeing landscape from a deaf perspective where the temporal immediacy that Voeglin assigns to sound is coterminous with image. The spatial and temporal detachment that ocularcentrism presumes is challenged by numerous scenes of sign-language sociality. In the deaf club sequence, young deaf people dance to music that they may not be able to hear but feel viscerally. While dancing, they conduct simultaneous signed conversations with their friends. In another film, *The Sea, The Stars, A Landscape*, various deaf characters communicate in ASL against the backdrop of cars honking, helicopters pulsing, sirens blaring. At one point, a deaf couple stands on a hill overlooking the Griffith Observatory. Their brief signed conversation is about the view, the smog, and the (surprisingly light) traffic. At the end of this sequence, now at night, a gay couple looks at the lights of the city, again from a high vantage. Using ASL, they discuss stars and planets while the camera focuses on the glittering lights of LA. The entire film is bookended by the "stars" of the film's title, from the observatory to city lights and stars at night. In each case, the city is interpreted from a deaf-centric vantage, one that literally "views" the urban landscape.

The city of Los Angeles is, to some extent, one of the stars of this project. It is not the touristic, palm-tree vistas of travel brochures but the bland, anonymous streets, neighborhoods and freeways that are its daily reality. O'Daniel sees the city both as a land and a soundscape of production, urban infrastructure, and social divisions. She provides captions for the sounds of this scape ("motor revving," "horns honking") to emphasize the fact. And just as the soundscape is bounded by captions, so the physical landscape of Los Angeles is bordered and sequestered by fences and barriers. In *The Sea, the Stars, a Landscape*, Nyke Prince drives through working-class neighborhoods of LA, and the city we see from her car window is dominated by fencing, walls, and commercial signage. Many of the scenes in this sequence feature houses heavily guarded by chain-link fences and barred windows, vistas seen through wire and foliage. At one point, Nyke stops at a stoplight, and the wall that we view from her car window is the glassed façade of a 99 Cent Store, its window filled to the ceiling with inexpensive products, an image that establishes a parallel between the protective fencing we have seen and the wall of commodities being displayed.

The fusion of landscape and soundscape in *The Tuba Thieves* serves to reorient sensations, creating gaps between sound and understanding. Asked by Kevin Appel about the function of such lacunae, O'Daniel describes them as a "lens" through which she sees everything:

> I recognize the *irony of switching senses* there and find real joy in that flip. . . . It's a different way of experiencing the relationship of one's self to one's body. There is sensitivity to visual, to sound, to touch that is to me so profound . . . but verbal language is less capable of summing up. (Interview; italics added)

O'Daniel stresses the fact that discontinuities in understanding displace the senses, rewiring sound as sight, reprocessing a visual image as a potential score, summoning language from silent nature. But why describe this as "ironic"? Perhaps her usage implicates the classic division of senses into discrete categories. When the category of sound, for example, no longer describes a particular piece of information, other senses fill in the blank. Hence by "flipping" senses, O'Daniel reconsiders the way we encounter a world whose self-presence can no longer be guaranteed through the usual channels.

"Switching senses" is very much the subject of *The Plants Are Protected*, a film whose narrative concerns a moving van full of exotic plants traveling from West to East Coast. The film is divided into three segments. The first is a closeup of the cab's interior with the sounds of rain and thunder in the background. A male figure opens the cab door and moves garbage off the passenger seat, leaves the cab and reenters, starts the engine and drives off. The date is revealed through a radio report announcing the impending arrival of Hurricane Sandy in 2012. We do not see the driver's face, only his lower body and hands. The second section is a series of close-ups of plants, and the third segment is an establishing shot of the entire interior of the truck, which we now see is carrying plants that shake slightly with the truck's movements. The camera pans slowly over the plants while a captioned voiceover begins a series of nasal consonants (/m/s) in upper and lower case. Captions suggest that this is the "language" of the plants made by "plant 1," "plant 2," and so forth. According to O'Daniel in various interviews, the vocal track is of Christine Sun Kim, responding to a number of cues supplied by the artist, who adds her own interpretation of the sound's source ("Third Plant: closed mouth sound").

At one point, O'Daniel adds the caption based on a letter to Andrei Tarkovsky that appears over the image of succulents and cacti. The plants jiggle and shake against the truck's movement as the camera pans slowly among and around them. When O'Daniel attempted to paste the quote from a PDF to a Word document, the formatting broke down, and spaces appeared between and among the words, creating a kind of textual stutter: "WATCH IT AS O NE WATCHES T HE STARS, OR T HE SEA AS O NE ADMI R. ES. A L ANDS C APE." Rather than correct the spacing, she decided to include the errors in the caption, perhaps to illustrate the provisional nature of all communication, especially among those deaf and hard-of-hearing persons who rely on captioning. Since the quotation advocates viewing film as one would view the night sky (the title of her previous 2011 film), its graphic fracturing nicely embodies the relationship between random points of light and the mythological figures that link human and infinite space. We call these figures constellations, but one might as easily speak of them as a kind of language.

The title of this segment, *The Plants Are Protected*, establishes an eco-political imperative of *Tuba Thieves*, the emphasis being on—in this case—plants displaced from their native desert landscape. The plants in the truck *are* protected from the elements yet are artificially isolated in pots, boxes, and containers of various sorts. Displacement of the natural landscape, as I've indicated, is framed by fences, divided by freeways, interrupted by culverts, buildings, and electrical wires. In one image from *The Sea, the Stars, a Landscape*, Nyke Prince stands on a promontory looking out at what we surmise is the ocean. Hearing members of the audience may hear the sound of waves; deaf members may read captions ("sound of wave crashing"), but the image never resolves on an image of the actual ocean. The highly refracted view of landscape in these sequences suggests that *The Tuba Thieves* is as much about the theft of landscape as of sound.

The demographic landscape depicted in the films is dominated by working-class and racially mixed (Black and Latinx) and deaf youth. We meet them in separate shots—Latinx teens looking through a chain-link fence at a dry culvert; a gay couple necking while overlooking the city at night; three deaf girls crossing the freeway on an enclosed pedestrian walkway, signing in ASL; Latinx and Black band members chatting on a bus. These figures dominate a landscape of economic and linguistic displacements that nevertheless marks a level of community that is otherwise invisible to city administrators and the Chamber of Commerce.

The Theft of Sound

Peter Szendy meditates on the history of listening, wondering who has a "right" to music and whether it is possible to transmit one's listening to others. Rather than focus on the music as the *end* of listening, Szendy is interested in the "regime of listening" itself and the juridical history of musical copying and plagiarism. For him, listening is a kind of theft, similar to what happens when a composer adapts or appropriates another work. He asks, What is the status of these various forms of listening—adaptation, copying, sampling, plagiarism—and do they constitute a form of theft? One of his examples is Mozart's famous transcription of Allegri's *Miserere*, a grand liturgical work whose performance was restricted to the inner sanctum of the Sistine Chapel. The musicians of the chapel were, as Mozart's father wrote, "forbidden under penalty of excommunication, to let the smallest part of this piece go, to copy it or communicate it to anyone" (qtd. in Szendy 9). Mozart, on a single hearing of it in Rome, was able to transcribe the entire work from memory and eventually perform it in Salzburg. Szendy explains that Allegri's "secret of Rome" was not the work itself but Mozart's listening to its performance. He stole not the work but the performance of the work and gave it a kind of secular life.

As applied to O'Daniel's project in *Tuba Thieves*, we might understand her work as a similar act of appropriation of sound in order to listen to what it tells her. Since her hearing loss is moderately severe, that listening must necessarily be partial and inexact, allowing her to interrupt narrative and acoustic continuities. As she says, "To be deaf or hard of hearing is constantly to be reconciling with experiences associated with sound and hearing and listening and deafness" (Interview with Kevin Appel). This theft of sound, according to Szendy, is not unlike what happens when a composer refashions an earlier work—Schönberg adapting Brahms, Bach readapting his earlier secular cantatas for later sacred works like the Mass in B Minor, Wagner and Liszt rescoring Beethoven's symphonies. The charged association with "theft" emphasizes the scandalous dethroning of one sense by another. Her adaptation of Cage's silent work is also a kind of critical "listening" since she fills his silence with visual and ambient noise and gives it a new narrative realization.[17] Her captioning of Christine Sun Kim's voice involves an acute listening to what deaf vocalization "sounds" like. The "regime of listening" is just that, a temporal field in which listening is revealed as a cultural form. When hearing is impossible or difficult, critical listening takes over and steals sensation from its hierarchical Aristotelian categories.

And this is where we need to return to O'Daniel's original impulse: hearing a story on radio about the theft of tubas and listening to its implications for a story about hearing loss. Like the big, ungainly instruments that provide the base line and rhythm for band music, O'Daniel's ever-expanding series of films and sculptures is, to adapt Henry James, a series of "large loose baggy monsters, with their queer elements of the accidental and the arbitrary."[18] The series remains incomplete and on-going as I write this, and so I have only registered some of the qualities already in evidence. But in the interstices of each film rests the difficulties experienced by the deaf and hard-of-hearing artist. She is, as she says, "constantly aware of how you are not catching something . . . . It can simultaneously be the most frustrating thing and the most profound thing at the same time."[19]

7

A Captioned Life

I feel sorry for the sky over the table on the right
—Ava captioning software transcription

"CC"

In a recent video, *Closer Captions*, Christine Sun Kim explores close captioning of diegetic sound in films. In her introduction, she complains that captioning of conversations is relatively unproblematic, but captioning of sounds—music playing, for example—is often rendered by a single word or phrase: *music, violin playing.* She imagines captions that would capture the texture, mood, and personality of the sound: "mournful music that sounds like crying in a bar." To remedy this, she created a short film of a single day, from dawn to night, depicting interior spaces and outdoor landscapes, crowds of people and scenes of nature. Each caption describes qualities and textures of sound that might occur in a scene. Some of the captions evoke the subject's experience—an image of the sky with clouds, the caption reading "the sound of sun entering the bedroom." The next image of trees seen through a window is captioned by an event inside the room: "electricity attempting to find its outlet." The disconnection between image and text speaks to Kim's view that captions may take on a life of their own, inspired by an image yet capable of registering associations created by the captioner. The video continues in this manner with scenes inside and outside, of natural landscape and crowded streets, each frame containing a caption that builds on potential auditory sources but often as not with free associations ("electricity attempting to find its outlet"). Against her complaint about the inadequacy of captions in rendering sounds ("they suck"), Kim provides a wry commentary on what else a scene might evoke—and what a caption often leaves out.

As with her 2015 work *Close Readings*, discussed in chapter 2, Kim here explores the limits of captioning while reimagining their function from a deaf perspective. These captions, as her title indicates, are "closer" to her own imaginings of what sound might "look" like. Sound is not absent from this video; toward the end, we see a crowd of young people standing on a street corner. The caption reads, "I sometimes see busy scenes in movies," followed by "captioned with only one musical note." For the first time in the video we hear a single note played by a chime or gong, which begins to repeat until an entire orchestra begins to play. Gradually, the sound diminishes to silence. Meanwhile, the image of the crowd remains constant—people coming and going, talking and gesturing. The visual contract with the soundtrack is broken, and a new registration of the acoustic properties of image created.

Kim's concern here is with the limits and possibilities of captioning sound in films.[1] She calls attention to the problem of rendering the subtle nuances of sound into text, turning, say, the voice of someone with a thick accent into standard English or resolving a bit of punning play into a single word. The wind of a hurricane is hardly rendered by a single word—*wind*—nor does the phrase *music playing* specify whether the music is playing in the background or as non-diegetic music used to paint the mood of a scene. Sean Zdenek refers to these distinctions as constituting the rhetorical function of captions, the way they orient and represent sound. Since captioners must decide what is important—what is "worthy of being captioned"—they play a key role in structuring the filmic text (1).

Kim's captions in *Closer Captions* are open, meaning that they are a component of the film itself and cannot be manipulated by the viewer. Subtitling of foreign movies would be the most familiar form that open captions—or in this case subtitles—take. In closed captions, on the other hand, the text is hidden from view until a mechanism in the computer or television is switched on or in theaters channeled to specific viewers through a captioning device. The "cc" acronym that appears on a television screen or remote device allows the viewer to access the captioning option when it is necessary. Captioned television has been a boon for deaf and hard-of-hearing (DHOH) persons, but hearing persons use captions for other reasons—to permit TV watching while a baby sleeps, to understand unfamiliar accents, or to watch a sports commentary in a noisy bar. And in the case of several of the artists I will discuss here, captioning has provided a critical lens on the persons for whom captioning is addressed and the language used *in* that address.[2] First, a bit of history.

The era of silent films, when dialogue was represented on intertitles that interrupted the visual narrative, was a golden age of captioning. Silent films, of course, were not entirely silent, often accompanied by pit orchestras or pianos with various sound effects added. But for DHOH persons, films during the silent era were equally accessible as for hearing persons.[3] When talkies came into prominence in the mid-1920s, deaf people who had relied on intertitles were suddenly left out of the movie-going experience. In the interim between the end of silent films and the rise of closed captioning, educators within the deaf community began subtitling films, beginning in 1949 with members of the Lexington School in New York, which created a series of "captioned films for the deaf." As Gregory Downey says, the popularity and success of these films led to activism from the National Association for the Deaf and many other agencies to advocate for state and federal legislation to promote the film captioning (41–42). This activism increased within the Deaf community during the 1960s, building on Movieola technology that had been used by Herman Weinberg for subtitling foreign films in the 1930s. But it wasn't until 1986 that a first run Hollywood film using captions—Randa Haines's *Children of a Lesser God*—was released in limited distribution. In that film, William Hurt plays a hearing educator at a deaf school who develops a romantic—if volatile—relationship with a deaf worker, played by Marlee Matlin. In the version distributed for general consumption, there were no captions; Matlin's signing was re-voiced by Hurt as part of his dialogue.

It was in the area of educational television and with the advent of closed-circuit technologies that captioning was tried out on a broader scale. Closed captioning was first demonstrated at the First National Conference on Television for the Hearing Impaired in Nashville, Tennessee, in 1971 (Downey 71). A second demonstration was held at Gallaudet College (now Gallaudet University) on February 15, 1972, where ABC and the National Bureau of Standards demonstrated closed captions embedded within a broadcast of *The Mod Squad* (ibid.). Closed captioning was first introduced to the larger public in 1972 with Julia

Child's television show, *The French Chef*, and since 1993 has been a required element of all televisions sold with screens larger than thirteen inches (ibid.). With the 1990 Americans with Disabilities Act, captioning was mandated in movie theaters and other public venues. Film viewers use various assistive devices for closed captions, whether the text appears on specially designed glasses, in hearing loops, or on hand-held screens attached to the armrest. Despite this considerable improvement for DHOH viewers, there is a great variance in access depending on whether the film is produced independently or by a large production company. This fact—that many films and a good deal of television information (ads, public service announcements, news briefings) are not captioned—means that accessibility required by the ADA remains unevenly distributed.

In public settings like classrooms or courtrooms, captioning is performed in real time by a stenographer or court reporter typing on a special phonetic keyboard whose transcription is projected onto a screen or computer within a few seconds of vocal delivery. Although CART, or communication access real-time translation (formerly, computer assisted real-time translation), is required under the terms of the ADA, its availability remains subject to varying factors. Accommodation is often limited based on institutional budgets, access to local captioners, and—most important—willingness of administrators to provide such accommodation. Depending on region, in the United States, the cost of a captioner for a public event may be as high as $100 an hour, and if two captioners are required, the cost doubles. The quality of captioning varies from case to case. A court reporter who is used to transcribing legal discussion may have difficulty in a specialized academic seminar where terminology, proper names, and crosstalk create obstacles.

Voice-recognition or voice-to-text software solves some of the problems mentioned above by relinquishing transcription to digital language-processing systems. The technical term for this transition is *transduction*, the process of turning sound waves into text, although as Jonathan Sterne observes, the transduction of sound into "something else" by a machine is the very principle of the ear (22, 33–34). Thanks to research in artificial intelligence, nanotechnology, statistics, computer science, linguistics, and other fields, natural language processing is able, with increasing sophistication, to program computers to recognize natural (human) languages. Machine-learning technologies draw on complex algorithms to identify foreign words, specialized jargon, and non-traditional grammar, incorporating novelty and eliminating error. This is a big advance over automatic speech recognition (ASR), which utilizes dialog design to anticipate a given utterance's meaning. We experience ASR in telephone calls to commercial and banking institutions ("What is my balance?" or "Enter your medical record number"). Some television captioning uses a technique known as "respeaking," where a commentator's words are repeated by a technician in the studio into a microphone and submitted to an ASR system that then translates words into text. The point in the latter is to correct the inevitable errors that occur with the fast-paced sports commentary or news interview and provide a cleaner version. But even here, errors can occur. The British government's Office of Communications, which oversees captioning accuracy for DHOH, noted that the "Archbishop of Canterbury" became the "Arch bitch of Canterbury" and in a weather report, "fog patches" became "mist and Fox patches." One report that said that a woman "had never been on a bus on her own" became "never been on a bus on heroin" (Pullman).

Although voice-to-text systems are improving, they remain somewhat ineffective, as anyone who has used a dictation device on a smartphone can attest. Errors abound unless the acoustic environment is highly controlled and speakers talk directly into the microphone. Since I use several dictation devices—on my smartphone, iPad, computer, and captioning telephone—I have become interested in the errors that such technologies produce, if only because in misstating what is said, they provide hilarious, often inventive substitutes. In one conversation, to take a recent example, a friend's reference to "avant garde poetry" became, "Atlantic Avenue lifeguard poetry." My friend went on to ask,

Is he asleep looking at this delicious drink, yeah, I mean if you, hello, next, frank, let me open my eyes. . . . I think I may never say anything.

However interesting the transformations, transcription errors illustrate the potential for error in any speech act. Some years ago, Noam Chomsky and George Miller showed that the clause "The good can decay many ways" differs from "The good candy came anyway" only because the final 's' of "ways" in the first case would be ungrammatical in the second. One can understand why any transcription system could be fooled by such slight phonological differences. When voice-recognition software makes an error, it reveals language—its structure, lexicology, pragmatics—in its unstable and frangible condition. It also illustrates class-and-race-inflected differences in assigning meaning, depending on how a given program is designed and by whom.[4]

What are the arts of captioning error? What is the rhetorical work of captions in constructing meaning and negotiating the constraints of space and time.[5] Or more to the point, how does Kim's recaptioning embody the limits of linguistic representation and the persons who are presumed to be its readers? Kim's video installation could be seen as an extension of conceptual art in which the "art object" is replaced, in Joseph Kosuth's terms, with "art as idea." Her deaf recaptions do not critique or satirize their status as art but use their medium to *speak* to specific constituencies about how language interpellates some subjects and isolates others. The linguistic turn in art, associated with figures like Kosuth, Lawrence Weiner, Bruce Nauman, Robert Morris, and On Kawara, replaces the image or object with the word and moves the descriptive caption from the wall of the museum into the picture frame, accompanied, in many cases, by its own wall caption.

In one of his 1966–68 *Art as Idea* series, Kosuth creates an enlarged photostat, white font on black, of a dictionary definition of the word *definition* that he then displayed in galleries and museums. Instead of the representation of an object or scene (or abstract design) the "work" is a reproduction of a definition of definition, or in the artist's terms, the "idea as idea." Kosuth explains that "art's unique character is the capacity to remain aloof from philosophical judgements. . . . Art indeed exists for its own sake" ("Art after Philosophy"). In this aestheticized context, language serves as a relatively inert vehicle for commentary on its function, its institutional placement, its discursive cultural role. For Kim, in contrast, language is a site of contestation where the putative norm of speech and hearing comes up against the bodies and signs of specific constituencies.

I have a hat but I don't

Bye bye shut up.
Shut up hey shut up.
But yeah more carrots more parsnips or carrots at the beginning
Mattel set 1 carat I cut up 3 carats in a parsnip but even still if you have
    34 pounds right be down 3 pounds of beef to one carrot juice
Family dinner totally good
the last time was the first time that I've done.
. . .

Go lack go lack use to her.
Cocoa and clear soup and oranges and oat-meal.
Whist bottom whist close, whist clothes, woodling
Cocoa and clear soup and oranges and oat-meal.
Pain soup, suppose it is question, suppose it is butter, real is, real is only,
    only excreate, only excreate a no since
. . .

Best Buy Fred email
you want to pay
okay for all you done I like it
boiler companies
this for flatbread
did you put my glasses on
when they're sauce
. . .

A single example of excellence is in the meat. A bent stick is surging and
    might all might is mental. A grand clothes is searching out a candle
    not that wheatly not that by more than an owl and a path. A jam is
    proud of cocoanut.
. . . .

reading is living with Liz dining room
covered with map
he and his roommate is a roommate was also a tee time for
Live in Ohio and we go down and see them so they all live in Taj Mahals
. . .

Alas a doubt in case of more go to say what it is cress. What is it. Mean.
    Why. Potato. Loaves.

I use a form of voice recognition software that captions conversations through my smartphone's microphone. It has become my major form of communication in public situations—doctor's offices, markets, government offices—but also serves as a lifeline to personal communications with friends and family. Although in this chapter I will be speaking about transcription *errors*, my captioning system, Ava, is remarkably accurate, often transcribing exact technical terms, foreign language words, and proper nouns. One of its particular advantages is that when others have it on their smartphones, their voices appear on mine in different colored fonts, giving me the illusion of a group conversation. Ava stores transcripts from these conversations that I can access later—a real benefit when trying to remember a doctor's comments or a contractor's estimate. But as with any form of transcription, errors creep in, and depending on the amount of ambient noise, distortion will interrupt the rendering of a given person's speech.

I have provided a few samples above of transcripts from recent conversations, interlaced with passages from Gertrude Stein's *Tender Buttons* (1913) to suggest that inaccuracies are often pretty interesting and that mis-captioning bears a close resemblance to avant garde writing (or vice versa).[6] "It's a good good person to go with a dark trail / Embassy map very cool / I have a hat but I don't" sounds more like late Beckett than last year's Thanksgiving dinner conversation, which is where it appeared. By linking Stein to captioning errors, I don't mean to suggest that her writing is error prone the way that voice-to-text captioning is; rather, I see her exploring the same kinds of associative processes and substitutions by which natural-language-processing captioning programs work. Finding the right word means sifting through dozens of possible synonyms while anticipating the next step in a syntactic sequence; metonymy trumps metaphor. But I want to keep the expressive force of "error" to think about its generative potential in complicating what we take to be the correct word. And I want to foreground the relevance of error to individuals who, for varying reasons, live in a state of linguistic precarity.[7]

In his well-known description of linguistic error, "Two Aspects of Language and Two Types of Aphasic Disturbances," Roman Jakobson argues that in any adequate study of communicational breakdown, "we must first understand the nature and structure of the particular mode of communication that has ceased to function" (95). Jakobson goes on to describe the importance of selection in combining more complex linguistic units. We draw from a "lexical storehouse" or code that speaker and interlocutor share in common. That storehouse is divided into two categories: combination—a sign's relation to other signs in the utterance—and selection—a choice among alternative signs, the substitution of *pig* for *fig*. We might say that combination refers to the present utterance whereas selection refers to potential substitute words in a virtual lexicon. People living with aphasic disorders fall into two categories: those who have difficulty selecting from among possible words or synonyms and those who have difficulty with larger grammatical units. These two categories of aphasia—selection and contiguity disorder—are Jakobson's terms for variants from normative communication, but they also describe two important rhetorical figures in literature, metaphor and metonymy. When an individual has difficulty selecting among possible synonyms, we may say that they live with a metaphoric deficit. The aphasic individual who has difficulty forming longer units or sentences of grammatically related words lives with a contextual or metonymic deficit. Either of what Jakobson calls "gravitational poles" may prevail in different literary genres. Russian folk lyrics or Romantic poetry may foreground the use of metaphor while the realist novel (*Anna Karenina* is his example) relies on elaborations of detail and setting for the richness of its development.

I rehearse this familiar formulation to emphasize that a cognitive or neurological disability may reveal "aspects of language," to adapt Jakobson's title, that may otherwise be invisible. I would extend Jakobson's focus on aphasic disorders to communicational errors that occur with hearing impairments. The DHOH individual attempting to process speech may draw on the same metaphoric and metonymic poles that attend other communicational disorders. For Jakobson, aphasic disorders are deficits in communication. For Freud, slips of the tongue are a psychopathology. But for DHOH persons, captioning errors may be a kind of poetry. Gerald Shea, whom I have discussed earlier and who is severely hard of hearing, calls the errors he makes in processing conversations "lyricals."

The rhetorical figure of catachresis is the general term for the misuse of words, the substitution of a word from one context to describe another. As James Berger notes, "If language is tropic, catachresis is the foundation of language, and the linguistically impaired figure in literature is the catachresis as character" (28). Berger is speaking of characters like Billy Budd or Benjy Compson, whose stammer and moaning mark their speech impediments but which, as a consequence, reveal truths that other characters refuse to see. We might say that there is also a catachrestic reception where utterances are heard differently, where homophonic and metonymic substitutions create new associative possibilities. Catachresis defines the fragmentary nature of what we call understanding. Some parts are understood clearly while others are lost due to ambient noise, a speaker's pronunciation or accent, distraction and disinterest. Even in the most straightforward conversation, communication tends to consist of partial elements—incomplete phrases, metacommunicative remarks ("Are you saying that . . ."; "What do you mean by that?"), grunts, affirmations ("Yeah, right"), facial gestures and body language. Sight tends to reinforce or confirm what we hear, and body language can turn an anodyne statement into an aggressive retort. In Steven Connor's terms, we hear through a process of "intersensoriality," in which "hearing tends to ask questions that get answered by evidence of the eyes" (154). Of course, a voice-to-text transcription cannot rely on visual cues in searching for the right word, nor can it test that word against an ongoing conversation that may provide context. But a faulty transcription may reveal the thin line that separates meaning from misunderstanding.

A Recipe for Disaster

In 1972, WGBH Boston produced an eight-part pilot series of Julia Child's *The French Chef* to be broadcast through select PBS affiliates. It was to be the first captioned television program, funded largely by a grant from the Department of Education for the Handicapped. In an irony that deaf persons know all too well, the project goal was less to address the needs of deaf people than to test hearing people's responses to open captions—to assess whether the sight of superimposed words would be too disturbing—and to "estimate the size of the audience captioned television can be expected to reach" (Downey 64). Corporate officials were concerned that captioning television for a small deaf minority would "drive away the vast and lucrative hearing majority" (Downey 69). Although this pilot project included open captions—available to any viewer without mechanical interface—closed captions that could be turned off or on by the user were being tested among select deaf populations at around the same time. Over the next twenty years, closed captioning in television and film became more sophisticated, leading to federal legislation that mandated closed captioning in televisions, movies, and other media. In 1998, the FCC required companies that distribute television programming to caption those programs.

The French Chef was an oddly appropriate program in which to test issues of accommodation since it had its own accessibility agenda: to make French cooking available to American viewers. Child's folksy, unfussy presentation made complicated French cuisine seem if not easy to cook at least possible. The artist Carolyn Lazard may have had these factors in mind when they (the preferred pronoun) created their 2018 video A Recipe for Disaster, which reproduces one of Child's videos—a demonstration of omelet making—with the original titles along with the artist's own superimposed text scrolling over the image. We hear Child's voice and see her captioned commentary at the bottom of the screen, but Lazard's text scrolls across the entire screen, offering a very different narrative. The contrast between Child's celebration of the omelet's versatility and Lazard's critical intervention complicates the issue of access by imagining multiple audiences, hearing and sighted, who may experience, as their caption indicates, "sensory failure" in parsing several levels of information. But why does Lazard's text stress "failure" or "violence" when the image is all about the ease and satisfaction of omelet making? What looks like a vehicle of accommodation—captions to facilitate understanding for DHOH persons—becomes a site for considering how "access" implies the normalization of deaf and disabled persons. "This is not," Lazard's caption explains, "about something elsewhere / this is not a scene of a couple on the beach / discussing their dinner in a restaurant / this is a white woman who cooks / while talking about how to cook / what you hear is what you get / and what you get is what you hear." Aimie Hamrae calls this kind of critical intervention "access knowledge" to describe how the principle of accommodation promised by universal design is something produced and structured by laws, architecture and design, but it is also something that produces individuals as well. What you get is what you hear, but what you see, as in Kim's Closer Captions, may be something else. The absence of captions produces the DHOH person; intervention into the captioning process produces a more critical viewer.[8]

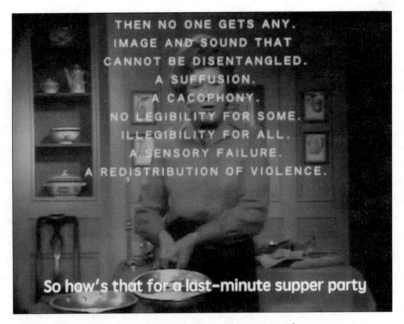

THEN NO ONE GETS ANY.
IMAGE AND SOUND THAT
CANNOT BE DISENTANGLED.
A SUFFUSION.
A CACOPHONY.
NO LEGIBILITY FOR SOME.
ILLEGIBILITY FOR ALL.
A SENSORY FAILURE.
A REDISTRIBUTION OF VIOLENCE.

So how's that for a last-minute supper party

Figure 7.1. Carolyn Lazard, from *A Recipe for Disaster* (2018)[9]

Lazard's text, "a redistribution of violence," is itself a rather violent interruption of Child's demonstration in order to divert expectations of what is being said onto another conversation, creating "A REDUN-DANCY FOR SOME / A CLARITY FOR OTHERS." But there is a further voice, a ghost voice that sometimes speaks over Child, describing what is happening on screen. It is an example of audio description, designed to aid sight-impaired persons in sorting the actions and events in the mise en scène.[10] Thus we have distributed voices, each vying for our attention along different sensory platforms. The critical nature of Lazard's text advocates a "media of medias / a new materialism / a way of making and consuming / that refuses translation." The original pilot project to make audible material available for DHOH audiences is repurposed now to reveal "a way of making and consuming / that refuses translation" by seizing on the fact of captioning as its medium. The basic elements of omelet making—eggs, butter salt—are compared to "3 materials image, sound, text" that comprise the video.

Lazard identifies as a disabled artist who lives with multiple autoimmune diseases who passes as able-bodied but who lives in what they call "biomedical purgatory." Many of their films, images and installations chronicle time spent in doctors' offices and waiting rooms hooked up to IVs and watching television on hospital monitors. A work like *Recipe for Disaster* foregrounds captioning's limits while expanding its epistemological force in structuring a putatively normal viewing experience. It may seem churlish for Lazard to critique what is otherwise a boon for DHOH persons who now have mandated access to television and movies, but their point is not to castigate WBGH or PBS or Child herself. Rather, as Emily Watlington says, "captions and visual descriptions are the fabric of the work, a site for criticality and creativity, not only a corrective." Or in Hamrae's terms, Lazard moves from "making" to "knowing," from acoustic and physical design to new understandings of what access implies and who is invited into accessible spaces.

Reading Affect: Liza Sylvestre

In chapter 2, I discussed Christine Sun Kim's recaptioning installation *Close Readings*, in which the artist asked several DHOH friends to recaption scenes from Disney's *Little Mermaid*. The captions that these viewers provided are radically different from those provided by the Disney company. The "deaf captions" responded to affective elements in a scene—how it felt for a deaf individual to reimagine Ariel's loss of voice and her fumbling attempts at sign language as tragic. In a similar sense, reading affectively is the subject for many of visual artist Liza Sylvestre's works. As someone with significant hearing loss and who has had cochlear implant surgery, she defines herself as an "individual who is medically, although not culturally deaf."[11] In her 2018 film *Captioned*, she creates what she calls a "self-commentary" on Howard Hawks's 1934 screwball comedy *Twentieth Century*, starring John Barrymore and Carole Lombard. Rather than captioning the film's famously hectic dialogue, she recorded her own reactions to every scene in the hour-and-half film.[12] The tension between fast-paced dialogue and reflective commentary is often startling and occasionally funny, creating an entirely different movie.

Sylvestre's choice of *Twentieth Century*, with its fast-paced verbal patter, might seem an odd choice for deaf captioning. Yet it is precisely the film's excess of talk that challenges the deaf captioner to seek

The spaces between the words are gone. Rapid. Rabid. Rage.

Figure 7.2. Liza Sylvestre, from *Captioned (2018)*[13]

meaning elsewhere. In the film, John Barrymore plays a beleaguered, self-enamored stage impresario, Oscar Jaffe, who transforms a lingerie model, Mildred Plotka (Carole Lombard) into the glamorous Lily Garland as the star of his play.[14] Flanked by his two befuddled assistants, Oliver Webb (Walter Connolly) and Owen O'Malley (Roscoe Kearns), Oscar tries to dominate Lily's acting career, badgering and hectoring her into conformity with his wishes. Despite her rising fame on stage, Lily is crushed by Oscar's domineering authority, ultimately causing her to flee New York for Hollywood and a film career. His directorial career declines without Lily, leading him to bankruptcy and a stint in jail. Meanwhile, Lily achieves fame in film, her face on the covers of magazines serving as a constant reminder to Oscar of his own failures. The two estranged figures, director and actress, meet accidentally on the Twentieth-Century Limited train going from Chicago to New York. Through a series of complicated ruses and masquerades, Oscar tries to lure Lily back into his fold, offering her a chance to appear in a new play in the role of Mary Magdalene. While faking a fatal illness,

Oscar convinces her to sign a contract. She agrees to the part, feeling that his former domineering self has changed, but the last scene shows that he remains a controlling, domineering male.

Sylvestre's headnote says that her captioned interpretations "include visual observations, plot assumptions/interpretations and also the thoughts that cross my mind as it wanders due to the boredom and strain of this event."[15] Such desultory wandering can be observed in one rather busy scene where Lily is being dressed by her maid, gesturing wildly while speaking to one of Jaffe's assistants. Sylvestre's caption reads, "I'm trying to follow her words and make sense of them . . . but it's not coming together. She keeps looking down and making theatrical gestures that change the shape of her lips. I need something I can rely on in order to make sense of things, so I notice how pointy and delicate her chin is" (Captioned 22'29"). Lombard's "theatrical gestures," so much an element of her stylized character, become an occasion to notice the shape of Lily's chin or lips, the sequins on Lily's dress or the sparkling lights of the star on Lily's dressing room door. She wonders why Jaffe has suits of armor in his office, and later, when he is being evicted from his theater along with the armor, she comments, "The suits of armor do have a purpose!" The removal of armor, hinting at Jaffe's lost virility, leads Sylvestre to notice a costume in the open doorway bearing a swastika insignia, a brief, haunting sign (in 1934) of things to come. Such minute observations bring thematic elements to the surface that would ordinarily be eclipsed by the dialogue. But when Sylvestre hears a fragment of that dialogue, her captions comment on the hearing process itself. At one point, responding to one of Jaffe's grandiose speeches, Sylvestre's caption reads, "I heard that line '. . . the last people in the world and the future of the human race depended on it.'" but goes on to reflect on the importance of context for DHOH persons: "This is the perfect example of how context is necessary for me when communicating verbally. Because there is a common phrase it's like there is a small part of my brain that is always expecting it. it's like a little hole of understanding that is a particular shape" (Captioned 49'23").

A "little hole of understanding" differentiates Sylvestre's concerns from Lazard's. The latter's captioning of Julia Child superimposes an ideological critique of how captions foreclose alternative meanings in the name of accessibility. Against Child's claim to make French cooking easier, Lazard makes its representation difficult to consume. Sylvestre's recaptioning focuses on her phenomenological encounter with the film, a record of reactions, asides, and associations. It shares some similarities with audio description provided for persons with sight impairment but focuses less on the details of what is on the screen than what those events trigger in her own mind. She understands the cartoonish nature of the film but often adds her own whimsical asides. When Jaffe jabs a pin in Lily's bottom to produce a scream, Sylvestre responds, "I feel like I'm watching a cartoon. The poor woman needs to get out of there." When that pin is ceremoniously displayed on a heart-shaped pin cushion as a memento of the scream's role in her acting career, Sylvestre's caption reads, "Seriously, the pin he stabbed you in the ass with?" When Jaffe turns away from Lily to utter a melodramatic speech, Sylvestre comments, astutely, "I hate people that don't look at me when they talk. In this scenario it seems like a power trip" (*Captioned* 24'54"). Such metacommentary brings out the gender dynamics of the film as rendered in visual terms—body language, movement, facial expression—that are always unacknowledged elements of conversation.

When I remarked that Sylvestre's captioning imposes an affective reading of the film in contrast to Lazard's more political version, I would amend that remark to say that her redirection of the plot back on her own reactions is in itself a political act. It calls attention to an alternate film hidden in the "talking film," one that implicates a deaf politics when captions are not supplied. The rapid repartee between characters in *Twentieth Century* effaces any hope of lipreading, leading to frustration: "The spaces between the words are gone. Rapid. Rabid. Rage." We have seen this expression of deaf rage earlier in Christine Sun Kim's Whitney installation where the absence of accommodations for DHOH persons is excoriated on the museum walls. Both Lazard and Sylvestre, in different ways, understand the power of film's visual information as what A. N. Whitehead calls prehension, a "lure for feeling" in the viewer (281). They also express impatience at the logic that presumes correspondence between caption and truth. By drawing on a highly stylized filmic genre, the screwball comedy, Sylvestre is able to undercut its overt comedy and create a film that maps her own role as participant observer.

Moments of Stillness: *Sound of Metal*

The recaptioning experiments of Christine Sun Kim, Carolyn Lazard, and Liza Sylvestre test the provisional nature of captions and the access they provide. Their work divides the viewer into several persons: one who hears the dialogue and one who reads the captions. The lack of sync between the two disorients transparency. The captions superimposed over the image are in a battle for intelligibility, offering an auto—and textual—critique of speech and sound. Who inhabits the space between visual and textual? In Darius Marder's 2021 film *Sound of Metal*, that space is occupied by a "hearer" who is subjected to the "sounds" and silences of metal. It is a film in which silence is as much the viewer's experience as it is that of the film's protagonist. One of the notable features of the film is that it is open captioned, meaning that the subtitles are burned onto the film, but there are significant moments of non-captioning that place the hearing viewer in close proximity to the film's protagonist.

Sound of Metal concerns a punk rock drummer, Ruben (Riz Ahmed), who loses his hearing and must confront the challenges this poses to his masculinity, his social and sexual relations, and, not insignificantly, his sobriety. While on a tour with his girlfriend, Lou (Olivia Cooke), his hearing suddenly drops out, and he becomes—understandably—angered and shaken, unable to process this volcanic change. The film mimics his hearing loss by cutting out the soundtrack from time to time, giving the film's listeners (and viewers) some sense of Ruben's disorientation.[16] Ruben and Lou are both recovering addicts, four years sober, for whom music and their relationship have been crucial for recovery. Now, Lou fears that Ruben will relapse as a consequence of hearing loss, and she works to place him in a sober-living community for deaf persons. The rehabilitation center is run by Joe (Paul Raci), a Vietnam War vet who grew up as a CODA (child of deaf adults) and who lost his own hearing in combat. Although Ruben initially repudiates his own deafness, he gradually comes to accept the support he receives and the version of tough love that Joe administers.

Despite his growing familiarity with sign language and the friendship he develops with the deaf rehab center, Ruben has not relinquished his desire to regain his hearing. He sells off his recording equipment and the big Airstream trailer that he and Lou used for their tours to raise money for a cochlear implant. After the operation, he returns to the sober-living community, hoping to continue living there, but Joe tells him that his decision may cure his hearing but not his mind. His continued presence at the farm would challenge the deaf protocols of the community by attempting to fix a condition that others do not deem a problem. What is important, Joe says, is to achieve a "moment of stillness" in which one is no longer trying to fix or remedy loss. Ruben sets out on his own, living for a time in a motel while his wounds, both physical and psychological, heal, and he contemplates his next move as a returning hearing person.

In the film's last act, Ruben flies to Paris to reunite with Lou, who is now living with her French father. It becomes clear that a former addict drummer was not exactly the father's idea of a perfect mate for his daughter, but he has changed his mind. He tells Ruben that ultimately, he had been good for her by helping her kick her habit. But the expected romantic denouement never happens. Ruben and Lou share an intimate moment, but both realize that there would be no going back to their erratic life on the road. Ruben is clearly out of his element in the bourgeois environment of Lou's father's home, his wealthy friends, and the French language. He finally leaves, and in the film's last scene, we see Ruben in a park staring ahead in a noisy urban soundscape. We don't know whether he will relinquish his cochlear implants for the deaf community (Joe has offered him a job as a teacher and counselor) or attempt to live as a hearing person. A church bell begins pealing, and Ruben takes out his implants, leaving the film with that extended, silent moment of stillness Joe imagined. The sound of metal—a church bell—rhymes with the first sound of the film—Lou's acoustic guitar—which bookend the movie, each iteration of metal promising very different ends.

Sound of Metal is, to all intents and purposes, a "silent film." Spoken dialogue is open captioned, and we often live inside Ruben's own soundless world. During the segment at the deaf rehab center, the members' sign language is not captioned, thereby instantiating Ruben's alienated—and perhaps the hearing viewer's own—perspective from Deaf World. To further the alienation effect of Ruben's hearing loss, director Marder and his sound designer, Nicolas Becker, created a soundscape that utilized Foley effects that replicate the mechanical output of cochlear implants. The thud of drums, muffled conversations, and the shrill electronic screeching of the implant itself occupy most of the soundtrack in the latter half. The film occasionally returns to what hearing persons might regard as "subjective sound," but it is entirely possible to watch the film without the soundtrack, filling in gaps in communication and providing one's own audio cues. Becker, who has experienced hearing loss, explains that as the film moves forward, "[subjective sound] becomes less and less strong. The more you go in the film, the more it comes back to typical levels. We come back to the kind of typical world that people know" (Reilly). Captioning in the film is erratic, translating spoken speech and sounds, but when ASL is signed, there is no captioning. Translation of sounds—"leaves rustling," "wind in grass," distorted chatter"—are minimal and often irritatingly intrusive.

In an interview with the filmmaker Alison O'Daniel, Marder refers to his sound perspective as "POH" or "point of hearing" ("The Noise Inside"). His inversion of the more familiar phrase, "point of view" reverses the usual ocularcentric treatment of film—"the gaze," the "camera eye," and the "viewer's perspective." What would happen if we viewed film from perspective of hearing—and *not* hearing? Of course, the term *hearer* implies an audist perspective, but Marder's film is also about the ideology of hearing and what it means to lose it. By adopting a "point of hearing," Marder redirects the gaze of the camera onto the soundscape and most importantly on the complex interplay of visual and acoustic information.

Ruben's hearing loss shifts that point of hearing onto other transformative aspects, most specifically his gendered and sexual relationships and perhaps his former addiction. In the opening scene, we see him in a hyper-masculine pose, bare chested, muscularly drumming at a frenetic pace. We see him going through his morning exercise routine, doing pushups and mixing health drinks, and when he loses his hearing, railing against soundlessness by smashing equipment, slamming his hand into walls, and shouting at Lou. Although it is never stated as such, he is of Middle Eastern descent, (the actor, Riz Ahmed, is Pakistani), and the otherness he experiences with hearing loss points up his alienation in both hearing and Anglo-centric worlds. Marder explained that when Riz Ahmed began to learn ASL, which utilizes facial and bodily expression, he had a momentary "shift of consciousness" when he "realized as a hearing person how guarded and locked inside we are" (O'Daniel "The

Noise Inside"). Being "locked inside" includes being contained as well by social attitudes about what it means to be masculine and a national subject.

Alison O'Daniel remarks on her experience as a hard-of hearing person watching the film without sound. She enjoyed the middle section of the film at the rehab center that is conducted primarily in ASL She used her knowledge of sign language to recognize the often humorous banter of conversations in sign, but when she turned on the sound, she was disappointed. "When I watched it with sound, it got in the way. I never would've caught that if I hadn't watched it again without sound" ("The Noise Inside"). In a sense, O'Daniel's silent viewing illustrates what the film's "point of hearing" might mean for multiple audiences. And as with Christine Sun Kim, Marder's film imagines distributed audiences, hearing and deaf and those in-between who must decode not only the film's visual language but it's acoustic language as well. Captions in the film occupy a middle ground between these two forms of language, a provisional space of access to meanings that exceed the words.

Missing Pictures

We have seen the pictures of our past, but the point is the caption.
—Vanessa Place, cover blurb, Robert Fitterman, *Holocaust Museum*

Thus far I have focused on films whose use of captions foregrounds the POH (point of hearing) that accompanies and frames visual media. By rearticulating the relationship between sound and sense, dialogue and its reception, these films make the problematic of hearing a central feature of plot. One could say the same for a number of recent films in which captioning and/or silence complicate film's presumptive reliance on sound as an adjunct of visual language: Zeinabu Irene Davis's *Compensation* (1999), Todd Haynes's *Wonderstruck* (2017), and John Krasinski's *A Quiet Place* (2018). In addition to offering an alternative to the sound-based film, these recent films reorient the relationship between sound and text, between the primordial "voice" that underwrites subjectivity and the distributed voice of media technology. As such, the recaptioning of films or, in the case of *Sound of Metal*, the silencing of sound, complicates the idea of captions as textual adjuncts to something else. This is not only a matter for film but, as my reference to Joseph Kosuth and conceptualism suggests, is a matter of the visual object itself, whether it may exist autonomously as an object or whether it is inscribed in discourses about it. And to return to my initial discussion, captioning errors, failures of translation, glitches in transduction bring to the surface the errant trajectories that thwart intention.

Vanessa Place's blurb for Robert Fitterman's *Holocaust Museum* that serves as my epigraph for this section summarizes the importance of descriptive captions in museums and exhibitions. Such explanatory commentaries offer historical, biographical, and thematic contexts for a painting or photograph, but they also limit and restrict what the viewer sees. Speaking of journalistic press images, Roland Barthes says that by explaining the image, the caption ultimately rationalizes and consumes it (15–31). Fitterman's book-length work consists of captions attached to photographs in the Holocaust Museum in Washington, DC. By omitting the image and displaying only the caption, Fitterman provides another answer to the question of what it means to write after Auschwitz. He implicitly ponders the problematics of summarizing materials in a museum memorializing Jews murdered in Nazi death camps. What possible descriptive device could explain or contextualize such images? Claude Lanzmann's answer in *Shoah* (1985) was not to display period photographs of the camps and their emaciated prisoners but to show contemporary interviews with survivors, local townspeople, and former guards. The focus in *Shoah* is the post hoc account of horror; Fitterman's solution is to make captions the point. For it is here in the institutional setting of a museum that the relationship between the desire to catalogue and describe meets the desire to exterminate and purify.

This chapter has been about captioning of verbal and sonic materials, but I want to extend the theme of "a captioned life" to include other kinds of captioning that promise clarification, elucidation, context. The museum, with its galleries, docent tours, special exhibits, and framing texts provides a space where the Holocaust can be recreated and memorialized through its excrescences—images, objects, documents. Fitterman's work must also be considered a museum, a recovery of material texts taken from the Holocaust Museum and displayed seriatim in a flat, impersonal rhetoric. Fitterman has selected only a small portion of the over eighteen thousand images in the museum's website. As Charles Bernstein says, "The absence of the images has a powerful effect, evoking the erasure of a people and a culture through the Systematic Extermination Process" ("This Picture" 36). Captions are divided into categories that are his own invention and not those of the museum. Of course, creating categories mimics the darker Nazi practice of enumerating and cataloguing—of clothing, teeth, shoes—that marks the horrific practices of the Final Solution. By keeping records, separating clothing and body parts, the human is erased and turned into an object.

Fitterman's captions maintain the museum's cataloguing imperative, however, by listing the photograph number and the image in stark, unadorned prose. In the section labeled "Jewelry," for instance:

Jewelry boxes made by prisoners at a Slovakian labor camp. [Photograph #72027] (79)

A female vendor offers jewelry, used clothing, and other items for sale on the street in the Warsaw ghetto [Photograph # 07528] (79)

Metal brooch designed in imitation of the ration card issued to Bela Bialer in the Lodz ghetto. [Photograph #N02815] (79)

The clinical descriptions of these stolen objects permit one to reflect on the close proximity of *jewelry* and *Jew*, a proximity that the Nazis exploited in demonizing Jewish wealth and by extracting gold from prisoners' teeth. Jews are reduced to things, their body parts, clothing, and accessories serving as cenotaphs. The same goes for a section devoted to the doors of gas chambers:

The door to the gas chamber in Dachau. It is marked "shower-bath." [Photograph #00276] (93)

Interior view of a gas chamber in the Mauthausen concentration camp. Original text reads: "This is the gas chamber, not how it looks like a shower room. Camp Mauthausen." [Photograph #23839] (93)

View of the door to the gas chamber at Dachau next to a large pile of uniforms. [Photograph #31327] (93)

A door to a gas chamber in Auschwitz. The note reads: Harmful gas! Entering endangers your life. [Photograph #14614] (93)

View [*sic*] a medical table used for removing gold teeth from prisoners at the Mauthausen concentration camp. Original caption reads: "This is the chamber where they knocked out gold teeth, after they were gassed by SS men." [Photograph #23836] (93)

Such descriptions are made all the more chilling by the inclusion of earlier captions added to the original photograph. These commentaries offer prior attempts at explaining the subject of the image from a much more engaged and empathetic respondent. Captions explain captions; "removing gold teeth" explains the caption included on an original photograph, "knocked out gold teeth," as if to provide a more neutral phrasing for the original caption's violent rhetoric.

The caption without its referent is a special kind of text. As Martin Glaz Serup says, "What happens to the caption when there is no longer a photograph to contextualize? When the caption is isolated it now refers to a referent that is no longer there" ("Captions without Images"). But of course, a photograph, by definition, is an image of a referent that is no longer there. The bare captions of Fitterman's book stand for the vertiginous problematic of representation itself, now shifted from the aesthetic to the sociopolitical sphere. Mimesis is joined to history in the most material way: through a book that refuses closure while exposing the attempt to memorialize through images. The inadequacy of representation in this case is perhaps the most accurate representation possible, reversing the parasitic relationship of text to image that Barthes finds in the "photographic message." The caption does not provide connotative information about the image—"to 'quicken' it with one or more second-order signifieds" (25). Rather, the caption denotes the condition of human erasure; the more accurate the description of bodies, objects, spaces, the more inaccurate its truth value.

It may seem that I have veered rather far from captioning errors, but in a way, *Holocaust Museum* illustrates an important strand of my concern. By signaling the impossibility of representing a source text—in this case a photograph—Fitterman's use of the Holocaust Museum's captions renders error as the main subject. Although this is a visual-textual example, it shares with other forms of sonic captioning the problem of original and supplement or, in Barthes's terms, denotated object and connotated commentary. But Barthes notes of the "photographic para-dox" "that here the connoted (or coded) message develops on the basis of a message *without a code*" (19). In terms of Fitterman's representation of the Holocaust, the absence of the code produces a reading of the historical record as a problematic of documentation itself. Denotation and connotation are imbricated in representing individuals who are not represented.

A Captioned Life

I want to return to my initial remarks about the use of voice-to-text soft-ware and what it has taught me about the "life" in my chapter title. In all my examples, captioning has been repurposed to render a life differently, whether to bring the life of a deaf viewer into perspective, as with Liza Sylvestre's, Carolyn Lazard's, and Darius Marder's films, or to exhibit how a life can be erased, as in Robert Fitterman's *Holocaust Museum*. Errors in captioning reveal the limits of human communication as a given and turn attention onto other portals of information. After a life of talk and audible conversation, I now conduct most of my social interaction via captioning, either through voice-recognition systems or through various forms of closed and open captioning on television, film, and on a captioning phone. And this shift is not simply an adaptation to information technologies but a reorientation of consciousness. What some might call a prosthesis becomes a component of the bodymind, just as the wheelchair for the person with a spinal cord injury becomes a component of the body.

In *Queer Phenomenology*, Sara Ahmed speaks of what happens when a person becomes disabled as a form of disorientation: "It is by under-standing how we become orientated in moments of disorientation that we might learn what it means to be oriented in the first place" (6). The presumption of oral conversation is challenged when rendered into text on a screen. The sight lines of conversation assume a greater importance when one needs to read lips. Disorientation produces a new awareness of what it means to be oriented in a hearing world, what expectations about human intercourse are taken for granted, and how those expectations marginalize others. In *Distressing Language*, I have used disorientation as a window onto various projects of meaning-making, my own and those of other artists and writers. It is a commonplace of modernist criticism to see the aesthetic as a mediation of the commonplace, the ordinary, the pre-reflective. The canonical terms for modernism—defamiliarization, alienation effect, estrangement—these are the disorientations by which the aesthetic body is supported, understood, and evaluated. A life in captions is another version of that mediated experience, now produced through a digital transfer of information with its inevitable glitches and errors.

In earlier work on poetry, I described the materiality of contemporary poems as a "palimtext" to stress the layered etiology of a poem, its historical and cultural sources, its evolution from notebook to chapbook to published poem to vocal recitation to mnemonic recreation.[17] I was inspired by looking at the notebooks and manuscripts of the poet George Oppen, who layered his revisions physically one on top of another using slips of paper and glue, the poem rising off the page as a midden of prior intentions. I saw the text as an archaeological dig into material forms and practices of which the final published version is only the latest sediment. Little did I realize that the palimtext would also describe the textualization of my own life, a life enriched by embracing error. Understanding the body of the text as a text of embodiment poses a new challenge for hermeneutics, forcing us as artists and critics to dig down into the matter of the body, hearing its distressing language as a kind of poetry.

Afterword

Redressing Language

I know words. I have the best words.
—Donald J. Trump

[E]rror . . . is the permanent chance around which the history of life and that of man develops.
—Michel Foucault

In this book, I have looked at the vicissitudes of error as a generative feature of art and literature, especially when it derives from conditions of bodily and sensory impairment. The arts of error in modernism—from Duchamp, Stein, and Dada to the aleatory compositions of Cage and Cunningham to the performances of Marina Abramović, Mary Duffy, and Karen Finley—offer new ways of thinking about what many might consider mistakes of grammar, harmony, logic, movement, and aesthetic purity. They also call into question the integrity of the body, its physical and psychic boundaries, its limits and capabilities. But error in art—Cézanne's violation of the retinal image mentioned in my introduction—is the very condition for modernist innovation, challenging the presumed integrity of a landscape by rendering it phenomenologically. "He [sic] is always astray in errancy," Heidegger's definition of being—dasein—also defines the modern artist who, in Keats's famous terms, lives in "uncertainties, mysteries, doubts without any irritable reaching after facts and reason."[1]

Artists and writers who live with a disability understand all too well what error means as it has been applied to those who, at least since Francis Bacon, have been described as "errors of nature."[2] They have used their experiences of complex embodiment to intervene into what society deems as natural, average, and self-evident. In Distressing Language, I have avoided separating disabled and nondisabled artists into discrete categories. I have done so to illuminate the aesthetic manifestations of error as a spectrum of capabilities across a wide range of projects and innovations. Surely it is time to remove the barrier that separates the "disabled artist" from the "artist." By placing the body at the center of this endeavor, I hope to explore the diverse manifestations of sensation and physical capability upon which the aesthetic relies. Aesthetics, as Terry Eagleton says, is "born as a discourse of the body" (13). When that body hears differently, speaks out of turn, moves in unconventional ways, new demands are placed on the generic categories by which cultural endeavor is defined. Error for the artists I discuss in this book is not a deviation on the bell curve but, as Foucault says in my epigraph, a "permanent chance around which the history of life" develops.

In my celebration of aesthetic error, I need to confront its more ominous implications in what some are calling a "post-truth" society.[3] In particular, what form does "truth" assume during a global health crisis such as the current COVID-19 pandemic? The issue is larger than health and epidemiology and concerns the very nature of truth as it has organized philosophical thought since the Enlightenment. As David Bates has written, "Philosophy begins to think about truth only when it arises as a problem" (vii). He goes on to emphasize how Enlightenment philosophers made error a key element in the pursuit of truth. For Locke, Condillac, d'Alembert, and others, truth is a goal, "not a possession," a destination to be pursued and searched out through rational inquiry and observation (ix). Progress is measured by the errors of judgment and proof left in its wake. In a passage that resonates with our concerns with disability and disease, Bates writes that "on the one hand, enlightenment is the cure for the 'disease' of irrationality, and on the other, enlightenment itself is the pathogen that must be combated with alternative concepts of truth and identity" (xi).

The skepticism about truth has been invigorated, if that is the proper term, by the current coronavirus pandemic and the rhetoric surrounding it. This rhetoric is not about finding a cure for a disease but about disputing its reality. For Donald Trump, the coronavirus pandemic was a phantom, produced by various enemies (China, Democratic governors, the Deep State) to frustrate his goals for power. When he was presented with scientific evidence about the virus's impact and the need for social distancing, he offered "alternate facts" that disputed data from scientists and epidemiologists, including representatives of the CDC and Department of Health and Human Services. Such detours from reality when turned into social policy had mortal consequences, as exemplified by the large numbers of infections that resulted from crowds who attended his rallies unmasked and packed into stands. As of this writing, COVID-19 has infected over forty million people in the United States and killed over six hundred thousand, with new spikes in infection reported daily. And yet on any given day for Trump, it was a "hoax," a carefully planned conspiracy, just another flu. At a rally, Trump claimed that "we are rounding the corner" on the coronavirus on the same day that the United States reported the highest infection rate since the beginning of the pandemic—a seven-day average of seventy-five thousand new cases. In a book called *Distressing Language*, it is important to apply my title to a world leader whose language is, to paraphrase William Burroughs, a "virus from outer space." The Trump era, as Janet McIntosh writes, "feels like a political emergency to many, but it also feels like a linguistic one" (1).

Diseases are disseminated by language as well as microbes. Paula Treichler, Cindy Patton, Douglas Crimp, and others said as much about the AIDS pandemic in the 1980s, recognizing that medical research for a cure was hampered by the Reagan administration and the Moral Majority's repeated insistence that the HIV virus was spread by "gay lifestyles":

> AIDS is not merely an invented label, provided to us by science and scientific naming practices, for a clear-cut disease entity caused by a virus. Rather, the very nature of AIDS is constructed through language and in particular through the discourses of medicine and science; this construction is "true" or "real" only in certain specific ways—for example, insofar as it successfully guides research or facilitates clinical control over the illness. (Treichler 11)

By speaking of truth "in certain ways," Treichler is not being a Trumpian relativist but a realist in thinking of how terms like *infection*, *sexual transmission*, and *virus* are spread by usage that infects policy decisions and social attitudes. "Sexual transmission," during the AIDS pandemic, was a shorthand for sexual acts among homosexual males, even though HIV transmission was also possible through infected blood transfusions and heterosexual contact.

What does error mean if there is nothing against which to measure it? Burroughs's strategy in *The Ticket That Exploded*, in which the virus metaphor appears, was to cut up or fold in passages from previous work, news reports, and advertising to detour mind control and Orwellian newspeak. Speaking of the strategies of the Nova police (as well as his own practice), Burroughs advises, "[Always] create as many insoluble conflicts as possible and always aggravate existing conflicts" (54–55). Burroughs's description could as easily describe disability activism such as the Capitol Crawl in support of the ADA, the Deaf President Now protests, and sit-ins in support of Section 504 of the Rehabilitation Act, in which deaf and disabled persons put their bodies on the line to disrupt normal functioning of institutions. Such activism becomes a model for many of the disabled artists I discuss in this book, where the boundary between politics and art dissolves. By distressing the language of power, they redressed its ability to shape the national discourse around ability.

Given what some have called "truth decay" during the Trump administration, my efforts in tracking error in poetry and art may be somewhat dated, a vestigial remnant of a time when truth claims could be tested, evaluated, and most important, *believed*. And it is significant that a good deal of this relativizing of truth is occurring around disease—a disability, after all—whose therapeutic is a "return to normalcy" at whatever cost. One early account of the relationship between disease and normalcy is provided by the philosopher of science and medicine Georges Canguilhem. In his major work, *The Normal and the Pathological* (1943), Canguilhem is critical of the pathologizing of disease—not because it doesn't exist but because it is imbricated in the biological reality of the human species.[4] As summarized by Rayna Rapp, for Canguilhem, "the choreography of normality and abnormality as mutually co-constitutive, the normative depending in large measure on the pathological, the outlawed, and the despised instance for its very taxonomic foundation" (469). Canguilhem's most sustained discussion of biological error occurs at the end of his book, where he complicates the presumed opposition of his titular terms as they apply to disease:

Disease is not a fall that one has, an attack to which one succumbs, but an original flaw in macromolecular form. If, in principle, organization is a kind of language, the genetically determined disease is no longer a mischievous curse but a misunderstanding. (279)

Canguilhem inverts the theological definition of error—a fall from grace—by locating it in the *bios*, in the molecular composition of the organism. Most significant for my concerns is his description of biological anomalies as "misunderstandings" within the structure of language. Canguilhem is speaking here of hereditary diseases such as sickle-cell anemia or hemophilia, but his view could be applied to any anomaly as a variation in bodily functioning. Biological norms are not fixed by a standard that identifies variants within a population but are created as a relationship between bodies and environments, a relationship of capabilities not of limits. Deviations from a standard become pathologies, errors that can be studied and categorized. What is "normal" is, in fact, the existence of error.

Canguilhem anticipates the social model of disability by understanding anomalies as defined by barriers and obstacles. Instead of seeing disease as a pathology, he understands it as a difference: "An anomaly is a fact of individual variation which prevents two beings from being able to take the place of each other completely" (137). As Stephen Talcott summarizes, "Canguilhem locates this distinction [between normal and pathological] in the living experiences of impotence before obstacles." To speak of a disease as a "misunderstanding" may be of little solace to the person living with—and dying from—COVID-19, but it is a way of removing the moral distinctions that philosophers and social scientists from Descartes to Durkheim have used to describe biological error. On the other hand, by seeing error as a constituent feature—indeed, the creator—of norms, much of the moral opprobrium surrounding disease is challenged.

It may seem that in contrasting Trumpian "alternate facts" with Canguilhem's error, I have confused a rhetoric of political opportunism with one of epistemology. For Trump, COVID-19 was and is a social reality he must hide and repudiate because it was inconvenient for his hold on power. For Canguilhem, disease is an anomaly, a difference that proves the norm: "Normativity, in the fullest sense of the word, is that which establishes norms" (126–27). Critical disability studies, occasionally with Canguilhem as source, has mounted a strong critique of the idea of an embodied norm, understanding it as a discursive system that underwrites compulsory able-bodiedness. Making this fact visible has been the project of many of the artists I discuss in this book, but it may be the province of much aesthetic practice in general. This may explain why I began with Duchamp, hardly an advocate for disability rights, whose treatment of error and chance foregrounds quotidian mutability into the creative process. Or rather, he takes the "risk" of error as a given in his transformation of aesthetic discourse.

The dire prophecies of a post-truth era, where all values seem knocked into the proverbial cocked hat, must be historicized as the products of a specific regime and person. But that person is a symptom—a function—of a much larger crisis of legitimation. More broadly, such a condition may be the result of a technological revolution in which increased access through the internet and social media and other digital platforms have neutralized information and created a vastly expanded public sphere of competing voices. Speech that bullies, infantilizes, threatens, shames, and invades privacy deadens the kinds of debate that Habermas felt was possible outside of—and resistant to—the state. Is freedom of speech possible when "speech" itself is in scare quotes, no longer tied to a speaker but to an algorithm or formula? In *Distressing Language*, I have occasionally referred to "distributed voicing" as a description of those voices clamoring for attention and validation. On the positive side, distribution carries with it an ideal of shared experience and dialogue, a democratization of voicing instead of the bullying pulpit. To distress and displace that voice becomes an imperative in much contemporary cultural production, but it is also a social imperative to recognize our interdependent and intersected identities, marking temporal movement through verbal echolocation rather than a Google map. When the voice is displaced from what is most familiar—in sign language poetry, in re-captioned film, in stammering, in textual appropriation and erasure—it may be revealed as the product, not the source, of systems of power.

ACKNOWLEDGMENTS

I subscribe to the Ancient Mariner theory of research, which is when you can't stop telling your tale of distressing language to anyone willing to listen. A book is not an albatross, but it does tend to hang about one's consciousness as a reminder of what you haven't read or considered. I have been fortunate in my listeners during the writing of this book, all of whom responded generously to portions of chapters and curtailed my more extravagant claims. First and foremost, I want to acknowledge the help and support I've gained from Peter Middleton, to whom this book is dedicated. He read and provided extensive commentary on many drafts and served as a vital sounding board for every aspect of my research. His own work on contemporary poetry, neurodiversity, hearing loss, and philosophy has been an invaluable resource. I also want to thank two former students and now good friends who helped launch this project. Corrine Fitzpatrick introduced me to the work of Christine Sun Kim many years ago, having worked with the artist on several projects. Amanda Cachia asked me to write a catalogue entry for her *Loud Silence* exhibition, through which I discovered the work of Alison O'Daniel and other deaf and disability artists. Amanda's PhD dissertation, which I read as a member of her graduate committee, remains one of the best introductions to disability arts.

Several of the poets and artists discussed in this book provided me with valuable commentary about their work and made images available for publication. Special thanks are extended to Alison O'Daniel, Christine Sun Kim, Catherine Yass, Bob Perelman, Charles Bernstein, Norma Cole, Joseph Grigely, Jena Osman, Liza Sylvestre, and Carolyn Bergvall. I could not have continued with this project without the input and support from friends in the disability and deaf studies community, especially Stuart Murray, Rosemarie Garland-Thomson, Rebecca Sanchez, Chris Krentz, Declan Gould, Joseph Straus, Jason Farr, Jeff Brune, Sarah Hayden, Maren Linnet, and Michael Bérubé. Special thanks to James

Berger for his conversations about related issues and whose book, *The Disarticulate*, has been a model for me in thinking about distressed language. My former colleague Carol Padden has been a wonderful friend and supporter who has generously helped me transition into life as a deaf academic. I am grateful as well to Anna Tucker, my faithful tutor, who has exhibited great patience in my achingly slow progress in ASL.

Conversations with colleagues at UCSD contributed, in various informal ways, to the writing of this book. Thanks to Charles Curtis, Ari Heinrich, Sheldon Nodelman, Susan Smith, Amelia Glaser, Meg Wesling, David Serlin, Page DuBois, Brian Goldfarb, Peggy Lott, Seth Lerer, and numerous graduate students who organized events through the Transdisciplinary Disability Studies program, especially Rachel Fox, Jenni Marchisotto, Cassandra Hartleby, Sean Compas, and Bias Collins. Other friends and colleagues who provided information about specific issues include Steven Connor, Rachel Blau duPlessis, John Daley, George Hart, Dee Morris, Rachel Kolb, Nina Eidsheim, Jessica Luck, Craig Dworkin, Gerald Shea, and Sarah Hayden. A big shout out to Thibault Duchemin and Pieter Doevendans, the cofounders of the dictation service Ava, who have answered many questions about natural language processing and whose app has been a communication godsend.

Portions of *Distressing Language* were delivered as talks or panel presentations, for which thanks go to the following organizers: Chris Krentz at the University of Virginia; Anne Ellegood at the Hammer Museum in Los Angeles; Yin Wang of the National Cheng Kung University, Taiwan; Ariel Resnikoff and Orchid Tierney at the Kelly Writers House at the University of Pennsylvania; Walt Hunter for his panel at the ASAP Convention in Oakland, "Situating Formalism"; Cassandra Hartleby for organizing a panel on "Deaf/Disability Studies" at the University of California, San Diego; Jessica Luck for convening a panel at the "Disability as Spectacle" conference at UCLA on "Disability Poetics and/As Spectacle"; Declan Gould and Judith Goldman at the University of Buffalo.

A version of chapter 2, "Siting Sound," appeared in the *Journal of Literary and Cultural Disability Studies*, vol. 15, no. 2, 2021. Thanks to Chris Krentz and Rebecca Sanchez who co-edited this special issue on deaf studies. A version of chapter 5, "Diverting Language: Jena Osman's Corporate Subject," appeared in *The Fate of Difficulty in the Poetry of Our*

Time. Thanks to co-editors, Charles Altieri and Nicholas D. Nace, for including it and to Northwestern University Press for publishing it.

My editors at NYU Press have been uniformly helpful and supportive. Special thanks to Eric Zinner for his interest in the book and Furqan Sayeed for seeing this book through its various stages of publication. I much appreciate the close attention to the book's production by Martin Coleman and my copyeditor, Richard Felt. I am especially grateful to Michael Bérubé, co-editor of the Crip: New Directions in Disability Studies series, for endorsing this project from the outset. I received two helpful readers' reports, one anonymous and the other by Jonathan Sterne. I am grateful to both for helping me see this book as a book.

Last and not least, thanks to my family—my wife, Lori, our children, Ryder and Sophie, and our grandson, Shiloh, whose love and support continue to sustain and enrich my life.

NOTES

INTRODUCTION

1 On "narrative prosthesis," see Mitchell and Snyder.

2 Seth Lerer provides a thorough overview of error in philology, rhetoric, and academic life in *Error and the Academic Self*.

3 Fashion distressing might be an example of what Raymond Williams characterizes as the "residual" aspect of cultural formation, what has "been effectively formed in the past but is still active in the cultural process" (22). Frederic Jameson has drawn on Williams to describe the "retro" phenomenon of much postmodern culture.

4 Mike Rowe of the Discovery Channel's *Dirty Jobs* show notes in a Facebook post that distressed jeans "foster the illusion of work. The illusion of effort . . . . They're a costume for wealthy people who see work as ironic." www.theguardian.com.

5 I adopt the practice among many disability theorists who use the term *bodymind* to recognize the coexistence of cognitive and physiological features. As Margaret Price says, conventional usage tends to separate "body" and "mind" but that for persons with disabilities, especially mental disabilities, "our problems are in no sense 'all in our minds'" (240).

6 I discuss Williamson's work in *Concerto for the Left Hand* 80–99.

7 Michele Friedner, drawing on Foucault's biopower and Paul Rabinow's biosociality, argues that small-*d* or biological deafness may be a "ticket of entry into the Deaf community." She does not see lower-and-upper-case-d/Deafness as mutually exclusive but mutually constitutive insofar as the constraints, medical and institutional, that have produced a strictly medical definition of deafness also produce the conditions for new forms of community, alliances, and solidarity. See Friedner's "Biopower, Biosocialtiy, and Community Formation."

8 On the application of ASL to modern and contemporary poetry, see Bauman.

9 "One the one hand, the phonic element, the term, the plentitude that is called sensible, would not appear as such without the difference or opposition which gives them *form* . . . *The (pure) trace is différance*. It does not depend on any sensible plentitude, audible or visible, phonic or graphic. It is, on the contrary, the condition of such a plentitude." Derrida, *Grammatology* 62.

10 Jane Bennett speaks in a related manner of "distributive agency" that fuses human and nonhuman materialities: "A theory of distributive agency . . . does not posit a subject as the root cause of an effect. There are instead always a swarm of vitalities

at play. The task becomes to identify the contours of the swarm and the kind of relations that obtain between its bits" (31–32). My version of distributed voicing obviously differs from Bennett's by locating distribution among or between subjects, but I am influenced by her theory to extend "voicing" to nonhuman objects.

11 Briankle Chang, speaking in the context of communication theory, provides another formulation of inner speech: "As the picture on the cover of [Derrida's] *The Post Card* illustrates there is always someone speaking behind one's back; there is always more than one voice speaking at the same time, so that one can no longer be sure what the message is or who is speaking to whom" (209).

12 On *Boomerang*, see Eidsheim, *Sensing Sound* 95–101. See also Wagner 59–80.

13 Krauss 50–64.

14 Krauss acknowledges that *Boomerang* has a critical function as a form of video art that "exploit(s) the medium in order to criticize it from within" (59). Maybe so, but she does not provide a further possibility that it is a use of video to criticize normative attitudes toward language and communication.

15 When that voice is mediated by and through disability, it is, in the words of disability media scholars, "dismediated" or "biomediated" as a way of describing the co-constitution of the different body through media. On biomediation, see Hagood; on "dismediation," see Mills and Sterne.

16 *Invalid Modernism* 159–66.

17 Patricia Parker disputes the common linkage of catachresis and metaphor, noting that in early rhetoricians like Quintilian, the former refers to "the practice of adapting the nearest available term to describe something for which no actual [i.e., proper] term exists" (60). Metaphor, in Parker's terms, involves "a transfer or substitution employed when a proper term does already exist and is displaced by a term transferred from another place to a place not its own" (60). In these terms, catachresis more properly defines the kinds of substitutions that appear as errors.

18 "The identity of words—the simple, fundamental fact of language, that there are fewer terms of designation than there are things to designate—is itself a two-sided experience: it reveals words as the unexpected meeting place of the most distant figures of reality" (*Death and the Labyrinth* 14).

19 In her entry "Deafness" in *Keywords in Sound*, Mara Mills notes that deafness exists on a spectrum—"deafnesses"—that complicates the usual binary deaf/hearing. The history of deaf communication "makes clear that sound is always already multimodal" and that although considerations of deafness have "yet to become a regular feature of sound studies deaf and hard of hearing people have long testified to the heterogeneity of ear-listening" (52).

20 For an excellent overview of the relationship of deaf and sound studies, see Friedner and Helmreich.

21 This is a major theme in Eidsheim's *The Race of Sound*.

22 Jack Spicer in "A Textbook of Poetry," the third book of *Heads of the Town, up to the Aether* (1960): "No, now he is the Lowghost when He is pinned down to words" (308).

1. POETICS OF MISHEARING

Epigraphs: Steven Connor, "Earslips"; Bob Perelman, *Essay on Style* 13.

1 Tzvetan Todorov notes that when Columbus encountered the Taino people in October of 1492, he mistook their word *cariba* (a word for the inhabitants of the Caribbean islands) for the caniba or the people of China (the Great Khan) that he expected to find there. A misheard syllable becomes a New World for some and a displacement for others (30).

2 K. Mar Hauksson, "Miscommunication Costs Norwegian His life," https://www.icenews.is.

3 *The Guardian*, 21 September 2017. www.theguardian.com. See also Sanchez.

4 The film alludes to an earlier period in 1915 when William Mulholland, the source of the Mulwray character, built an aqueduct to divert water from the Owens Valley to Los Angeles. The film also refers to the failure of another of Mulholland's projects, the St. Francis Dam in 1928, that flooded poor and Latinx communities in Los Angeles.

5 On Duncan's relationship to de Angulo, see Fass 283. Also see Duncan's interview with Bob Callahan in the pamphlet *the Netzahualcoyotl News*, Summer, 1979.

6 On error in Duncan, see Reynolds.

7 Peter Middleton, "Inner Listening," unpublished paper.

8 Email correspondence, 20 November 2017.

9 Ibid.

10 Wright is an unapologetic oralist, having learned to read lips and to speak after losing his hearing at age seven and having been educated in oral schools in England. His autobiography, *Deafness*, is a strong endorsement for lipreading, but it is unfortunately rather critical of Deaf culture and sign language.

11 Remark made at her poetry reading at University of California, San Diego, 1995.

12 © 2002 by The Regents of the University of California. Published by the University of California Press.

13 Bush's claim to lipread truth turned out to be ironic, since in 1990, he passed a bill that included raising taxes.

14 I am grateful to Jessica Luck for alerting me to "Bad Lip Reading" videos.

15 In a *Rolling Stone* interview with Tim Dickinson, the anonymous producer said that he became interested in lip reading when his mother, then in her forties, lost her hearing. "BLR marveled at the way his mom, of necessity, became an expert lip reader. He would sometimes sit around at night, watching TV with the sound off trying to pick up the skill himself. I was terrible at it." Tim Dickinson, "Exclusive: The Bad Lip Reader Speaks." www.rollingstone.com.

16 Ibid.

17 Ibid.

18 It is appropriate that the one deaf character in *Ulysses* appears in the chapter "Sirens," whose organ is the ear and whose art is music. For a full discussion of blindness and deafness in the novel, see Linett, *Bodies of Modernism* 119–21.

2. SITING SOUND

Epigraph: Larry Eigner, 140.

1 This is a standard seating format at many deaf institutions and events. Classrooms at Gallaudet University, the only institution of higher education for deaf students, are arranged in a U-shape to facilitate visual conversation.

2 In his entry "Space" in *Keywords in Sound*, Andres J. Eisenberg provides a synoptic survey of the ways that sound and space are linked. Sara Hendren, an artist and design researcher, describes the architectural setting at Gallaudet University as an example of DeafSpace, a design principle that governs the organization of common rooms, furniture, hallways, doorways, and almost every aspect of the lived environment around individuals using sight for communication. See her chapter "Room" in *What Can a Body Do?*

3 Brenda Brueggemann has described this conference, which I also attended, and its goals in *Deaf Subjects* 47–53. Many of the issues raised at the conference are covered in Bauman et al.

4 Cook has put his suggestion into practice in segments featuring him in Judy Lieff's video documentary *Deaf Jam*. Signing his poetry, Cook pulls words out of the air and throws them into space.

5 I discuss Evgen Bavcar's work in chapter 6 of *Concerto for the Left Hand*.

6 The original French title, *Le Partage du sensible*, suggests a sharing, rather than a partition, of the senses.

7 On Bell and deafness, see Brueggemann *Deaf Subjects* and Sterne *The Audible Past*. For a thorough study of Bell's problematic relationship to deaf persons see Katie Booth, *The Invention of Miracles: Language, Power, and Alexander Graham Bell's Quest to End Deafness*.

8 © Christian Marclay, courtesy White Cube, and Fraenkel Gallery, San Francisco.

9 I have discussed the "tapevoice" in "Technologies of Presence Orality and the Tapevoice of Contemporary Poetics" (*Ghostlier Demarcations*).

10 Language writing would seem to offer the most overt challenge to the self-present voice, as would experimentation in digital poetry.

11 Rebecca Sanchez discusses relationships between deaf persons and their interpreters on very much this point. She notes the "peculiar intimacies that emerge when one engages another human as a prosthetic voice" ("Creating Shared Spaces").

12 Brenda Brueggemann, in chapter 1 of *Deaf Subjects*, has usefully adapted the work of Donna Haraway to describe this interstitial condition of deaf users of technology as that of a "deaf cyborg."

13 "Christine Sun Kim, a Selby Film."

14 "Christine Sun Kim, a Selby Film."

15 It has become obligatory for writers on issues of deafness to distinguish between small-*d* deafness (the audiological condition) and capital-*D* Deaf culture, sometimes expressed by a slash: d/Deaf. I prefer to use the small *d* most of the time to

represent both contexts, feeling that one cannot separate the physiological fact of deafness from the meanings society imposes upon it. But when I am addressing the cultural meaning of deafness—deafness as community—I then use the capital *D*.

16 On sound in deaf poetry, see Davidson "Hearing Things."

17 As Joseph Strauss says, "Hearing does not necessarily involve a one-to-one mapping of sense perceptions onto a single sensory organ; rather, hearing can be a much more multi-sensory experience" (*Extraordinary Measures* 167).

18 © 2015 MoMA PS1; Photo Pablo Enriquez.

19 Cf. Emily McDermott, "The Aural Artist," in *Interview Magazine* for one such account.

20 The emphasis on redirecting the sound sphere challenges the commonality of the public sphere as defined by philosophers from Plato to Habermas and Rancière. Habermas's public sphere, in which conversation produces a social space different from the state, is now established on a spectrum between deaf artist and hearing audience, not to alienate one from the other but to see sound through different eyes.

21 Credit: MASS MoCA.

22 Kim discusses the process of creating *Close Readings* in an interview with Jeppe Ugelvig O ("Sonic Identity Politics").

23 Credit: Conrado Johns.

24 On Kim's use of notation, see Holmes 196–99.

25 Credit unknown.

26 Credit: Erica Leone.

27 Credit: Erica Leone.

28 Credit: White Space Beijing and Yang Hao 杨灏 (capital d).

3. MISSPEAKING POETICS

1 Cheney's claim was, in fact, a link in what the philosopher Hilary Putnam calls a "chain of authentication" that relied on links between Vice President Cheney, National Security Advisor Condoleezza Rice, and Secretary of State Colin Powell, along with various foreign leaders. What Adam Hodges calls the "symbolic power" of the presidency—in this case George W. Bush—was buttressed by affirmations from others who supported his final claim of links between Saddam Hussein and Osama bin Laden (61–62).

2 I have somewhat distorted Louis Althusser's formulation of "internal distance" in art that he, drawing on Pierre Machery, describes as the way that art "presupposes a *retreat*, an *internal distantiation* from the very ideology from which their novels [Balzac and Solzhenitsyn are his examples] emerged. They make us 'perceive' (but not know) in some sense *from the inside*, by an *internal distance*, the very ideology in which they are held" (222–23).

3 Cole, "SPEECH PRODUCTION: Themes and Variations" (*Beauty Is a Verb* 261). "Speech Production" also appears in Cole's collection *Natural Light*.

4 Cole says that the books she displayed in the "Living Room" were all published before 1960. Email conversation, 30 January 2019.

5 Norma Cole, author statement on *Collective Memory* (unpublished).

6 Jennifer Bartlett, "Preface," *Beauty Is a Verb* 15.

7 Email correspondence, 24 January 2019.

8 "'Our ways of making nonsense will depend upon our ways of making common sense', writes Susan Stewart (1979: viii); 'the nature of nonsense will always be contingent upon the nature of its corresponding common sense'" (qtd. in McHale 7).

9 He poses as Humpty Dumpty, who says, contra Alice, "When I use a word . . . it means just what I choose it to mean—neither more nor less."

10 Bergvall, "Overview." *Say, "Parsley."* www.carolinebergvall.com.

11 Jacques Derrida summarizes the spatial and verbal implications of the term: "[The Ephraimites] were known for their inability to pronounce correctly the *shi* of *shibboleth*, which became for them, in consequence, an *unpronounceable name*. They said *shibboleth*, and at the invisible border between *shi* and *si*, betrayed themselves to the sentimental at the risk of their life. They betrayed their difference by showing themselves indifferent to the diacritical difference between *shi* and *si*; they marked themselves with their inability to re-mark a mark thus coded" (*Sovereignties in Question* 22–23).

12 "2 Stopped for Speaking Spanish Sue U.S." *The New York Times*, Sunday, 17 February 2019, National, p. 26.

13 Celan invokes the shibboleth in another poem, "In Eins" (1962), which features some of the same language: "Im Herzmund / erwachtes Schibboleth," adding to "shibboleth's" references to Viennese workers movement and Spanish Republic, a reference to 13 February 1962 memorializing "Peuple / de Paris" who demonstrated against the OAS.

14 Image credit: © Doris Salcedo / Photo © Tate.

15 The shibboleth is an example of what some are calling "biological citizenship," the biological presuppositions that often determine national belonging. As Nikolas Rose and Carlos Nova say, "Histories of the idea of race, degeneracy, and eugenics, and those of demography and the census, show how many citizenship projects were framed in biological terms; in terms of race, blood lines, stock, intelligence, and so forth" (440).

16 See her description of the installation at www.carolinebergvall.com.

17 Shell's book, *Stutter*, chronicles a large number of persons with a stammer—from Moses and Hamlet to Marilyn Monroe and James Earl Jones.

18 In several readings available on YouTube, Scott reads from *Blert* with only an occasional pause or stammer, but for the most part, he reads without hesitation.

19 Scott's reference to the swallow may conjure the mythological figure of Procne in Eliot's *The Waste Land*, who is transformed into a swallow after serving her son as a meal to her husband, Tereus. She is reacting to the rape of her sister, Philomela, whose tongue is cut out to prevent her from revealing her rape by Tereus. The

swallow's call as an alternative form of expression is referenced in James Drake's installation *Tongue-Cut Sparrows*. In this work, the artist displayed video projections of three women relatives of prisoners in an El Paso jail standing on a sidewalk across from the prison using home-made sign language to communicate with their loved ones inside. I am grateful to Adelaide Morris for alerting me to Drake's 1998 installation at Artpace, San Antonio, Texas. www.artpace.org.

20 Roman Jakobson's well-known 1956 study of aphasic disorders makes a similar point—that speech disturbances expose "new insights into the general laws of language" (96). Out of his distinction between similarity and contiguity disorders among aphasics, he is able to develop a general theory of tropes like metaphor and metonymy. On the larger implications of this for modernism, see Berger 231–35.

21 Lawrence Abu Hamdan, *Conflicted Phonemes*, 2012. Exhibition view: Lawrence Abu Hamdan. *The Voice before the Law*, Hamburger Bahnhof—Museum für Gegenwart, Berlin, 2019. © Lawrence Abu Hamdan, courtesy Maureen Paley, London / Staatliche Museen zu Berlin, Nationalgalerie, Baloise Group / Mathias Völzke.

22 Stevens, "The Idea of Order at Key West."

4. "TONGUE-TIED AND / MUSCLE / BOUND"

Epigraph: Larry Eigner, *The Collected Poems of Larry Eigner*. Subsequent references to Eigner's poetry are based on this edition. Pagination is sequential throughout all four volumes. Used by permission of the publisher, Stanford University Press. In quoting Eigner's poems I have retained the poet's favored Courier typewriter font.

1 Ferris, "The Enjambed Body." Ferris's essay from 2004 is one of the first attempts to study representations of embodiment and disability in poetry. More importantly, he uses his own body and shorter left leg to discuss prosodic terms like *enjambment* as they derive from bodily metaphors.

2 David Mitchell and Sharon Snyder provide a similar formulation. Speaking of their book *The Biopolitics of Disability*, they say that it "attempts to push all the way through the sleeve of impairment to explore how disability subjectivities are not just characterized by socially imposed restrictions, but, in fact, productively create new forms of embodied knowledge and collective consciousness" (2).

3 This emphasis featured centrally in reviews of the Stanford four-volume *Collected Poems*, which features typeface based on Eigner's own Courier font from his 1940 Royal typewriter. In a generous selection from the Stanford edition, *Calligraphy Typewriters*, the editors continue this graphic convention and include as a frontispiece a photograph of Eigner's typewriter. I have written about Eigner's typewritten page in "Missing Larry" in *Concerto for the Left Hand* 116–41.

4 Jessica Luck in "Larry Eigner and the Phenomenology of Projected Verse" provides an excellent reading of Eigner's relationship to Olson's projectivism. She notes that "Eigner usefully highlights some tensions in 'Projective Verse' between Olson's emphasis on the ear and speech and a more multisensory, often visual notion of an open-field poetics" (467). She shows how the essay leans towards ob-

jectivism in its emphasis on word as thing. The word should be "shaped as wood can be when a man has his hand to it" (Olson qtd. 467).

5 Robert Grenier notes that when Eigner moved into his Berkeley home, he ate communally with several other family members, which initially caused problems. "Larry learned not to monologue (when he 'spoke') and not to *only be silent* (whereas he had been conditioned to 'listen' / 'stop speaking'), but to *Participate* in what was being said, by talking and listening" (*Collected Poems* 1350).

6 In his chapter on Eigner, "The Eigner Sanction," in *Narrowcast*, Lytle Shaw coins the term *slow time*.

7 As Alison Kafer summarizes, "Crip time emerges here as a wry reference to the disability-related events that always seem to start late or to the disabled people who never seem to arrive anywhere on time" (*Feminist, Queer, Crip* 26).

8 Watten, "Missing 'X,'"; Luck, "Larry Eigner."

9 Dust jacket note for Eigner's *Another Time in Fragments*.

10 "Inner speech" is most often associated with the work of Lev Vygotsky. In *Thought and Language*, he is critical of Piaget's theories of the inherent egocentrism of childhood language and posits that the earliest speech of the child is social, that private speech derives from social speech.

11 The concept of inner speech is anticipated in Merleau-Ponty's *The Phenomenology of Perception* in the chapter on "The Body as Expression and Speech." "Thought is no 'internal' thing and does not exist independently of the world and of words. What misleads us in this connection and causes us to believe in a thought which exists for itself prior to expression, is thought already constituted and expressed, which we can silently recall to ourselves and through which we acquire the illusion of an inner life. But in reality this supposed silence is alive with words, this inner life is an inner language" (183).

12 See Volosinov, *Marxism and the Philosophy of Language*.

13 John Hendrickson, "What Biden Can't Bring Himself to Say." *The Atlantic* (January/February 2020). www.theatlantic.com.

5. DIVERTING LANGUAGE

1 Louis Zukofsky in "An Objective" defines *predatory intent* thus: "An idea—not an empty concept. An idea—its value including its meaning. The desk, i.e. as object including its value—The object unrelated to palpable or predatory intent" (16).

2 On Laurie Anderson's version of Longfellow, see Fredman 83–99.

3 The poem's rather flat, legalistic prose describes the various ways in which corporations can be analogized to persons. Such analogical thinking, as Osman says in a note at the end of *Corporate Relations*, "reanimates age-old ideas of a mind-body split" and instantiates modernist ideas of the body as a machine (73).

4 An earlier version of this chapter appears in this volume.

5 Much of the failure of the defense by the solicitor general's office rested with the claim that under McCain-Feingold, Congress could ban not only television

advertisements but books as well. Samuel Alito seized on this claim, asking the solicitor general, Malcolm Stewart, whether the publication of a campaign biography during an election season could also be banned. Stewart admitted that if the book advocated for a particular candidate, the government could criminalize it. Thus the conservative majority showed how the denial of Citizens United's right to broadcast *Hillary: The Movie* was tantamount to governmental censorship. On Chief Justice John Roberts's influence over the *Citizens United* case, see Jeffrey Toobin, "Money Unlimited," *The New Yorker*, 21 May 2012, 36–47.

6 This is a very different perspective from Robert Lowell's memorializing of the monument to Robert Gould Shaw in "For the Union Dead," a public art that "sticks like a fishbone / in the city's throat" (Lowell 136).

6. MISSING MUSIC

Epiraph: Alison O'Daniel, "Generative Misunderstanding," interview with Anne Ellegood.

1 My section title comes from Michael Palmer's 1977 book, *Without Music*, inspired by Philip Glass's memoir, *Words without Music*. Poems in the volume also refer to collaborations between the poet and the choreographer and dancer Margaret Jenkins and her company, who often danced without music or to Palmer's texts. Schönberg is quoted in Szendy 127.

2 I discuss these aspects in "Cleavings," in *Concerto for the Left Hand*.

3 Small defines musicking in the infinitive: "To music is to take part, in any capacity, in a musical performance, whether by performing, by listening, by rehearsing or practicing, by providing material for performance (what is called composing), or by dancing" (108).

4 On music within the Deaf community, see Jones "Imagined Hearing." She focuses on the work of the rock band Beethoven's Nightmare and the rappers Sean Forbes and Signmark. I would also mention Anna Mae Lentz's poem "Eye Music," which describes her love of music even though she is deaf. Using an expressive display of ASL, she signs her memories of driving trips with her parents when younger, watching the movement of telephone lines from her parents' car that mimic the lines of a musical stanza. Her signing compares the rhythmic movement of the lines as the car moves forward to various instruments. The same is true of Patrick Greybill's "Paradox," which represents his memory of seeing a black singer singing a blues song while being accompanied by a pianist, the poet's hands imitating the rhythm of the piano while signing the lyrics of the song "Where Is the Man I Love."

5 My examples in this chapter are taken largely from the Western compositional tradition, but a much more comprehensive case could be made about musical value by looking at improvisation in jazz or the role of dance in the music of indigenous peoples. On the role of "Motion and Feeling through Music," see Keil and Feld. I might also add Nathaniel Mackey's epic prose work *From a Broken*

Bottle Traces of Perfume Still Emanate, an epistolary novel based on members of a jazz group, the Mystic Horn Society, whose conversations about various jazz performances, performers, and innovations constitute the closest thing to a textualized music—what one might call "musical ekphrasis"—that I know.

6 Although it is associated with Romanticism, the harp's antecedents would include classical and biblical references—Hermes's invention of the lyre upon hearing the wind playing across string stretched across a tortoise shell, King David's harp that, as described by Thomas Hankins and Robert Silverman, "sang in the wind when he hung it before his tent at night" (89). Hankins and Silverman's account of the aeolian harp in *Instruments and the Imagination* is the best account of the instrument's various cultural meanings. I am grateful to Joseph Sterne for alerting me to their chapter.

7 Catherine Yass comments on the means of the piano's suspension: "The piano was suspended from a number of materials. First there were flat yellow cords to prevent damage to the piano. Once they were clear the cords were connected to four chains. The four chains came together and were suspended from a giant hook, which was in turn suspended from the crane by a thick metal cable or wire. The piano was suspended from four points to keep it level. The pair of yellow cords wrapped round underneath the piano emerging at the four points." Email correspondence, 9 September 2020.

8 Email correspondence, 23 November 2018.

9 Credit: Catherine Yass.

10 Paul Carter refers to this as a "communicational contract that listening implies" ("Ambiguous Traces" 44).

11 O'Daniel comments on the subsequent events following the thefts: "The schools have been able to replace them depending often on community support to raise money and sometimes they just go without tubas or use donated, beat up ones. At Centennial HS—the school I have collaborated with the most—Kendrick Lamar, an alum, replaced their stolen tubas with beautiful new ones." Email correspondence, 27 December 2017.

12 Sam Quinones, who covered the thefts for the *LA Times*, felt that tubas were selected because of their importance in the Mexican banda industry, both in Los Angeles and in Mexico, in which the tuba is a primary—and costly—instrument. http://articles.latimes.com.

13 Credit: Mina Singh.

14 A corollary issue in thinking about 4′33″ and its relationship to an audience is the degree to which O'Daniel's version is a "performance" of it. Since she appropriates it in a larger work and adds visual elements not in the original score, does she violate copyright by staging it (there is a published score for the piece)?

15 O'Daniel confirms the importance of Oliveros: "I was indeed trying to employ Deep Listening, but set up a conceptual experiment for myself to see if I could do this without the ears. Eventually, I started to understand this process as allowing the serendipitous, but frequently opaque reference materials to drive narrative . . .

listening as a process of connecting the dots." Email communication, 27 December 2017.

16 On Oliveros and deep listening, see LaBelle 158–59.

17 O'Daniel did get permission from the Cage estate to "perform" 4'33". Email conversation, 8 December 2018.

18 Henry James, preface to *The Tragic Muse*.

19 Appel interview.

7. A CAPTIONED LIFE

1 Kim elaborates on this problem in a conversation with Raymond Antrobus and Meg Day. "Inventions in Sound," *BBC Radio 4*, www.bbc.co.uk.

2 For a thorough overview of closed captions as they are used by both hearing and deaf persons, see Zdenek.

3 Charlie Chaplin befriended the deaf California artist Granville Redmond and included him in a number of his silent films, including *City Lights*. He also introduced him to other Hollywood directors with whom he played bit parts. In one film, *You'd Be Surprised* (1926), Redmond was cast as a coroner who witnesses a murder and who poses as a deaf valet in order to uncover the plot. He and the film's protagonist, played by Raymond Griffith, use fingerspelling to communicate, and for once, as Alexander Pach wrote in *The Silent Worker*, "deaf people put it over the hearing for what they spell is not put on the screen in title form so this part the hearing people miss" (qtd. in Redmond 161).

4 Chris Krentz related to me that in a graduate seminar a captioner rendered "Europeans" as "you're a penis." Given the seminar's subject—Milton—one wonders why this word was the inevitable substitute.

5 In speaking of rhetorical function of captions, I am paraphrasing a passage in Sean Zdenek's *Reading Sound* in which he recognizes that although much thought has been given to the visual and acoustic elements of film and video, little attention has been given to "the possibility that captions might be potent and meaningful as other kinds of texts we study in the humanities" (xiii).

6 Passages quoted by Stein are from the "Food" section of *Tender Buttons*: "Orange in" (344), "Cups" (338), "Chicken" (341).

7 I realize that the arts of captioning error are a subset of AI computer error more generally. Writers have made active use of this phenomenon. The work of flarf poets, to take one example, involves using Google searches to create hybrid poems based on juxtapositions of unlikely terms. Michael McGee's *My Angie Dickinson*, for example, uses the search term *Angie Dickinson* combined with fragments of Emily Dickinson's poems to create mashups of contemporary pop culture and nineteenth-century diction.

8 Hamrae defines "access knowledge" as "a regime of legibility and illegibility [that] emerged from interdisciplinary concerns with what users need, how their bodies function, how they interact with space, and what kinds of people are likely to be in the world" (5). It grows out of universal design as defined by Ronald Mace,

which describes the need for an accessible environment. "Access knowledge" moves the phrase from the sphere of architecture away from a normalizing, standardizing narrative to an epistemological sphere that considers for whom and for what intent design is intended.

9 © Carolyn Lazard and Essex Street.

10 In their overview of audio description, Georgina Kleege and Scott Wallin describe the procedure as "the process of translating visual information into words for people who are blind or have low vision. Typically such description has focused on films, museum exhibitions, images and video on the internet, and live theater."

11 "Artist's statement," 2016. www.lizasylvestre.com.

12 In her *Captioned* film series, Sylvestre bases her captions on a first viewing. "I watch the films in my editing software with my cochlear implant and add my captions as they 'come to me' in the moment. So the juxtapositions are coincidental." As a consequence, her position outside "the normative film dynamic" allows her "to more clearly see many of the cultural shortcomings prevalent in the films." Email correspondence, 13 August 2020.

13 Credit: Liza Sylvestre.

14 The movie was based on a never-produced Broadway play, *Napoleon of Broadway*, by Charles Bruce Millholland. Adapted by Ben Hecht and Charles MacArther in 1932 as *Twentieth-Century*, which ran for 152 performances.

15 "Captioned. Twentieth-Century." www.lizasylvestre.com.

16 The film's sound designer, Nicolas Becker, placed sound-cancelling devices in Ahmed's ears that could create the experience of hearing loss as he was acting. Becker also developed recording technologies that imitated Foley effects, "distortions that replicate the mechanical output of cochlear implants, and [track] Ahmed's body for physical sounds" (Reilly).

17 I discuss the poetic "palimtext" in *Ghostlier Demarcations* 64–93.

AFTERWORD

Epigraphs: Donald Trump, 2016 Republican Convention nomination acceptance speech; Michel Foucault, introduction to Georges Canguilhem's *The Normal and the Pathological*, pp. 22–23.

1 Keats, Letter to George and Thomas Keats, December 1817, *Selected Poems and Letters* 261.

2 The phrase occurs in Bacon's *Novum Organum*: "In the Eighth Rank of Prerogative Instances: we will place Deviating Instances such as the Errors of Nature, or Strange and Monstrous Objects in which Nature deviates and turns from her ordinary course" (II: 193).

3 The term *post-truth* was canonized by the *Oxford Dictionary* in 2016, which named it 2016's word of the year. Although the phrase is often attributed to the Donald Trump administration, it was used in the 1990s to describe the waning of truth following Watergate and the Iran-Contra scandal. Lee McIntyre provides an excellent overview of the various forms and manifestations of post-truth think-

ing, noting that it refers less to the absence of truth than to the authority of what "feels" like truth. "As a catch-all phrase 'post-truth' seemed to capture the times. Given the obfuscation of facts, abandonment of evidential standards in reasoning and outright lying that marked 2016's Brexit vote and the US presidential election, many were aghast. If Donald Trump could claim—without evidence—that if he lost the election, it would be because it was rigged against him, did facts and truth even matter anymore?" (1–2).

4 A good survey of Canguilhem's theorization of error can be found in Talcott.

WORKS CITED

Adorno, Theodor. *Aesthetic Theory*. Translated by Robert Hullot-Kentor, U of Minnesota P, 1997.

Ahmed, Sara. *Queer Phenomenology: Orientation, Objects, Others*. Duke UP, 2006.

———. *The Promise of Happiness*. Duke UP, 2010.

Allison, Raphael. *Bodies on the Line: Performance and the Sixties Poetry Reading*. U of Iowa P, 2014.

Althusser, Louis. "A Letter on Art." *Lenin and Philosophy and Other Essays*, translated by Ben Brewster, Monthly Review Press, 1971, pp. 221–27.

Altieri, Charles, and Nicholas D. Nace. *The Fate of Difficulty in the Poetry of Our Time*. Northwestern UP, 2018.

Alworth, David. *Site Reading: Fiction, Art and Social Form*. Princeton UP, 2016.

Apter, Emily. "Shibboleth: Policing by Ear and Forensic Listening in Projects by Lawrence Abu Hamdan." *Say Shibboleth!: On Visible and Invisible Borders*, edited by Boaz Levin, Hanno Loewy, and Anika Reichwald, Bucher Verlag, 2018, pp. 138–50.

Arendt, Hannah. *The Origins of Totalitarianism*. Harcourt, 1976.

Attali, Jacques. *Noise: The Political Economy of Music*. Translated by Brian Massumi, U of Minnesota P, 1992.

Bacon, Francis (Lord Verulum). *Novum Organum or True Suggestions for the Interpretation of Nature*. William Pickering, n.d.

Baggs, Amanda. "In My Language." YouTube Video, 2007. www.youtube.com.

Barry, Robert. "'Sound Is Expensive': An Interview with Christine Sun Kim." *The Quietus*, 6 February 2017. http://thequietus.com.

Barthes, Roland. "The Photographic Message." *Image—Music—Text*, translated by Stephen Heath, Hill and Wang, 1977, pp. 15–31.

Bartlett, Jennifer, Sheila Black, and Michael Northern, editors. *Beauty Is a Verb: The New Poetry of Disability*. Cinco Puntos, 2011.

Bartlett, Jennifer, and George Hart. *Momentous Inconclusions: The Life and Work of Larry Eigner*. U of New Mexico P, 2020.

Bates, David. *Enlightenment Aberrations: Error and Revolution in France*. Cornell UP, 2002.

Bauman, H-Dirksen L. "Getting out of Line: Toward a Visual and Cinematic Poetics of ASL." *Signing the Body Poetic: Essays on American Sign Language Literature*, edited by H-Dirksen Bauman, Jennifer L. Nelson, and Heidi M. Rose, U of California P, 2006, pp. 95–117.

Bauman, H-Dirksen L., and Joseph J. Murray. "Deaf Studies in the 21st Century: 'Deaf-Gain' and the Future of Human Diversity." *The Disability Studies Reader*, 4th ed., edited by Lennard J. Davis, Routledge, 2013, pp. 246–60.

Baumann, H-Dirksen L., Jennifer L. Nelson, and Heidi M. Rose, editors. *Signing the Body Poetic: Essays on American Sign Language Literature*. U of California P, 2006.

Bennett, Jane. *Vibrant Matter: A Political Ecology of Things*. Duke UP, 2010.

Berger, James. *The Disarticulate: Language, Disability, and the Narratives of Modernity*. New York UP, 2014.

Bergvall, Caroline. *Meddle English: New and Selected Texts*. Nightboat, 2011.

———. "Say, 'Parsely.'" *Fig*, Salt Publishing, 2005, pp. 49–60.

Bernstein, Charles. "A Defence of Poetry." *All the Whiskey in Heaven: Selected Poems*, Farrar Straus Giroux, 2010, pp. 213–15.

———. "Artifice of Absorption." *A Poetics*, Harvard UP, 1992, pp. 9–89.

———. "This Picture Intentionally Left Blank." *Pitch of Poetry*, U of Chicago P, 2016, pp. 34–47.

Booth, Katie. *The Invention of Miracles: Language, Power, and Alexander Graham Bell's Quest to End Deafness*. Simon and Schuster, 2021.

Branca, Sid. "A Sound That You Like: Christine Sun Kim's Fingertap Quartet." *Badatsports*, 16 November 2015. www.badatsports.com.

Brueggemann, Brenda Jo. *Deaf Subjects: Between Identities and Places*. New York UP, 2009.

Burroughs, William, *The Ticket that Exploded*. Grove, 1967.

Cachia, Amanda Louise. *Raw Sense: Choreography, Disability, Politics*. 2017. University of California, San Diego, PhD dissertation.

Canguilhem, Georges. *The Normal and the Pathological*. Zone, 1991.

Carruth, Hayden. *The Voice That Is Great within Us: American Poetry of the Twentieth-Century*. Bantam, 1970.

Carter, Paul. "Ambiguous Traces, Mishearing, and Auditory Space." *Hearing Cultures: Essays on Sound, Listening and Modernity*, edited by Veit Erlmann, Berg, 2004, pp. 43–64.

Celan, Paul. "Shibboleth." *Memory Rose into Threshold Speech: Paul Celan: The Collected Earlier Poetry*, translated by Pierre Joris, Farrar, Strauss and Giroux, 2020, pp. 144–46.

Chang, Briankle G. *Deconstructing Communication: Representation, Subject, and Economies of Exchange*. U of Minnesota P, 1996.

Chen, Mel. *Animacies: Biopolitics, Racial Mattering, and Queer Affect*. Duke UP, 2012.

Cheng, William. *Just Vibrations: The Purpose of Sounding Good*. U of Michigan P, 2016.

Chinatown. Directed by Roman Polanski, Paramount Pictures, 1974.

Chomsky, Noam, and George A. Miller. "Introduction to the Formal Analysis of Natural Languages." *Handbook of Mathematical Psychology*, edited by R. D. Luce, R. R. Bush, and E. Galantev, vol. 2, Wiley, 1963, pp. 269–322.

Cole, Norma. *Natural Light*. Libellum, 2009.

———. "Speech Production." *Beauty Is a Verb: The New Poetry of Disability*, edited by Jennifer Bartlett, Sheila Black, and Michael Northern, Cinco Puntos, 2011.

Coleridge, Samuel Taylor. *The Complete Poetical Works of Samuel Taylor Coleridge*, edited by Ernest Hartley Coleridge, vol. 1, Oxford UP, 1962.

Connor, Steven. "Earslips: Of Mishearings and Mondegreens." www.stevenconnor.com.

———. "Edison's Teeth: Touching Hearing." *Hearing Cultures: Essays on Sound, Listening and Modernity*, edited by Veit Erlmann, Berg, 2005, pp. 153–72.

Creeley, Robert. "The Language." *The Collected Poems of Robert Creeley, 1945–1975*, U of California P, 1982. p. 183.

"Cultures of Reading." *PMLA*, vol. 134, no. 1, January, 2019.

Davidson, Michael. *Concerto for the Left Hand: Disability and the Defamiliar Body*. U of Michigan P, 2008.

———. *Ghostlier Demarcations: Modern Poetry and the Material Word*. U of California P, 1997.

———. "Hearing Things: The Scandal of Speech in Deaf Performance." *Concerto for the Left Hand: Disability and the Defamiliar Body*, U of Michigan P, 2008, pp. 80–99.

———. *Invalid Modernism: Disability and the Missing Body of the Aesthetic*. Oxford UP, 2019.

———. "Technologies of Presence Orality and the Tapevoice of Contemporary Poetics." *Ghostlier Demarcations: Modern Poetry and the Material Word*, U of California P, 1997, pp. 196–223.

Deaf Jam. Produced and directed by Judy Lieff. Kanopy, 2011. www.judylieff.com.

Derrida, Jacques. *Of Grammatology*. Translated by Gayatri Chakravorty Spivak, Johns Hopkins UP, 1974.

———. *Sovereignties in Question; The Poetics of Paul Celan*. Fordham UP, 2005.

———. "The Flowers of Rhetoric." *Margins of Philosophy*, translated by Alan Bass, U of Chicago P, 1982, pp. 245–57.

Dickinson, Emily. *Emily Dickinson's Poems as She Preserved Them*, edited by Cristanne Miller, Harvard UP, 2016.

Diderot. "*Paradoxe sur le Comédien*." *Oeuvres*, Gallimard, 1951, pp. 1003–58.

Dowling, Sarah. *Translingual Poetics: Writing, Personhood Under Settler Colonialism*. U of Iowa P, 2018.

Downey, George J. *Closed Captioning: Subtitling, Stenography, and the Digital Convergence of Text with Television*. Johns Hopkins UP, 2007.

Duchamp, Marcel. *Dialogues with Marcel Duchamp*. Edited by Pierre Cabanne, translated by Ron Padgett, Viking, 1971.

Duncan, Robert. "Crosses of Harmony and Disharmony." *The Collected Poems and Plays*, edited by Peter Quartermain, U of California P, 2014, pp. 39–42.

———. "The Truth and Life of Myth: An Essay in Essential Autobiography." *Collected Essays and Other Prose*, edited by James Maynard, U of California P, 2014, pp. 139–94.

Eagleton, Terry. *The Ideology of the Aesthetic*. Basil Blackwell, 1990.

Eidsheim, Nina Sun. *Sensing Sound: Singing and Listening as Vibrational Practice*. Duke UP, 2015.

———. *The Race of Sound: Listening, Timbre and Vocality in African American Music*. Duke UP, 2019.

Eigner, Larry. *Another Time in Fragments*. Fulcrum Press, 1967.

———. *Areas, Lights, Heights: Larry Eigner Writings 1954–1989*. Edited by Benjamin Friedlander, Roof, 1989.

———. *Calligraphy Typewriters: The Selected Poems of Larry Eigner*, edited by Curtis Faville and Robert Grenier, U of Alabama P, 2017.

———. *The Collected Poems of Larry Eigner*. Edited by Curtis Faville and Robert Grenier, 4 vols., Stanford UP, 2010.

Eisenberg, Andrew J. "Space." *Keywords in Sound*, edited by David Novak and Matt Sakakeeny, Duke UP, 2015, pp. 193–207.

Eliot, T. S. *The Use of Poetry and the Use of Criticism: Studies in the Relation of Criticism to Poetry*. Harvard UP, 1961.

Empson, William. *Seven Types of Ambiguity*. New Directions, 1966.

Fass, Ekbert. *Young Robert Duncan: Portrait of the Poet as Homosexual in Society*. Black Sparrow, 1983.

Feldman, Morton. "The Anxiety of Art." *Give My Regards to Eighth Street*, edited by B. H. Friedman, Exact Change, 2000, pp. 21–32.

Felstiner, John. *Paul Celan: Poet, Survivor, Jew*. Yale UP, 1995.

Ferris, Jim. "The Enjambed Body: A Step Toward a Crippled Poetics." *Georgia Review*, Summer, 2004. https://thegeorgiareview.com.

Fitterman, Robert. *Holocaust Museum*. Counterpath, 2013.

Friedner, Michele. "Biosociality, Biopower, and Community Formation: How Biopower Is Constitutive of the Deaf Community." *Sign Language Studies*, vol. 10, no. 3, 2010, pp. 336–47.

Friedner, Michele, and Stefan Helmreich. "Sound Studies Meets Deaf Studies." *The Senses and Society*, vol. 7, no. 1, 2012, pp. 72–86.

Foucault, Michel. *Death and the Labyrinth: The World of Raymond Roussel*. Translated by Charles Ruas, Doubleday, 1986.

———. Introduction. *The Normal and the Pathological*, by Georges Canguilhem, Zone, 1991, pp. 7–24.

Fredman, Stephen. "Laurie Anderson in the Reagan Era." *American Poetry as Transactional Art*. U of Alabama P, 2020.

Freud, Sigmund. *The Psychopathology of Everyday Life*. Translated by Alan Tyson, Norton, 1960.

Garland-Thomson, Rosemarie. *Extraordinary Bodies: Figuring Physical Disability in American Culture and Literature*. Columbia UP, 1997.

Glennie, Evelyn. "How to Truly Listen." TED Talk, 2003. www.ted.com.

Goldsmith, Kenneth. *Head Citations*. The Figures, 2002.

Gravendyk, Hillary. "Chronic Poetics." *Journal of Modern Literature*, vol. 38, no. 1, 2014, pp. 1–19.

Grigely, Joseph. *St. Cecilia*. Frances Young Tang Teaching Museum and Art Gallery at Skidmore College Contemporary Museum, 2007.

Hagood, Mark. "Disability and Biomediation: Tinnitus as Phantom Disability." *Disability Media Studies*, edited by Elizabeth Ellcessor and Bill Kirkpatrick, New York UP, 2017, pp. 311–29.

Halberstam, Judith. *The Queer Art of Failure*. Duke UP, 2011.

Hamden, Lawrence Abu. "Conflicted Phonemes." *Say Shibboleth!: On Visible and Invisible Borders*, edited by Boaz Levin, Hanno Loewy, and Anika Reichwald, Bucher Verlag, 2018, pp. 129–37. Also on his website: www.lawrenceabuhamdan.com.

Hammer, Langdon. "Voice and Erasure in Srikanth Reddy's *Voyager*." *The Fate of Difficulty in the Poetry of Our Time*, edited by Charles Altieri and Nicholas D. Nace, Northwestern UP, 2018.

Hamrae, Aimi. *Building Access: Universal Design and the Politics of Disability*. U of Minnesota P, 2017.

Hankins, Thomas J., and Robert J. Silverman. "The Aeolian Harp and the Romantic Quest of Nature." *Instruments and the Imagination*, Princeton UP, 1995, pp. 86–112.

Hannon, Molly. "How Christine Sun Kim, Deaf Sound Artist, Hears Everything." *Daily Beast*, 1 June 2016. www.thedailybeast.com.

Harmon, Kristen. "Addressing Deafness: From Hearing Loss to Deaf Gain." *PMLA Profession*, 2010, pp. 124–30.

Hart, George. "'Enough Defined': Disability, Ecopoetics, and Larry Eigner." *Contemporary Literature*, vol. 51, no. 1, 2010, pp. 152–79.

———. *Finding the Weight of Things: Larry Eigner's Ecrippoetics*. U of Alabama P, 2021.

Hayles, N. Katherine. *How We Became Posthuman: Virtual Bodies in Cybernetics, Literature, and Informatics*. U of Chicago P, 1999.

Heidegger, Martin. *Being and Time*. Translated by John Macquarrie and Edward Robinson, Harper and Row, 1962.

Hejinian. Lyn. *My Life and My Life in the Nineties*. Wesleyan UP, 2013.

Hendren, Sara. *What Can a Body Do? How We Meet the Built World*. Riverhead, 2020.

Hodges, Adam. *When Words Trump Politics: Resisting a Hostile Regime of Language*. Stanford UP, 2020.

Holmes, Jessica. "Expert Listening beyond the Limits of Hearing: Music and Deafness." *Journal of the American Musicological Society*, vol. 70, no. 1, 2017, pp. 171–220. doi10.1525/jams.2017.70.1.171.

Howe, Susan. "Melville's Marginalia." *The Nonconformist's Memorial*, New Directions, 1993, pp. 83–150.

Jackson, Derrick Z. "Cheney's Misspeaking Streak." *The Boston Globe*, 17 September 2003. archive.boston.com.

Jain, Sarah Lochlann. "Living in Prognosis: Toward an Elegiac Politics." *Representations*, vol. 98, no. 1, 2007, pp. 77–92.

Jakobson, Roman. "Two Aspects of Language and Two Types of Aphasic Disturbances." *Language and Literature*, edited by Krystyna Pomorska and Stephen Rudy, Harvard UP, 1987, pp. 95–120.

James, Henry. *The Tragic Muse*. 1890. Penguin, 1995.

Jones, Jeannette DiBernardo. "Imagined Hearing: Music-Making in Deaf Culture." *The Oxford Handbook of Music and Disability Studies*, edited by Blake Howe et al., Oxford UP, 2016, pp. 54–72.

Joyce, James. *Finnegans Wake*. Penguin, 1967.

————. *Ulysses*. Random House, 1986.

Kafer, Alison. *Feminist, Queer, Crip*. U of Indiana P, 2013.

Kahn, Douglas. *Noise, Water, Meat: A History of Sound in the Arts*. MIT Press, 1999.

Kearney, Douglas. *Mess and Mess*. Noemi, 2015.

Keats, John. *Selected Poems and Letters by John Keats*. Edited by Douglas Bush, Houghton Mifflin, 1959.

————. *The Poems of John Keats*, edited by Jack Stillinger, Harvard UP, 1978.

Keil, Charles, and Steven Feld. *Music Grooves: Essays and Dialogues*. U of Chicago P, 1994.

Kim, Christine Sun "Art Talk with Sound Artist Christine Sun Kim." Interview with Paulette Beete. *Art Works Blog*. National Endowment for the Arts, 27 March 2017. www.arts.gov.

————. "Christine Sun Kim: A Selby Film." https://vimeo.com.

————. "I Performed at the Super Bowl. You Might Have Missed Me." *The New York Times*, 3 February 2020. www.nytimes.com.

————. "Signs of Friendship: A Conversation between Christine Sun Kim and Renée Hlozek." Ted Blog. www.blog.ted.com.

————. "Sonic Identity Politics with Christine Sun Kim." With Jeppe Ugelvig O. *Dis*, vol. 20, January 2016. www.dismagazine.com.

————. "The Enchanting Music of Sign Language." TED talk, 2015. www.ted.com.

Kim-Cohen, Seth. *In the Blink of an Ear: Toward a Non-Cochlear Sonic Art*. Bloomsbury, 2009.

Kolb, Rachel. "The Brain's 'Instantaneous Inventions': Exploring the Discursive Normalcy and Pathology of Mishearings." Unpublished paper.

Konnikova, Maria. "Excuse Me While I Kiss This Guy." *The New Yorker*, 10 December 2014. www.newyorker.com.

Kosuth, Joseph. "Art after Philosophy." *Ubu Web*. www.ubu.com.

Krauss, Rosalind. "Video: The Aesthetics of Narcissism." *October*, vol. 1, 1976, pp. 50–64.

Kleege, Georgina, and Scott Wallin. "Audio Description as a Pedagogical Tool." *Disability Studies Quarterly*, vol. 35, no. 2 (2015). https://dsq-sds.org.

Krentz, Christopher. *Writing Deafness: The Hearing Line in Nineteenth-Century Literature*. U of North Carolina P, 2007.

Kushalnagar, Raja. "Who Owns Captioning?" *Disability, Rights, and Information Technology*, U of Pennsylvania P, 2017, 183–97.

LaBelle, Brandon. *Background Noise: Perspectives on Sound Art*. Continuum, 2006.

Lazard, Carolyn. *A Recipe for Disaster*. www.carolynlazard.com.

Lerer, Seth. *Error and the Academic Self: The Scholarly Imagination, Medieval to Modern*. Columbia UP, 2002.

Linett, Maren Tova. *Bodies of Modernism: Physical Disability in Transatlantic Modernist Literature*. U of Michigan P, 2017.

Lorde, Audre. *The Cancer Journals*. Aunt Lute, 1980.

Lowe, Lisa. *Immigrant Acts: On Asian American Cultural Politics*. Duke UP, 1996.

Lowell, Robert. "For the Union Dead." *The Selected Poems of Robert Lowell*, Farrar, Strauss and Giroux, 1986, pp. 135–37.

Luck, Jessica Lewis. "Larry Eigner and the Phenomenology of Projected Verse." *Contemporary Literature*, vol. 53, no. 3, 2012, pp. 461–92.

Lyall, Sarah. "Caution: Art Afoot." *The New York Times*, 11 December 2007. www.nytimes.com.

Mackey, Nathaniel. *From a Broken Bottle Traces of Perfume Still Emanate*. Vol. 1–3, New Directions, 2010.

Magee, Michael. *My Angie Dickinson*. Zasterle, 2006.

Marclay, Christian. Interview with Ben Neill. *Bomb*, 1 July 2003. www.bombmagazine.org/.

———. *Things I've Heard*. Fraenkel Gallery, 2013.

McAlpine, Erica. *The Poet's Mistake*. Princeton UP, 2020.

McDermott, Emily. "The Aural Artist." *Interview*, 14 December 2015. https://www.interviewmagazine.com.

McHale, Brian. "Making (Non)sense of Postmodern Poetry." *Language, Text and Context: Essays in Stylistics*, edited by Michael Toolan, Routledge, 1992, pp. 6–35.

McIntosh, Janet. "Introduction: The Trump Era as a Linguistic Emergency." *Language in the Trump Era: Scandals and Emergencies*, edited by Janet McIntosh and Norma Mendoza-Denton, Cambridge UP, 2020, pp. 1–43.

McIntyre, Lee. *Post-Truth*. MIT Press, 2018.

McRuer, Robert. *Crip Times: Disability, Globalization, and Resistance*. New York UP, 2018.

Melnick, David. *Men in Aida*. *Imagining Language: An Anthology*. Edited by Jed Rasula and Steve McCaffery, MIT Press, 1998, 284.

Merleau-Ponty, Maurice. *The Phenomenology of Perception*. Translated by Colin Smith, Routledge, 1962.

Mills, Mara. "Deafness." *Keywords in Sound*, edited by David Novak and Matt Sakakeeny, Duke UP, 2015, pp. 45–54.

Mills, Mara, and Jonathan Sterne. "Biomediation—Three Proposals, Six Tactics." *Disability Media Studies*, edited by Elizabeth Ellcessor and Bill Kirkpatrick, New York UP, 2017, pp. 365–78.

Mitchell, David, and Sharon Snyder. *Narrative Prosthesis: Disability and the Dependencies of Discourse*. U of Michigan P, 2000.

———. *The Biopolitics of Disability: Neoliberalism, Ablenationalism, and Peripheral Embodiment*. U of Michigan P, 2015.

Muldoon, Paul. "Cuthbert and the Otters." *One Thousand Things Worth Knowing*, Farrar, Strauss and Giroux, 2015, pp. 3–12.

Mullen, Harryette. "From A to Z: Conversations on Sleeping with the Dictionary." *Looking up Harryette Mullen: Interviews on Sleeping with the Dictionary and Other Works*, edited by Barbara Henning, Belladonna, 2011, pp. 45–46.

———. *Muse and Drudge*. *Recyclopedia: Trimmings, S*PeRM**K*T, and Muse and Drudge*. Graywolf, 2006, pp. 97–178.

———. *Sleeping with the Dictionary*. U of California P, 2002.

Nguyen, Viet Thanh. "The Ideas That Won't Survive the Coronavirus." *The New York Times*, 19 April 2020, Review, pp. 10–11.

O'Daniel, Alison. "Generative Misunderstanding: Alison O'Daniel Interviewed by Anne Ellegood." *Bomb*. www.bombmagazine.org.

———. Interview with Kevin Appel. *Issue* (2018). https://issuemagazine.com.

———. "The Noise Inside: Writer/Director Darius Marder on *Sound of Metal*. *Filmmaker Magazine*. www.filmmakermagazine.com.

Olson, Charles. "Maximus to Gloucester, Letter 15." *The Maximus Poems*, U of California P, 1983, pp. 71–75.

———. "Projective Verse." *Collected Prose*, edited by Donald Allen and Benjamin Friedlander, U of California P, 1997, pp. 239–49.

Osman, Jena. *Corporate Relations*. Burning Deck, 2014.

———. *Public Figures*. Wesleyan UP, 2012.

———. *The Character*. Beacon, 1999.

Oxford University Press. *The Oxford Annotated Bible with the Apocrypha*. Oxford UP, 1965.

Packard, Cassie. "Deaf Artist Christine Sun Kim Is Reinventing Sound." *Vice*, vol. 3, 2015. https://www.vice.com.

Padden, Carol, and Tom Humphries. "A Different Center." *Deaf in America: Voices from a Culture*, Harvard UP, 1988, pp. 38–55.

———. *Deaf in America: Voices from a Culture*. Harvard UP, 1988.

Palmer, Michael. "The Danish Notebook." *Active Boundaries: Selected Essays and Talks*, New Directions, 2008.

Parker, Patricia. "Metaphor and Catachresis." *The Ends of Rhetoric: History, Theory, Practice*, edited by John Bender and David E. Wellbery, Stanford UP, 1990, pp. 60–73.

Perelman, Bob. "Essay on Style." *7 Works*, The Figures, 1978, pp. 13–20.

———. *The Marginalization of Poetry: Language Writing and Literary History*. Princeton UP, 1996.

Perloff, Marjorie. "Language in Migration: Multilingualism and Exophonic Writing in the New Poetics." *Unoriginal Genius: Poetry by Other Means in the New Century*, U of Chicago P, 2010, pp. 123–45.

Philip, M. NourbeSe. *Zong! As Told to the Author by Setaey Adamu Boateng*. Wesleyan UP, 2008.

Pound, Ezra. *The Cantos of Ezra Pound*. New Directions, 1973.

Price, Margaret. *Mad at School: Rhetorics of Mental Disability and Academic Life*. U of Michigan Press, 2011.

Puar, Jasbir K. "Prognosis Time: Towards a Geopolitics of Affect, Debility and Capacity." *Women and Performance*, vol. 19, no. 2, pp. 161–72.

———. *The Right to Maim: Debility, Capacity, Disability*. Duke UP, 2017.

Pullum, Geoffrey. "Speech Recognition vs. Language Processing." *The Chronicle of Higher Education*, 23 May 2013. www.chronicle.com.

Rancière, Jacques. *Aesthetics and its Discontents*. Translated by Steven Corcoran, Polity Press, 2009.

———. *The Politics of Aesthetics: The Distribution of the Sensible*. Translated by Gabriel Rockhill, Continuum, 2004.

Rapp, Rayna. "Gender, Body, Biomedicine: How Some Feminist Concerns Dragged Reproduction to the Center of Social Theory." *Medical Anthropology Quarterly*, vol. 15, no. 4, 2001, pp. 466–77.

Raworth, Tom. "South America." *Tottering State: Selected and New Poems. 1963–1983*, The Figures, 1984, p. 54.

Redmond, Granville. *Granville Redmond: The Eloquent Palette*. Edited by Scott Shields and Mildred Albrond, Crocker Art Museum, 2020.

Reed, Brian. *Nobody's Business: Twenty-First Century Avant Garde Poetics*. Cornell UP, 2013.

Reilly, Dan. "How *Sound of Metal* Reimagined the Silence in Hearing Loss." *Vulture*, vol. 12, 2020. www.vulture.com.

Retallack, Joan. "The Poethical Wager." *The Poethical Wager*, U of California P, 2003, pp. 21–47.

Reynolds, Sean. "'I Could Not Let Eu Go: Robert Duncan Falls for the Wrong Verb." *Journal of Modern Literature*, vol. 37, no. 1, 2013, pp. 90–106.

Riley, Denise. "'A Voice without a Mouth:' Inner Speech." *Qui Parle*, vol. 14, no. 2 , 2004, pp. 57–104.

Roberts, John. *The Necessity of Errors*. Verso, 2011.

Rose, Nikolas, and Carlos Novas. "Biological Citizenship." *Global Assemblages*, edited by Aihwa Ong and Stephen J. Collier, Blakwell, 2005, pp. 439–63.

Sachs, David. "A Philosophical Resistance to Freud." *Dialectica*, vol. 44, nos. 1/2, 1990, pp. 203–14. www.jstor.org.

Salcedo, Doris. "Transcription." www.tate.org.

Sanchez, Rebecca, "Creating Shared Spaces with Every Form of Language." *How We Get to Next*. https://howwegettonext.com.

Saussure, Ferdinand de. *Course in General Linguistics*, edited by Charles Bally and Albert Sechehaye, translated by Wade Baskin, McGraw Hill, 1959.

Scalapino, Leslie. *The Public World/Syntactically Impermanence*. Wesleyan UP, 1999.

Scott, Jordan. *Blert*. Toronto: Coach House, 2008.

———. "Interview, Part 1." You Tube. www.youtube.com.

Serup, Martin Glaz. "Captions without Images." *Jacket 2*. jacket2.org.

Shannon, Claude. *The Mathematical Theory of Communication*. U of Illinois P, 1998.

Shaw, Lytle. "The Eigner Sanction: Keeping Time from the American Century." *Narrowcast: Poetry and Audio Research*, Stanford UP, 2018, pp. 71–104.

Shea, Gerald. *Song without Words: Discovering My Deafness Halfway through Life*. DaCapo, 2013.

Shell, Marc. *Stutter*. Harvard UP, 2003.

Shelley, Percy Bysshe. *Shelley's Poetry and Prose*. Edited by Donald H. Reiman and Neil Fraistat, Norton, 2002.

Sheridan, Richard Brinsley. *The Rivals. The School for Scandal and Other Plays*. Penguin, 1988.

Siebers, Tobin. *Disability Aesthetics*. U of Michigan P, 2010.

Silliman, Ron. *What*. The Figures, 1988.

Small, Christopher. *Musicking: The Meanings of Performance and Listening*. Wesleyan UP, 1998.

Smith, Gregory G, editor. *Elizabethan Critical Essays*. 2 vols. Oxford UP, 1959.

Smith, Roberta. "Seeing (and Playing) Music of Everyday Life. *The New York Times*, 8 July 2010. www.nytimes.com.

Sng, Zachary. *The Rhetoric of Error from Locke to Kleist*. Stanford UP, 2010.

Spicer, Jack. "A Textbook of Poetry." *My Vocabulary Did This to Me: The Collected Poetry of Jack Spicer*, edited by Peter Gizzi and Kevin Killian, Wesleyan UP, 2008, pp. 299–313.

Stauffer, Jill. *Ethical Loneliness: The Injustice of Not Being Heard*. Columbia UP, 2015.

Strauss, Joseph. *Extraordinary Measures: Disability in Music*. Oxford UP, 2011.

Stein, Gertrude. "Composition as Explanation." *Gertrude Stein, Writings 1903–1932*, edited by Catherine R. Stimpson and Harriet Chessman, Library of America, 1998.

———. *Tender Buttons. Gertrude Stein, Writings 1903–1932*, edited by Catherine R. Stimpson and Harriet Chessman, Library of America, 1998, pp. 313–55.

Sterne, Jonathan. *The Audible Past: Cultural Origins of Sound Reproduction*. Duke UP, 2003.

Stevens, Wallace. "The Idea of Order at Key West." *The Collected Poems of Wallace Stevens*, New York: Knopf, 1968, 128–30.

Sylvestre, Liza. *Captioned. Twentieth-Century*. http://www.lizasylvestre.com/captioned.

Szendy, Peter. *Listen: A History of Our Ears*. Translated by Charlotte Mandell, Fordham UP, 2008.

Talcott, Stephen. "Georges Canguilhem and the Philosophical Problem of Error." *Dialogue*, vol. 52, no. 4, 2013, pp. 649–72. www.cambridge.org.

Taylor, Talbot J. *Mutual Misunderstanding: Skepticism and the Theorization of Language and Interpretation*. Duke UP, 1992.

Todorov, Tzvetan. *The Conquest of America*. Translated by Richard Howard, Harper, 1982.

Tomlinson, Charles. *Selected Poems*. New Directions, 1997.

Treichler, Paula. *How to Have Theory in an Epidemic: Cultural Chronicles of AIDS*. Duke UP, 1999.

Tudor, David. "An Interview with David Tudor by John David Fullemann." Stockholm, 31 May 1984. https://davidtudor.org.

Twilley, Nicola. "Seeing with Your Tongue." *The New Yorker*, 15 May 2007. www.newyorker.com.

United States of Poetry. Larry Eigner segment. KQED Video: Washington Square Films, 1996. https://www.youtube.com.

Voegelin, Salomé. *Listening to Noise and Silence: Towards a Philosophy of Sound Art*. Continuum, 2010.

Volosinov, V. N. *Marxism and the Philosophy of Language*. Seminar Press, 1973.

Vygotsky, Lev. *Thought and Language*. Translated by Alex Kozulin, MIT Press, 1986.

Wagner, Anne. "Performance, Video, and the Rhetoric of Presence." *October*, vol. 91, 2000, 59–80.

Watlington, Emily. "Critical, Creative, Corrective, Cacophonous, Comical: Closed Captions." *Mousse*, Essays Mousse 68. http://moussemagazine.it.

Watten, Barrett. "Missing 'X': Formal Meaning in Crane and Eigner." *Total Syntax*, Southern Illinois UP, 1985, pp. 168–90.

Weidman, Amanda. "Voice." *Keywords in Sound*, edited by David Novak and Matt Sakakeeny, Duke UP, 2015, 232–45.

Whitehead, Alfred North. *Process and Reality: An Essay in Cosmology*. Harper & Row, 1957.

Williams, Raymond. *Marxism and Literature*. Oxford UP, 1977.

———. *Politics and Letters: Interviews with* New Left Review. Verso, 2015.

Wittgenstein, Ludwig. *Tractatus Logico-Philosophicus*. Translated by D. F. Pears and B. F. McGuinness, Routledge, 1961.

Wright, David. *Deafness: An Autobiography*. Harper Perennial, 1993.

Wright, Sylvia. "The Death of Lady Mondegreen." *Harper's*, November 1954, pp. 48–51.

Yergeau, Melanie. *Authoring Autism: On Rhetoric and Neurological Queerness*. Duke UP, 2018.

Zdenek, Sean. *Reading Sounds: Closed-Captioned Media and Popular Culture*. U of Chicago P, 2015.

Zukofsky, Louis. "An Objective." *Prepositions: The Collected Critical Essays of Louis Zukofsky*. U of California P, 1981, pp. 12–18.

INDEX

Page numbers in *italics* indicate Figures.

ABOUT THE AUTHOR

MICHAEL DAVIDSON is Distinguished Professor Emeritus at the University of California, San Diego. His most recent books include *Concerto for the Left Hand: Disability and the Defamiliar Body* (2008) and *Invalid Modernism: Disability and the Missing Body of the Aesthetic* (2019). He is the author of eight books of poetry, the most recent of which is *Bleed Through: New and Selected Poems* (2013). He is the editor of *The Collected Poems of George Oppen* (2008).